SHADOW
TRADES

"International business texts typically focus upon everyday corporate activities and the various political, legal, and cultural environments to which they must adapt. These books do consider illicit practices, such as counterfeiting, that threaten companies, as well as some ethical, social responsibility, and sustainability issues, but generally tilt toward the sunny side of global commerce... In *Shadow Trades,* author Amos Owen Thomas introduces readers to a wide range of much more controversial, often despicable, business conduct that flourishes on a worldwide scale... – **Terrence H. Witkowski, Professor of Marketing, Director, International Business Program, College of Business, California State University**

"Shadow Trades takes on the existence and growth of illegal markets from a business perspective... Related dark markets are examined, using careful analysis of available data, as are the relationships among legal and illicit markets, businesses, and government activity in alternately ignoring or facilitating this largely hidden activity. The consequences of this situation for legitimate business and broader economic development are discussed, as are the actions that might be taken to improve the contemporary situation globally. Good insights into some bad behaviour, and the reasons why it continues to thrive." – **Jay S. Albanese, Professor and Criminologist, Virginia Commonwealth University, Richmond. Author, *Handbook of Transnational Crime & Justice***

"The legitimate global capitalist financial and business world lives in creative co-existence with its dark alter ego. As this book demonstrates, these shadow trades haunt capitalism and complicit government as viruses. These co-inhabit spaces with hosts such that management, healthcare and environmentalism have their converse in exploited labour, organ harvesting and waste dumping. Amos Owen Thomas is bold enough to take a fierce analytical torch to this murky admixture in a book that will become a mainstream source for business and business educators." – **David Weir, Professor of Enterprise and Director of External Engagement, Huddersfield University**

"*Shadow Trades* makes a great addition to the literature on CSR and Business Ethics, filling one of the gaps that have existed in management knowledge. I believe that there are still no credible books in this area for education and training purposes on the market. Dr Thomas' book will certainly be a welcome addition to what we have now at business schools around the globe." – **Samuel O Idowu, Deputy CEO, Global Corporate Governance Institute; Co-editor, *Encyclopaedia of Corporate Social Responsibility***

"This is a very important book on a subject typically ignored in management education. The author's unique perspectives and insights make for a vital contribution to our knowledge. It is important for students and the general public to understand these challenges, so I hope the book gets some traction in academia and beyond." – **Laurence Chalip, Professor, Director, School of Sport, Recreation, and Tourism Management, George Mason University, Virginia**

Compelling and original, *Shadow Trades* exposes the criminogenic nature of international capitalism. The spectres of fraud, violence and coercion lurk on every page. Essential reading for all scholars of critical globalization studies.' – **Leo McCann, Professor of Management, University of York**

"Driving directly to the heart of crime, greed and desperation, the author explains the interactions between leading world countries and companies profiting from illegal activities to economically disadvantaged countries mired in political conflict and military rule. *Shadow Trades* describes how UN, laws, international conventions and interventions are circumvented by ingenious yet, corrupt means to the detriment of every living creature on this planet." – **Colleen Clarke, Professor Emeritus, Minnesota State University, Mankato; Author, *Stealing History***

"Amos Owen Thomas addresses a fascinating collection of cross border business activities that provide a rich source of material for discussing business ethics and corporate social responsibility. By highlighting these examples of cross border activity that are either illegal or at the margins of social acceptance, the book provides a unique source for reflecting on contemporary international economic value creation with a dark side.' – **Johan Lindeque, Assistant Professor of Strategy, University of Amsterdam Business School**

"Professor Amos Owen Thomas's book *Shadow Trades* makes a tremendous contribution to uncovering an important phenomenon of economy that has been little known." – **Tony Fang, Professor, Stockholm Business School, Stockholm University; Emerging Markets Cross-Cultural Research Group**

"It is assumed that globalisation fosters only legitimate trade and hence there is not much in the international business literature about the dark side. This timely book sheds much needed light on issues such as human trafficking, money laundering, waste management and arms trade. For instance it provides an excellent critique of the push and pull migration theories underlying irregular migration and illuminates our understanding of its global human resource implications. *Shadow Trades* is a very interesting and novel book and a must-read for academics, practitioners, government official, policy makers and social activists." – **Yaw Debra, Professor, School of Management, Swansea University; Chair, Academy of International Business – Africa chapter**

Amos Owen Thomas

SHADOW TRADES

The Dark Side of Global Business

Los Angeles | London | New Delhi
Singapore | Washington DC | Melbourne

Los Angeles | London | New Delhi
Singapore | Washington DC | Melbourne

SAGE Publications Ltd
1 Oliver's Yard
55 City Road
London EC1Y 1SP

SAGE Publications Inc.
2455 Teller Road
Thousand Oaks, California 91320

SAGE Publications India Pvt Ltd
B 1/I 1 Mohan Cooperative Industrial Area
Mathura Road
New Delhi 110 044

SAGE Publications Asia-Pacific Pte Ltd
3 Church Street
#10-04 Samsung Hub
Singapore 049483

Editor: Matthew Waters
Assistant editor: Jasleen Kaur
Production editor: Rachel Burrows
Copyeditor: Sarah Bury
Proofreader: Brian McDowell
Marketing manager: Abigail Sparks
Cover design: Francis Kenney
Typeset by: C&M Digitals (P) Ltd, Chennai, India
Printed in the UK

Library of Congress Control Number: 2020941911

British Library Cataloguing in Publication data

A catalogue record for this book is available from the British Library

ISBN 978-1-5297-4320-3
ISBN 978-1-5297-4319-7 (pbk)

At SAGE we take sustainability seriously. Most of our products are printed in the UK using responsibly sourced papers and boards. When we print overseas we ensure sustainable papers are used as measured by the PREPS grading system. We undertake an annual audit to monitor our sustainability.

It is difficult to get a man to understand something, when his salary depends upon his not understanding it.

Upton Sinclair (*I, Candidate for Governor: And How I Got Licked*, 1935)

CONTENTS

LIST OF TABLES

LIST OF FIGURES

ABOUT THE AUTHOR

Amos Owen Thomas was a docent/reader in international business at Stockholm University until his recent retirement and remains associated with the Emerging Markets Research Group of its Stockholm Business School. For almost 30 years he served at eight universities in Australia, the Netherlands, the UK, Namibia, Singapore and Papua New Guinea. In that time, he also taught and researched for short periods in about 30 countries in East Asia, Central Asia, Middle East, Western Europe and South America. Prior to academia, Amos was employed or consulted for 15 years in business, government and non-profit sectors in a few countries around the Asia-Pacific region.

CHAPTER 1
CHARTING THE BORDERLESS

Credit: jgeheest/pixabay

Quest to Query

Evidence of shadow trades is often hidden in plain sight, in the products and services we avail ourselves of in contemporary societies worldwide. These could be the workers in nail bars, fast-fashion in department stores, fruit in supermarkets, transplant surgeries in hospitals, chocolate confectionary, jewellery, ubiquitous smartphones, and so on endlessly. So how does one extricate the illicit operations such as exploited labour, conflict minerals, arms sales and tax evasion from the legitimate organisations that deliver these? Does lack of economic opportunity, discrepancy between law and enforcement, and high prices for desired goods and services stimulate the growth of shadow trades? If illicit trade is symbiotic with or parasitic on legitimate corporations, are there gradations in legitimacy and what could be the catalysts for change? This book represents a long quest, over a decade in gestation, prompted by periodic exposés in news-magazines and television-documentaries which led to a search for further sources of information, such as were available. Inter-government and non-government organisations have done laudable work researching and advocating on issues related to shadow trades such as in arms, drugs, organ harvesting, and conflict minerals that know no borders. Of late, a few authors and editors have written and compiled research on selected illicit operations and transnational crime, though seldom on illicit operation intersects with legitimate entities from a critical global business perspective, as this book seeks to.

Scanning the Horizon

Timeless Trades

Nothing is altogether new about a dark side to global business since illicit practices have existed side-by-side with legitimate trade in goods and services down through history. The trans-Atlantic slave trade of the 17th to 19th centuries was an intrinsic part of legitimate trade in cotton, sugar and other goods between the so-called Old World and New. Similar trade in humans existed across the Sahara and from Arabia down the east coast of Africa alongside trade in salt, gold and textiles. In Asia, opium was exported by colonial powers from India to China in exchange for tea and silk, among other legitimate products desired in Europe. Armed conflicts have often been waged to gain control of the sourcing and logistics of natural resources to support industry and economy. The current deficit in business research would seem to imply that such trades no longer exist, are relatively insignificant today, or at least do not impinge on legitimate global business. Yet the very globalisation of markets in the late 20th and early 21st centuries, through lowered barriers to the movement of finance, information, goods and people worldwide, is at the heart of the burgeoning shadow trades as well. Just as in the past and regardless of extant laws prohibiting these, the illicit businesses today share the same supply chains and are being incorporated into goods for legitimate markets, with this entwining characterising the shadow trades.

Despite all the focus on explicating international trade in recent decades, scant attention has been paid to the concurrent growth of a dark side in human trafficking, money laundering, waste dumping, arms exporting and the like, although such trade taints many legitimate global businesses. These are not just ethical issues for sociologists, political scientists, geographers, environmental engineers and lawyers alone to concern themselves with, but for political advocates of free trade, business academics and management practitioners as well. Drawing on information on these trades in the public domain, the news media, as well as other academic sources in the social sciences, humanities, even physical and medical sciences, this book endeavours to analyse the catalysts of present-day shadow trades in terms of economic differentials, corporate culpability and government negligence. While some secondary data are available on the shadow trades, given their nature, these are of necessity estimates needing to be triangulated or otherwise harmonised for reliability. Primary data remains far more limited given the significant risk, cost and opacity challenging all who attempt its collection, whether researchers or journalists, but this deficiency ought to be no barrier to revealing the dark side to global business and addressing the accompanying socio-economic injustice.

Attention Deficits

Much has been published about the liberalisation of international trade and its generally positive benefits for regional economies and multinational corporations involved. Yet scarce mention is made of the unofficial and dubious trades that thrive within the same world economy. Although illicit and legitimate businesses are inextricably intertwined, whether by design or default, scant research has been done in the business and management disciplines, with the possible exception of economics and finance on the arms trade and money laundering. Within academia, research on some exemplars of the shadow trade phenomenon are published, primarily by researchers mostly from the social sciences and sometimes the natural sciences. Drugs smuggling and human trafficking have received considerable attention in criminology and public policy. Toxic waste dumping and human organ harvesting are largely covered by the environmental and medical sciences, respectively. While there have been books focusing on specific shadow trades, such as the arms industry, sex trade, art smuggling and human trafficking, these have largely been written by journalists. It is regrettable that these trades have seldom been addressed collectively, not least from a business perspective. Given this relative indifference to the shadow trades, this book highlights the opportunity for academics to collaborate with industry, civil society and government towards tackling the environments that enable as well as the business models underpinning them.

By and large, public and corporate advocates of the free market in international trade do not appear to address the immorality of shadow trades that thrive within its far-flung operations across borders. It has taken civil society activists and non-government organisations to spearhead the requisite of social responsibility and sustainability to which corporations are being held. Perhaps legitimate businesses need likewise to be educated into distancing themselves from illicit ones that nonetheless share the same supply chains, financial institutions, communications technologies and favourable trade treaties, tarnishing consumers and citizens alike. Far more than corporate social responsibility narrowly defined and practised, the need is for corporate advocacy, even activism, against all forms of shadow trade – including those at some geographic or economic distance from one's own industry. If corporations seem recalcitrant in distancing themselves and governments negligent in monitoring the shadow trades, then civil society and non-government organisations have a vital role to play in goading the former entities into responsible action against these pernicious businesses. That current approaches of regulation, law enforcement and charity do not adequately address the growth of the shadow trades is manifestly evident. It would make for a refreshing change if business and other social science academics would be radically outspoken on socio-economic justice issues, and actively involved against the scourge of shadow trades still ongoing in the 21st century.

Conscience Cognizant

The aim of business research into the dark side of global business ought to be primarily for equipping people in their roles as citizens, consumers, workers, union officials, government policy-makers and administrators, business executives and civil society groups to work better at addressing the very real human fallout. But a major impediment to research has been the lack of transparency about the shadow trades for the obvious reasons of their illicit and illegal nature. It is extremely difficult to separate the contribution of unethical transactions to legitimate sectors of the economy, such as mining and transplant surgery. Furthermore quasi-legal industries including arms sales and waste dumping tend to avoid declaring or to under-declare their transactions so as not to attract public attention. Still, scope exists instead for research of particular shadow trades or illegal business or at least illicit operations in a particular country or between countries, based on secondary data obtained in cooperation with governmental and non-governmental sources plus innovative primary data-gathering, and all subject to rigorous critical analysis. Examining the borderless networks of the shadow trades ought to serve to motivate all stakeholders in the legitimate economy to retaliate with similar creativity.[1] This book's call for research is predicated on having findings that serve ultimately to bring about positive social change and economic justice, not merely inputs for an academic sub-discipline.

Theories of business ethics generally do not encompass the shadow trades, but only legitimate enterprises that might face ethical conundrums in some part of their operations. The cases that graduate students and in-service executives are exposed to in business ethics courses seem to have somewhat neat demarcations of the extent of culpability of the firm, which are far from accurate reflections of the real world of global business. It would be convenient if the shadow trades introduced above could be clearly distinguished from legitimate ones, but that is plainly not the case. Thus the average consumer is invariably ignorant that the perfectly legal products and services on the market that he or she uses may have the taint of illegitimate businesses and/or illicit operations. While proponents of shadow trades might exploit loopholes in the diversity of legal systems governing commerce across national borders, there is near-universality of moral standards that should apply to their consequent victims. Thus more comprehensive models and realistic cases need to be generated, if business, government and civil society decision-makers are to be adequately equipped to operate worldwide against shadow trades. Recognisably, such educative endeavours could prove challenging to establish with multi-constituent products globally, and to work effectively in developing and emergent economies, even among their affluent consumers.

Gauging Quantum

Figures Reckoned

The quantum of any shadow trade, whether money laundering, human trafficking, organ harvesting, contraband smuggling, toxic waste disposal, conflict minerals or small-arms sales, makes them significant global businesses in their own right. Although each might seem miniscule *vis-à-vis* the legitimate international trade in merchandise and commercial services, the inroads of such shadow trades into those sectors of the world economy taint numerous products and services, and unwittingly their end-users, consumer and industrial. The major impediment to uncovering these shadow trades is the characteristic lack of transparency of illicit businesses across borders, although commendable research has been done by non-government organisations (NGOs) and inter-government organisations (IGOs). Less than 5 percent of the millions of containers tend to be physically inspected and 80 percent of international trade uses open account transactions that provide the facilitating financial institutions with little information on amounts and identities. Further documentation of this dark side of global business comes via investigative journalism in the news media, rather than business media, but generally not from academic publications. Nonetheless estimating the extent of these shadow trades is foundational for ethical engagement to mitigate their adverse societal impact by action directed at undermining their business model as the key.

Estimates of shadow trades such as human trafficking, organ harvesting, resource plunder and small-arms sales typically have a range of value (Table 1.1). Further estimates for these and other shadow trades covered in this book such as waste disposal, tax evasion and large arms will be dealt with in their specific chapters. The largest – counterfeiting and drugs trafficking – have received considerable research attention elsewhere and so are not dealt with in depth here except for their intersects with the shadow trades covered. Money laundering, corruption and organised crime tend not to be estimated separately given their overlap with, and/or derivation from, other shadow trades.

Table 1.1   Selected shadow trades: annual value[3]

TYPE OF TRADE	ESTIMATED ANNUAL VALUE [USD]	ESTIMATED ANNUAL VALUE [EUR]
Counterfeiting	923.0 billion-1.6 trillion	808.9 billion-1.4 trillion
Drug trafficking	426.0-652.0 billion	373.3-571.4 billion
Human trafficking	**152.2 billion**	**133.4 billion**
Illegal logging	**52.0-157.0 billion**	**45.6-137.6 billion**
Unregulated fishing	**15.5-36.4 billion**	**13.6-31.9 billion**
Illegal mining	**12.0-48.0 billion**	**10.5-42.1 billion**
Crude oil theft	**5.2-11.9 billion**	**4.6-10.4 billion**
Illegal wildlife trade	**5.0-23.0 billion**	**4.4-20.2 billion**
Small arms trafficking	**1.7-3.5 billion**	**1.5-3.1 billion**
Cultural property trafficking	**1.2-1.6 billion**	**1.1-1.4 billion**
Organ trafficking	**840.0 million-1.7 billion**	**736.0 million-1.5 billion**
TOTAL	**1.6-2.2 TRILLION**	**1.4-1.9 TRILLION**

Note: Shadow trades marked in bold are featured within this book, while some of the others are alluded to

Copyright © Global Financial Integrity, 'Transnational Crime and the Developing World,' 2017. Used with permission.

The value of shadow trades might seem miniscule vis-à-vis global merchandise exports which totalled USD17.4 trillion, while commercial services were USD5.25 trillion and e-commerce USD27.7 trillion, as accounted by the World Trade Organization (WTO)[2]. However, as this book will argue, it is highly problematic to separate the contribution of illicit transactions to legitimate sectors of the world economy such as mining, agriculture, finance and health industries. Even quasi-legal sectors of the capitalist world system, such as arms sales and waste dumping, have much incentive to under-declare their transactions so as not to attract public attention and rancour. For obvious reasons the illegality and secrecy surrounding substantial parts of shadow trades constitute a major hurdle to formal research and the collection of definitive statistics. Nonetheless given the high socio-economic costs to the countries impacted, the virtual silence – whether incidentally, accidentally or deliberately – on involvement of legitimate business in various shadow trades ought not continue unchallenged.

Media Mentions

Notable examples of shadow trades that have come to international attention through the media include forms of resources mining in conflict zones used to fund civil wars, such as in West and Central Africa. Diamonds, other gems, gold, other metals and rare earths are not easily detected in their transport across borders and hence they are useful also in laundering profits and funding purchases of arms and military equipment. Arms industries in the industrialised world, subsidised and supported diplomatically by their governments as being legitimate, yet periodically make the headlines over corruption. Less is made in the media of their connection with well-publicised conflict, refugees and consequent human trafficking and people smuggling. Yet another shadow trade is the growing and smuggling of hard drugs such as cocaine from Bolivia and Columbia via other Latin American and Caribbean states into North America, or heroin from Afghanistan and Myanmar via Central Asian countries into Europe. Likewise, some of this goes to fund warlords, insurgencies and ethnic strife to the detriment of the people's lives and their countries' economies. Relatively little mention is made of the shadow trade in medical tourism and questionable pharmaceuticals which, while raking in profits for their suppliers, risk the lives and health of users, resulting in an economic and social cost borne usually by governments of the least developed countries. Pure shades of black and white in international trade rarely exist, as many legitimate businesses might be involved partially, indirectly or possibly unwittingly in illicit operations, and vice versa.

Although the media are the most common source, the dearth of regular news and investigatory documentaries on the shadow trades could represent a form of self-censorship, as their owners fear offending advertisers and business audiences. Instead the preference is on positive features that promote the consumption of goods and positive attitudes towards corporations, rather than to seem to allege the participation of multinational corporations in the shadow trades, even if unwittingly. Media corporations may also be parts of conglomerates that include other businesses sensitive to investigatory journalism covering the shadow trades that might implicate them, and apply direct or informal pressure on editors and journalists to stay silent. In some countries, journalists are at risk, in much the same way as activists, of assault, kidnap, murder and disappearances when investigating illicit operations that feed into shadow trades and thus seeking to raise awareness among society and government of their harm. By no means do the shadow trades covered by this book comprise an exhaustive list; there are many linkages between various trades, both legitimate and illicit, that have yet to be investigated by the media as well as research organisations.

Wronging Rights

What might seem like harmless, if hypocritical, protection of local industry in the industrialised world via tariffs and non-tariff barriers can and does have dire consequences for the developing world. Combined with neo-colonial access by corporations from the industrialised world to developing world markets for their manufactured goods and specialist services, the extraction of the latter's resources for production regularly decimates their economies. Oftentimes government attempts at combating the shadow trades are targeted at the vulnerable poor caught up at the extreme end of the supply chains, such as the peasant farmers, illicit distillers, smuggler 'mules' and street pedlars, all minions who are readily replaceable in the trade. Meanwhile the wealthy elite and influential businesspersons profiting from the borderless value-chain of drugs are left relatively untouched by law enforcement. All efforts at stemming the tide of shadow trades via public policy, stricter laws, bilateral agreements and market mechanisms seem doomed to failure unless the broader issues of socio-economic discrepancy and imperialistic domination of the world economy are adequately addressed. What is seldom acknowledged is the fact that such social injustice and economic violence invariably comes back to haunt the industrialised countries, such as through the problems of irregular migration, drug smuggling, terrorism and climate change.

   As an instance of unthinking strategy proving counter-productive, national security concerns upon the global war on terror launched by the US government after 9/11 came into conflict with the neo-liberalism it espoused worldwide following the dissolution of the Soviet Union about a decade earlier. Measures to monitor shadow trades, the latter conflated as a means of financing terrorism, were developed in the US context which then cordoned off legitimate world economic activity as well. Notably, the gravity economic model traditionally used to explain international trade, both illicit and legitimate, has been found to be a major determinant of trade-based money laundering, implying that criminals use the practice to hide from stricter regulations.[4] Transposed to the different context of the Middle East and North Africa, this paradigm criminalises informal funds transfers, driving borderless flows from legitimate trades into the dark market where these become available for financing terrorism.[5] Since laws to combat terrorism financing have clamped down on the use of financial institutions, criminal syndicates are now disguising their funds through transnational transactions that falsify prices and quantities. Nevertheless legitimate trade itself can be a conduit for the illegitimate, although this has yet to receive sufficient attention apart from advice to government about the warning signs such as companies doing business in high-risk countries or in high-risk products, and shipping products inconsistent to their business.[6]

Viewing Askance

Economic-Commercial Cynicism

Supply chains involving trafficked people or coerced labour, together with other shadow trades such as minerals from war zones, dumping toxic wastes from manufacturing process or discarded products, pollutants left in the country of production often result in products that are marketed legitimately in both industrialised and developing countries. Multinational corporations typically outsource production to developing countries to have a competitive edge in international markets, and many do not adequately audit the human resources practices of their contractors and other suppliers lest it affect their profitability. Denial of the existence today of labour exploitation and resource looting, and that even legitimate businesses might be complicit in shadow trades via the latter's borderless supply chains, is little different from the approach of colonial regimes and imperialistic traders that opposed the abolition of slavery over the past few centuries in various parts of the world. Corporations may have been convinced about the necessity of their social responsibility and seem reasonably complaint with Triple Bottom Line reporting. Nonetheless, much of their efforts have been reactionary and cursory in protecting their own reputational equity and financial profitability, rather than proactive in instituting change in the management of transnational operations within their industry and the countries they operate in.

If shadow trades are facilitated by the same factors as legitimate global business, then policies designed to impact one will invariably affect the other. Some scholars have persuasively argued that deviant globalisation is inextricably entwined with legitimate business in the world economy, and thus cannot be eliminated without severe, somewhat unpredictable consequences to the latter.[7] In fact, instead of being the target of moral outrage, often expressed patronisingly by influential voices in industrialised economies, these shadow trades may be the primary means by which those in developing countries can participate in and profit from the neo-liberal world economy, largely meeting pent-up demand by circumventing the regulatory environments of the trading economies. Given their borderless networks, any expectation that national regulation along with enforcement will, in and of itself, limit or eliminate shadow trades might well be futile. However, if the shadow trades can be seen not just as feeding off legitimate business, but also as competitive sectors, then the latter could prove capable of undermining the former.

Political-Legal Negligence

Illicit operations are sometimes tolerated by governments in the hope that participating businesses, both domestic and foreign, bring economic benefits which are best not interfered with. Thus minimal prosecutions of criminal syndicates for shadow trades might signal political corruption rather than low incidence of their borderless operations. Composite assessment based on victim surveys, perception of business consultancies, homicides, corruption rankings, and estimates of the black economy proposes that organised crime is most prevalent in countries where the rule of law is lax and the resultant high cost of doing legitimate business disadvantages advancement.[8] Crime syndicates based in various countries do trade with each other worldwide, as well as with legitimate businesses. Chinese triad gangs are said to have sold their trafficked people to Italian mafia for service in Naples sweatshops, while the Columbian Cali cartel is alleged to have negotiated drug distribution franchises in Asia with the Chinese triads, and the Russian and Italian mafia might even jointly own a commercial bank. While all such quasi-national syndicates dabble in a range of objectionable trades, it is also alleged to be with some deference to relative expertise or comparative advantage, with the Nigerians specialising in credit-card and bank fraud, Columbians at counterfeiting, Chinese at human trafficking and Russians at business scams.[9] Thus by no means do the shadow trades listed in this book constitute an exhaustive list, for there are many linkages and intersects between various global businesses and transnational operations, both legal and illicit.

Whether for political expedience or economic self-interest the industrialised world tends to raise barriers to trade which work to the detriment of both their own countries and those of the developing and emergent world through fostering conditions for shadow trades. If remote regions, mountainous terrain, circuitous river deltas that facilitate cross-border transportation for shadow trades are near impossible to police, do the interventions need to be done at the urban centres of trade? Could governments instead nationally or regionally penalise businesses with dubious links to shadow trade by undermining their financial profitability? But are accomplices in shadow trades merely entrepreneurs driven by necessity, even if they are eventually seduced by the returns for taking high risks? Might public policy and market forces be transformed to favour the legitimate corporations over the shadowy ones? Would rewarding those businesses that endeavour scrupulously not to have such links in their transnational supply chains with incentives and tax breaks suffice? Or should that be done by consumers being made more aware of shadow trades and being driven to demand accountability by businesses, rewarding those that do respond with customer loyalty, despite any cost premium?

Extending Boundaries

Comprehending to Apprehend

Should the legal penalties for human trafficking, smuggling and bonded labour be raised to match those of trading in contraband drugs? Could allowing financial reward for organ donations, live or cadaveric, in industrialised countries eliminate the present global market for body parts from developing and emergent countries? Would factoring the full cost of recycling or disposal into the product price reduce the demand for new and more products and thus the waste dumping in developing and emergent economies? Could social justice, pacifist and non-violence movements mitigate the onset of war and civil strife, and thus the need for arms to settle conflicts and enforce peace? Might international legislation for greater transparency of trans-national financial transactions mitigate money laundering, including that related to the other shadow trades? Many corporations trumpet their green credentials about being eco-friendly and sustainable while being less than candid about their transgressions, and are routinely found out to be green-washing with dire business consequences. In the case of shadow trades, there has been no similar pressure yet for corporations to declare their non-involvement, let alone for governments to take proactive action. This book embodies the hope that corporations, governments and non-profit organisation will be nudged to advocate for socio-ethical justice and thus the shadow trades could be addressed by all countries across whose borders these operate worldwide.

Forerunners and Lineage

Over the past decade or so there has been a steady trickle of academic and general books related to shadow trades which deserve acknowledgement so that this latest contribution to be put in context, albeit none have been from within the field of global business with which all these trades invariably intersect. Already cited in this chapter was a pioneering and highly influential book which addresses rather concisely a few more illicit trades than this present book does. Although now over a decade and a half old and understandably dated, relatively little has changed since.[10] In the 2000s another volume about transnational threats[11], also already acknowledged, foregrounded national security issues from a somewhat US-centric standpoint, whereas the present volume takes a borderless socio-economic stance.[12]

The 2010s saw, first, the publication of a book focused on the global arms trade, which provided comprehensive news reportage on this single shadow trade,[13] a topic covered as an in-depth chapter in this present volume. Then a best-seller demonstrated thoroughly the linkage between the drug trade and money-laundering, particularly in Europe and the Americas.[14] Money-laundering in particular is covered in the present volume on a more global scale, as are – to a limited extent – its links to the drug trade. Another book published in the same year adopted a public policy perspective towards a similar range of trades as in this book,[15] although the latter brings a business-oriented one as well. While there was a book published that may appear the closest to the present book,[16] it adopted highly quantitative economic modelling instead of the qualitative critique in this one. An edited volume on organised crime[17] indeed delivers on its promise, although this present tome on shadow trades highlights instead the wider involvement of legitimate business in borderless supply chains. More recently, a book brought a historical perspective to the illegitimate trades and their collective consequences, with a focus on just one,[18] while the present volume deals with various shadow trades in turn and majors on their possible mitigation. Perhaps the latest tome related to shadow trades is another edited volume which explores some similar arenas as the present sole-authored one, albeit from the scholarly viewpoint of the international political economy discipline.[19] The book you now hold in your hands adds yet another voice to this gradually growing chorus, one that adopts an interdisciplinary and business perspective on these and other shadow trades while especially commending interventions to mitigate their impact.

Since the mid-1990s, through presentations at conferences and seminars, this book's author began to call for colleagues worldwide within the general business disciplines to address this gap in our knowledge and these received seemingly positive response. However, when expanded versions of those conference papers were submitted to academic business journals, the muted response from their editors and reviewers betrayed a lack of interest. First and foremost, I was informed that such papers might be better submitted to journals in other social sciences related to the issues in each trade or criminology in general. Secondly, even though scant business literature and theoretical frameworks are available on the shadow trades *per se* to the best of my knowledge, their apparent lack in those articles submitted was queried. Appeals that these submissions were primarily a call for researchers to develop such literature and theory, not a seminal work, seemingly failed to convince the gatekeepers to established knowledge. Thirdly, their dependence on secondary data and dearth of primary data deemed the articles unacceptable for publication despite the implied assumption that hard primary data on these dubious borderless networks can be obtained without great risk to life and limb. Without funding from corporations, governments or universities worked in over the years, this research has been a private quest. It took the advice of an editor visiting from another major publishing house for me to begin compiling those articles towards a short e-book instead. It is due to the perseverance of a commissioning editor at its present publisher that you now hold this much more substantial printed tome in your hands, completed many years on.

Interrogating Legitimacy

Addressing this dark side of global business requires uncovering its causes and catalysts, perpetrators and facilitators, vested interests and beneficiaries. While international crime is strictly defined legally as activities that nation-states perpetrate on other nation-states or parts of their own and others, shadow trade is perpetuated by corporations, organisations, informal groups and even individuals. These take advantage of regional political-economic integration, trade treaties, and renewed nationalism in new states, break-away provinces, dysfunctional or non-functioning states in an increasingly globalised world. The uncritical promotion of international trade as the means of co-opting developing countries into the capitalist world economy on the questionable promise of equitable trade terms and sustainable economic growth needs challenging. While there is no consensus of definition, the shadow economy is often treated as synonymous with, and seldom differed from, the black, hidden and underground trades[20]. As characterised in this book and to be defined in the next chapter, shadow trades are less hidden and can be associated indirectly with legitimate businesses, as much as to illegitimate ones, though these links are still seldom readily accessible to assess comprehensively. Nonetheless a fair amount can be known or reasonably conjectured about the nurturing contexts for these pernicious businesses and the complex borderless network of their illicit operations in which governments and corporations may be complicit, either explicitly or unwittingly. By exploring their antecedents, dynamics and consequences, this book aims to uncover what we know already or might yet need to know, as well as what we can learn from their *modus operandi* that could be of value to legitimate businesses for distancing themselves from, and competing against, illegitimate ones.

Shadow trades are far from independent of the legitimate world economy but benefit from, participate in and contribute to it or, in other words, are symbiotic, parasitic, or possibly both. Thus understanding their business structure, supply chains, operations and markets, especially the sources of their profitability, may be more instrumental in undermining their growth, even their existence in the long term. After reviewing the ethical imperative, subsequent chapters on selected shadow trades seek to make the case for why governments, academia and corporations alike can no longer treat the issues of socio-economic justice they raise as being of peripheral import. These shadow trades, ranging from human trafficking and organ harvesting to arms sales and money laundering, are subsumed under broader categories as per the chapter titles, illustrate the shades of illegitimacy, extent of integration into the world economy and varied impact on people and societies. After tracking the links between these and with yet other borderless networks, a tentative typology by relative legitimacy of entities and operations involved is proposed. Finally by explicating the intersections between shadow trades and various business sub-disciplines, this book addresses how the present dearth of business-related research and managerial interventions on shadow trades might be overcome.

Structure and Purpose

Agenda for Audiences

In uncovering the shadow trades, the objective of this book is to draw attention to what is often hidden in plain view, namely from everyday products and services, to technologies and the supply chains that undergird them. It is not intended to be comprehensive on each trade or all possible shadow trades, but has been selective of certain trades to illustrate the breadth and depth of the issue. There are indeed a few books and many articles on particular trades by specialists in related disciplines and practice, and this book lays no claim to similar in-depth expertise in any specific shadow trade. However, it draws attention to the imperative of bringing interdisciplinary knowledge to bear on tackling all shadow trades and to not remain within academic research silos. Given the difficulty of obtaining data, the estimates cited in it may not necessarily be the most up to date, but these nonetheless serve simply to make a point. What this book aims to do, first, is to demonstrate that these trades are sizeable and successful businesses in their own right and deserve study of their management, marketing and financial models. Secondly, it raises the unacknowledged inroads of shadow trades into mainstream business, debunking any notion that there is a clear hard line between legitimate and illegitimate businss sectors within the world economy. Thirdly, this book proposes that understanding the business models behind these shadow trades might hold a key to undermining their growth, rendering them less effective or at least mitigating their socio-economic impact.

While undoubtedly written by an academic, this book is not meant solely for other educators and researchers, but also expectantly for practitioners like business executives, policy-makers, government officials and social activists, among others, concerned with bringing about significant change on the shadow trades. Ambitiously, it seeks to serve as a cross-over resource, from academic handbook to practitioner guidebook, advocating the translation of knowledge into awareness and then advocacy and action through adopting an accessible and jargon-free style for readability and ease of citing in strategies or policies. Overall, the orientation of this hybrid book is towards applied ethics, rather than moral philosophy, in the tradition of public intellectualism instead of ivory-tower theorising. It is certainly written with a mature audience of graduate students and middle managers in mind, in the hope that as current and potential business, political and civil society leaders they will be sensitised to such issues as and when encountered. Most crucially, this author hopes by so doing to motivate the application of expertise to undermining their business models, and thus contribute towards at least diminishing these shadow trades, if not their eventual eradication. In bringing together diverse shadow trades for analysis from an inter-disciplinary perspective, this book further constitutes a call to action by thoughtful citizens and consumers, leaders and managers, worldwide.

Scope and Coverage

Extant knowledge

The chapter following on in this book, entitled 'Darkness Enlightened', makes an overarching analysis of the issue of shadow trades within global business in terms of extant related knowledge. To achieve this in the light of limited business sources, this second chapter surveys the inter-disciplinary literature related to the shadow trades and defines such related concepts as legitimate trade, tainted industry, business ethics, political economy, neo-colonialism, socio-economic justice, corruption and non-transparency. The subsequent six chapters deal with broadly-categorised shadow trades in turn, progressing from those that are more personal in impact, such as human migration and organ transplant, and culminating with those that are more impersonal, such as the arms industry and financial outflows. In terms of structure, each of these chapters begins with an overview and then a section portraying a brief history of a particular shadow trade before noting its contemporary manifestations as per media portrayal and public perception. The sections following that seek to delineate the magnitude and nature of that trade, with definitions and statistics, supplemented by exploration of each borderless network reach and related narratives. The penultimate section of each chapter attempts analysis of the antecedents, concomitants and consequences of the trade and proposes interventions for resolution, often accompanied with a schematic diagram for clarity. The concluding section comprises the commentary by the author on what we know and how we could act, and is followed by a section providing further resources to peruse. Most chapters are appended by a 'Dim Domain' quasi-case that illustrates a particular practice or set of phenomena within that shadow trade and raises some rhetorical questions for reflection and/or controversial issues for debate.

Selected trades

The first chapter on a specific shadow trade is the third in this book on 'Irregular Migration and Labour Exploitation'. It outlines locations and persistence of trafficking, bondage, coercion and smuggling of persons as well as their subsequent exploitation, not only in the developing and emergent but also in the industrialised world, using definitive estimates from reports by international organisations, inter-government and non-government, as well as information from reliable media and academic sources. It seeks to model the antecedent push-pull factors, such as civil strife, trade policies, climate change and poverty, and consequent links to specific types of work in selected industries. The fourth chapter on 'Transplant Tourism and Organ Requisition' points out the role of economics and culture in sourcing body parts and the role of global diaspora in the location of surgery which has generally gone unnoticed. It concludes by evaluating means of raising local supply and dampening the global demand for human organs as strategic responses to this dubious trade. The fifth chapter is on the shadow trade of 'Resource Pilferage and Environment Degradation' and traces the sourcing of metals, precious stones, rare earths, oil, timber, wildlife, cultural heritage, and other valuable materials, particularly from conflict zones in developing and emergent countries. Invariably this shadow trade results in livelihood disruption, humanitarian law violations, even war crimes by government forces, separatist movements, warlord militias, criminal syndicates, terrorists and other armed groups.

In the second half of the book, the sixth chapter on 'Waste Transhipment and Hazardous Recycling' charts how this process encompasses everything from household trash, e-waste and organic waste to industrial chemicals, ship-breaking and nuclear by-products. Growth of this shadow trade is fostered by both the increase of waste generation in the industrialised world and disposal needs due to stringent environmental laws, as well as the investment opportunity and political corruption that this waste represents for the developing world. This shadow trade, more than any other, has major implications for climate change as well as its mitigation. The seventh chapter on 'Arms Conveyance and Military Contracting' identifies major arms exporter and importer countries, forms of government support, mechanics of arms transfers, commercialisation of military services as well as the socio-economic costs of war and legal liability. Despite the efforts of some inter-government and non-government organisations to develop initiatives on arms control, though not on mercenary forces, this shadow trade is thriving. The final chapter on a specific shadow trade is the eighth, on 'Financial Sleight and Money Laundering', which documents how kleptocrats of dysfunctional states in the developing world, crime syndicates, terrorist organisations, traffickers and smugglers, among others, have been able to launder their ill-gotten income and/or move funds abroad surreptitiously. It queries the collaboration of the legitimate banking sector with corrupt politicians and organised crime – as well as multinational corporations and mega-rich individuals – in depriving especially developing countries of their lawful revenues by exploiting tax loopholes and using financial havens.

Perusing suggestion

Given their diversity, each chapter on a related cluster of shadow trades may be read independently and it may be a strategy for one's reading to begin with the one that is of greatest personal or organisational interest. At the very least, though, all perusal should be done in conjunction with the first and last chapters, which set the various trades within broader economic and social contexts. Besides, it will soon be evident upon reading even a couple of chapters that there are links to shadow trades covered in other chapters, as well as far more trades than can be covered in a single volume. Thus the penultimate chapter on 'Tracking Cross-Currents' identifies further shadow trades that will have to be tackled in future, many of them tied to or extensions of the ones covered in this book. While still not comprehensive, shadow trade categories within that chapter should serve as a catalyst for all readers – whether managers, consultants, activists and researchers – to explore those trades most relevant to their own geo-political, socio-economic and industrial sector contexts. In education and training contexts, each of that penultimate chapter's sections and subsections should provide multiple further topics for specialist/guest lectures, project presentations, term papers or research seminars.

The concluding chapter on the 'Imperative for Engagement' attempts to draw together the linkages between the various shadow trades and propose a tentative typology to serve as a foundation for action on overcoming their adverse consequences for people and the environment. It aims to demonstrate the intersects between each shadow trade and other related ones as well as legitimate global business, raising issues that are critical for all societies, governments and industry to address. The quest for objective information according to strict standards of the physical sciences may be somewhat unrealistic in the applied social sciences. Rather, informed opinion based on extant knowledge, across the most reliable sources available, ought to suffice as the basis for intelligent debate and thoughtful decision-making. By design, this final chapter unapologetically uses somewhat polemic language in spelling out the ways that individuals and organisations might be challenged to bring about radical socio-economic change, through collective action on the prevalence of shadow trades. With such a format this book endeavours to be a source of knowledge and inspiration to corporate executives, political leaders, government officials, inter-government organisations, civil society, non-government agencies, scholars, citizens and consumers alike, to grapple independently as well as collaboratively with how these shadow trades may be addressed.

Evidence and Nomenclature

Before concluding this introductory chapter, a word must be said about the integrity of data incorporated and classificatory terminology and illustrative cases in the constituent chapters of the book. As acknowledged earlier in this chapter, definitive information is scarce, given the very nature of shadow trades, but there have been valiant efforts by inter-government and non-government organisations, research institutes and established news media. In a post-truth age, this book has endeavoured to provide recent secondary data and reliable estimates from the most reputable sources available at the time of research and writing, including original extracts from their reports, all duly cited and/or with permissions obtained for authencity. As data are continuously being updated in our information-rich world, whatever is cited in this book ought to be treated only as illustrative and instructive of the phenomenon. The avid reader ought to be able to track down newer information as it becomes available online after this book is published, either at the sources cited or through the further resources listed. It is hoped that this book will spur commitment to the collection and collating of more data, and that there will be the greatest interest in applying that information, such that a later edition might even be redundant. If the intermediate chapters seem somewhat theory-light, this is a deliberate decision and undertaken without apology because of the book's proclivity towards encouraging advocacy, activism and action among its readership. Throughout this applied social science book, the emphasis will be on creating knowledge and insight through action research involving evaluating judicious interventions, rather than merely theoretical conceptualisation.

Furthermore, readers should note that the terms 'industrialised', 'emergent' and 'developing' in reference to economies, countries and worlds are used throughout this book as an approximate classification of economic development, of which there are many. Needless to say there are alternative terminologies – such as 'First World/Third World', 'Middle Income/Low Income', 'North/South', 'Post-Industrial/ Least-Developed' – to describe them. Suffice it to say that all of these overlap along a continuum and the categorisations of countries vary, and certain countries have been in a flux between these levels over time. The use of the particular designations in this book are merely to make certain arguments about the shadow trades and are not meant to pronounce value-judgement on the status and role of any country or economy. Although the terms 'international', 'global', 'transnational' and 'multinational' do have differences in precise definition, there is not always consensus. Thus, these are often treated synonymously by the media, management books and occasionally in academic literature too. For the sake of simplicity, yet clarity and differentiation in this book, such descriptors are used alongside the entity most aptly so described; hence its consistent use of conjoint terms: 'international trade', 'global business/markets', 'world economy', 'multinational corporation' and 'transnational operation' including crime. Generally in this book, the terms 'legitimate/ illegitimate' are used to qualify entities such as organisations, corporations and governments, while the synonymous terms 'licit/illicit' are used to describe their operations, such as transactions, logistics and sourcing, all with reference to the ethical criteria most applicable. Both the terms 'legitimate' and 'licit' are closely allied to legality, though the terms 'moral' and 'ethical' represent a higher set of values and attitudes, such that a practice might well be legal but still highly unethical. The terms 'ethical/unethical' will routinely be used of entities and their actions, while the terms 'moral/immoral' will tend to be assigned to persons and values expressed. Finally, the term 'borderless' is generally reserved in this book for references related to 'shadow trades' which are typically undertaken by a flexible network of corporations, groups and individuals comprising a mix of legitimate and illegitimate actors, adaptively utilising both illicit and licit operations across single or multiple provincial, national, regional and international borders.

Dedication and Commendation

The gist of this legacy project of the author on the shadow trades has been shared with the literally thousands of people across all continents that this author had the rare privilege to teach over a three-decade career and from whom he has learnt much in turn about their historical, political, geographic, economic, societal and cultural contexts. This book is certainly in appreciation for the one-in-a-few-hundred learners who have kept in touch intermittently after graduation or tracked me down decades later to update about their careers and lives since. Their tales affirm my conviction that education is invaluable to transforming the world incrementally, even if society in general does not always appear to recognise its true worth to fund adequately. Most of all, this tome is dedicated to an even more select group who embraced this non-conformist of a professor, a misfit socialist in capitalist schools, and warmed to his inter-disciplinary, cosmopolitan, critical and socio-economic justice perspectives without worrying needlessly whether these would be examinable with evident bias, and continue to show curiousity about this obscure research shared once with them in prior nascent form.

This book certainly owes a debt to the rare exceptional colleagues who subscribe to the notion of academic freedom, indulged my eclectic interests that they did not quite comprehend and yet did not discourage this unconventional pursuit of the shadow trades, even long years after we had parted ways institution-wise given my peripatetic career. There have also been 'friends indeed' both inside and outside academia who proved 'friends in deed' during bouts of stress and illness over the years. They certainly know who they are, though if not, I would be glad to affirm my gratitude personally. All the same this book owes little to those peers prone to disdain any endeavours outside their areas of expertise, and especially the odd supervisor who could not grasp the principle in academia of being first among equals. One can only hope these few come to recognise themselves so someday, just as distinctly as many others around them well could. May this work be an encouragement to all of us academics to support each other in working inter-disciplinarily and proactively on issues outside the mainstream with a view to having greater societal relevance and enduring impact.

Finally, this book is commended to the leaders today in the business, government and the non-government sectors in the hope that they will be 'conscientisised' or have their conscience spurred to act on knowledge about these shadow trades and others yet. If collaborative efforts against the shadow trades are to prove effective, these need to be both bottom-up as much as top-down by individuals and groups within corporations, government and civil society working in solidarity across borders. Given the risks, it will take courage in challenging dated paradigms and conventional wisdom, confronting socio-economic injustice and unethical practices, speaking truth to power and taking radical stances, as and when needful. Should the present leaders of society remain unmoved, whether by this book or through other media, then perhaps graduate students as the leaders of tomorrow, along with all life-long learners, will catch the vision of being ethically-driven global citizens, becoming champions for advocacy, activism and action against all shadow trades prevalent within our world economy.

Endnotes

1. Naim, M. (2005). It's the illicit economy, stupid. *Foreign Policy*, (151), 96.
2. WTO (2018). *World Trade Statistical Review 2018*. Geneva: World Trade Organisation. [www.wto.org/english/res_e/statis_e/wts2017_e/wts17_toc_e.htm – accessed 15 July 2018].
3. Extracted from Havoscope (2019). The Black Market. [www.havocscope.com/ – accessed 09 August 2019].
4. Ferwerda, J., Kattenberg, M., Chang, H. H., Unger, B., Groot, L., & Bikker, J. A. (2013). Gravity models of trade-based money laundering. *Applied Economics, 45*(22), 3170–3182.
5. Warde, I. (2007). The war on terror, crime and the shadow economy in the MENA countries. *Mediterranean Politics, 12*(2), 233–248.
6. Delston, R. S., & Walls, S. C. (2009). Reaching beyond banks: how to target trade-based money laundering and terrorist financing outside the financial sector. *Case Western Reserve Journal of International Law, 41*, 85.
7. Gilman, N., Goldhammer, J., & Weber, S. (eds.). (2011). *Deviant Globalization: Black Market Economy in the 21st Century*. London and New York: A&C Black.
8. Van Dijk, J. (2007). Mafia markers: assessing organized crime and its impact upon societies. *Trends in Organized Crime, 10*(4), 39–56.
9. Lupsha, P. (1996). Transnational organized crime versus the nation-state. *Transnational Organized Crime, 2*(1), 21–48.
10. Naim, M. (2010). *Illicit: How Smugglers, Traffickers and Copycats are Hijacking the Global Economy*. New York: Random House.
11. Thachuk, K. (ed.). (2007). *Transnational Threats: Smuggling and Trafficking in Arms, Drugs, and Human Life*, 3–22.
12. Glenny, M. (2008). *McMafia: Crime without Frontiers*. London: Bodley Head.
13. Feinstein, A. (2011). *The Shadow World: Inside the Global Arms Trade*. Johannesburg and Cape Town: Jonathan Ball Publishers.
14. Saviano, R. (2016). *Zero Zero Zero: Look at Cocaine and All You See is Powder, Look through Cocaine and You See the World*. London: Penguin Random House/Allen Lane.
15. Efrat, A. (2012). *Governing Guns, Preventing Plunder: International Cooperation against Illicit Trade*. New York: Oxford University Press.
16. Storti, C. C., & De Grauwe, P. (eds.). (2012). *Illicit Trade and the Global Economy*. Cambridge, MA and London: MIT Press.

17. Albanese, J., & Reichel, P. (eds.). (2013). *Transnational Organized Crime: An Overview from Six Continents*. Thousand Oaks, CA: Sage Publications.

18. Shelley, L. I. (2018). *Dark Commerce: How a New Illicit Economy is Threatening our Future*. Princeton, NJ and Oxford: Princeton University Press.

19. Talani, L., & Roccu, R. (eds.). (2019). *The Dark Side of Globalisation*. London: Palgrave Macmillan/Springer.

20. Schneider, F. (2008). Shadow economy. In C. K. Rowley (ed.). *Readings in Public Choice and Constitutional Political Economy*. Boston, MA: Springer. pp. 511–532.

CHAPTER 2
DARKNESS ENLIGHTENED

Credit: Chuttersnap/Unsplash

Overview in Introduction

Shadow trades would seem well framed within the disciplines of business ethics and corporate social responsibility, being as these are the intersection of illicit operations and legitimate organisations. Decades ago, a literature survey of business ethics issues deserving further research attention listed organised labour, social dumping, tobacco promotion, the arms trade, international finance and wealth concentration.[1] Some issues raised then may seem rather quaint today having faced severe constraints in industrialised economies, but many are still persistent in developing and emergent economies. Given the paucity of academic publications on those topics two decades on, that academic call seems to have gone largely unheeded. Another business journal showcased scholarly articles predicting pertinent future ethics issues merely as workplace behaviour, payment for order flow, disadvantaged consumers, and organisational corruption, whistle-blowing and financial restatement among others.[2] Most of these ethical issues may well be pertinent in industrialised economies but have less relevance than more serious ones, such as labour exploitation, resource depletion, arms trade and tax evasion for the rest of the world. Thus, relevant inter-disciplinary literature, including from the political economy and critical theory traditions, needs to be reviewed in order to set shadow trades within the wider context of globalisation, neo-liberalism and disparities of development within capitalist world economy.

Trade Backdrop

Development Paradigms

Critical to an understanding of the phenomenon of shadow trades is the global context of countries at different levels of economic development. While the initial paradigm for development espoused certain socio-demographic and structural prerequisites, the experience of developing countries undermined these theories and demonstrated their a-historicity, paternalism and ethno-centricity. For one thing, capitalism grew out of the peculiar European monarchical/feudal system of the 16th–19th centuries, and for another, the path of the industrialised world subsequently was not without social and economic crises.[3] Whether politically, economically, socially or culturally, the developing world is not comprised of homogeneous countries, let alone potential clones of the industrialised world. Taking a more critical approach, dependency theorists argue that underdevelopment is caused not by socio-cultural factors but by political-economic ones. This updates Marx, who explained historical transformation of societies through the growth of capitalism, which in turn was due to the exploitation of the working class, a model which Lenin expanded to incorporate the relationship between imperial powers and their colonies.[4]

In a determined defence of capitalism against dependency theories, Berger, like many others, seeks to persuade that the efficient productive power and high standard of living of the masses generated in industrialised countries are being replicated in those developing countries which are well incorporated into the world capitalist system.[5] He contrasts these developments of Third World replicating First World ones through economic integration with his control case of the industrial socialism of the Second World, a questionable choice, and postulates that there is an intrinsic link between socialism and inefficient economic and authoritarian political systems. Although capitalism promotes a class system which permits social mobility, individual autonomy and democratic processes, he acknowledges that these are slow processes given the traditional culture and society of the Third World. What Berger does not address, though, is the soft power of capitalism via the commercial media and advertising that shapes a consumerist culture, even if just aspirational by the middle and lower classes. Arguably this neo-colonises developing countries, keeping their economies dependent on an industrialised world model of development through aid, investment, markets and trade.

The alternatives left open to developing countries were to isolate themselves from the capitalist world system or seek to have the terms of international trade radically revised. The former alternative was attempted by those countries which sought to set up an alternative socialist world system which has not been given due credit for standing up to the neo-colonialist dominance by the US.[6] The latter solution of a capitalist world economy was pursued via the General Agreement on Tariffs and Trade (GATT), resulting in the World Trade Organisation (WTO), which gained impetus with the end of the Cold War. But dependency theorists are sceptical of the value of GATT for developing countries, especially those in financial strife coming increasingly under the hegemony of the World Bank (WB) and International Monetary Fund (IMF). After all, the developing countries' lobbying over the 1970s and early 1980s for a post-colonial New International Economic Order (NIEO) through the United Nations was impeded by the US and other industrialised countries which preferred GATT as their platform since, in the latter, the developing countries are not able to act as a collective.[7] Neo-liberal prescriptions then for economy-restructuring, privatisation, deregulation, free markets and the like have been demonstrably poorer in promoting economic turnaround than the Keynesian ones of WB/IMF founding, but there is no democratic accountability to all member countries. With the US government being their largest funder through its Treasury Department, also notably headquartered in that city, the WB and IMF agenda is considerably driven by the former's imperialistic foreign policy, the three entities together constituting the Washington Consensus on managing the world economy.

Core versus Periphery

Based on the experience of Africa and Asia post-independence, Wallerstein formulated world-system theory, a variation of dependency theories.[8] This argues that there exists a world economic system through which capitalist industrialised or core countries, and their multinational corporations, exploit developing or periphery countries through low prices for raw material and high prices for finished goods. As part of the system, semi-periphery countries were both dependent on the core countries and exploitative of the periphery ones, which arguably could be equated with the emergent economies of today. In his prognosis, global integration of this system in favour of the inequitable status quo between nation-states would result in resistance, fragmentation and its ultimate collapse, but for the buffer of semi-peripheral states. Critics from the classical economics school would argue instead for the theory of comparative advantage, which holds that all countries involved are better off through unrestricted trade than if they did not trade at all.[9] Therefore, peripheral countries choose to trade with the core because they find it to their advantage to do so, core countries need not coerce them to do so, and peripheral countries are not necessarily exploited when core countries progress.

Criticisms of world-systems theory revolve around its simplistic one-dimension analysis of causality, namely economic exploitation. Some have put forward alternative models of geo-political factors, primarily citing political power rivalry between nation-states. In contrast to Wallerstein's view of a monolithic world capitalism, and in lieu of Marxist and non-Marxist periodisation, Lash and Urry offer a three-stage model of the development of capitalist economies: liberal, organised and disorganised.[10] The present 'disorganisation' of capitalism in the industrialised countries they attribute to globalising processes from above, such as multinational corporations and international financial markets, decentralising processes from below, such as the decline of mass industries, devolution of government and dispersion of populations, and transformation from within. With the onset of the post-industrial age, national governments have become co-players along with multinational corporations (MNCs), non-government organisations (NGOs) and other inter-government bodies (IGOs) on the world political and economic stage.

Guises of Colonialism

Historic colonialism is defined as domination and subjugation of territory or country by another with imperialistic ambitions to gain political and economic advantage internationally. Colonial powers imposed artificial boundaries that inhabitants never fully accepted, divided ethnic groups or enclosed ethnic rivals within their territories which then persisted, amalgamated on independence as post-colonial nation-states. Post-colonial theorists celebrate new forms of political power in the new era but ignore cultural and historical contexts, and tend to paradoxically advocate resistance to the colonial legacy even while admitting an indebtedness.[11] Cultural hegemony by the new political and intellectual elite of the post-colonial order enables them to sustain local dominance, promoting a cosmopolitan worldview that convinces the oppressed that their subordination is inevitable and justifiable.[12] In some countries local political and economic elites were astute to co-opt, collaborate and compete with global businesses for their own development ends to become emergent economies, while in others the exploitative trade relations went unchallenged, resulting in continued dependency and underdevelopment. Hence most ex-colonies experienced 'pseudo-independence', given the privileged and entrenched position of imperialistic business interests and historic trade links, which often underlie the shadow trades.

Neo-colonialism can thus be characterised as subtle political and economic control over a country, through persistence of the colonial structures, foreign investment, currency pegging, financial loans and development aid. Notably, Sartre posits that this use of capitalism, economic globalisation and cultural imperialism to dominate a country precludes the necessity for exercising military or political intervention.[13] Even though their forms of colonialism differed considerably, trade patterns of Britain and France with their colonies remained largely unchanged after independence.[14] Dominance of the free-market world economy by multinational companies, trade treaties that reaffirm economic difference, regional struggles supported by former colonial powers and widespread corruption in their sponsored local regimes underscore the fact that colonialism does not cease upon political independence. Even the measurement of the corruption as the perception of business leaders in industrialised economies, represents a neo-colonial approach to investment decisions,[15] as is their ambivalence towards the growth of emergent economies.[16]

The emergent economies have been significant in investing with developing countries, notably India and China in Africa to the tune of hundreds of billion US dollars annually, financing governments, extracting resources, sending entrepreneurs and marketing their products, thus making them neo-colonialists with attendant influence without political interference.[17] Notably, China's Belt and Road Initiative (BRI) seeks to provide infrastructure to developing countries for intercontinental trade by land and sea, though the generosity invariably should result in indebtedness, dependency and hegemony. This would seem to confirm Wallerstein's notion of semi-periphery countries in the capitalist world economy exploiting the periphery on behalf of the core or industrialised countries, and for their own political economy objectives. Underlying all these, dominance is predicated on a free-market system being held as the prime means for economic development, even though industrialised countries, such as those in Northern Europe, in particular of social-democratic leanings, demonstrate the successful implementation of the alternative economic model, which includes high social spending and taxes without undermining global competitiveness. The relationship between neo-colonialism and globalisation is seldom detailed, yet essential to understanding the context of the shadow trades.

Vantage Advantage

Global Standpoint

Integration of the world technologically, economically and politically, and the apparent breakdown of barriers between countries, is said to characterise the current era.[18] Globalisation has been typified as the time–space compression of the world and an intensification of global consciousness.[19] Developing countries depend on industrialised ones for investment and technology, while industrialised countries need developing ones for their minerals, agriculture and energy resources, as well as markets for their own industrial and consumer goods. Hence it is assumed by neo-liberalism that any person or entity can compete with others in the pursuit of private business interests. In reality, free markets are scarcely what they claim to be, because this is the rhetoric of political players that exercise economic imperialism over a territory and worldwide capital accumulation.[20] The group of the top seven industrialised countries (G7) and the international financial and trade institutions (IMF, World Bank, WTO) and multinational corporations effectively control the world economy, to the detriment of most developing countries which cannot compete. While the reduction in trade barriers, better communications networks, capital mobility and increased integration of economies they advocate are meant to work for the good of all countries, these have not alleviated but perpetuated socio-economic injustice.

Although claimed otherwise, globalisation holds greater benefit for industrialised countries than for developing countries through related series of phenomena which are characteristic of neo-liberal economic policies. In an empirical test of world-systems theory, Peacock and colleagues demonstrated that over time there has been increasing divergence in economic development and wealth distribution between the core, semi-periphery and periphery countries, and that there was convergence only among core countries.[21] There must be acceptance that developing countries cannot follow the pattern of development of the industrialised world because of their previous imperialistic subjugation or present neo-colonial dependence. Robertson and Pinstrup-Andersen demonstrate how acquisition of land in developing countries as industrial country investments in development, whether for food or biofuels, constitutes a form of neo-colonialism,[22] typically disenfranchising peasants and contributing to human migration flows in search of livelihood. Even the seemingly positive formalisation of worldwide fair-trade certification[23] and food safety[24] for connecting developing world producers with ethical industrialised world consumers can be seen as having the tinge of neo-colonial paternalism. Consequently, the prevailing system of international trade and investment appears to favour the 'haves' over the 'have-nots' among its constituent nation-states and has perpetuated, even exacerbated, the economic disparity between industrialised and developing worlds that constitutes the worldwide context for much of the shadow trades.

Critical Endeavour

The wide-ranging changes in geo-political, social and economic environments world-wide over the late 20th and early 21st centuries have given rise to managed liberalism and capitalist democracy as the dominant paradigms worldwide. Thus, in business studies, critical theorists have not been able to make inroads into the disciplinary establishment, skewed as it is towards positivist empiricism and rational choice theory. Consequently, ahistoricity of learning, repackaging of knowledge for business consulting and individuation of change characterise their sub-disciplines.[25] This is certainly evident in the absence of a critical approach to international trade, which continues to be promoted as the prime means of exporting the liberal economic model and integrating trading nation-states into the capitalist world economy. Nonetheless, the meta-theoretical work of Honneth invariably compels rethinking questions of fact versus value, freedom versus determinism, and similar age-old ontological dualities.[26] This approach to social justice, in terms of the innate human capacity for reason, allows for understanding the causes of affective and corporeal experiences of the world, as well as for querying the dominant discourses on the same.

Given critical theory's continued marginality, there remains a reluctance by its proponents to go beyond sociological explanation, for instance of harmful inequities, to normative explication of emancipation, as indeed ought to be the case with the shadow trades. Progressivism from a parochial nationalism to cosmopolitan globalism, as had been anticipated by some political philosophers, has not occurred in reality, apart from token efforts at prosecuting 'crimes against humanity' through international courts of justice. Writing on harm in world politics, Linklater proposes that it was the capacity of nation-states to inflict widespread human suffering as demonstrated in the World Wars that established, and has since dominated, the discipline of international relations.[27] This ethical or critical perspective may be of particular relevance to the analysis of the shadow trades typically occurring between industrialised and developing/emergent economies. The present system of sovereign countries could be inappropriate to tackling these worldwide issues, including the resultant suffering of victims in the latter economies. Despite the absence of world wars, the notion of all countries subscribing to mutual moral responsibilities, not just towards fellow national citizens but to wider humanity and world environment, has not taken root.

Encompassing Ethics

Focus on Foibles

Perusal of academic business journals with an interest in ethics reveals a somewhat conservative list of topics covered. Human resource-related issues include electronic surveillance of employees, ethical decision-making and work values. Yet virtually nothing has been published within management journals about human trafficking, child labour, indentured workers, and other forms of inhumane people management. Ethical concerns are also touched on in marketing journals, such as green consumption, product placement in children's films, disadvantaged consumers, online auction fraud, and fair-trade buying. However, little is mentioned about the marketing of blood diamonds, military arms, transplant tourism and even toxic waste, all ostensibly meeting the needs and wants of global consumption and production. Finance-related articles have covered financial reporting, performance of socially-responsible investments, tax evasion, insider trading, and so on. Still, money laundering, economic kleptocracy, financial secrecy or heritage looting receive far less attention. Strategy issues have included codes of ethics, social responsibility, bribery and corporate philanthropy. There have been some recognitions of the need to incorporate the illicit side of globalisation into the political economy discipline,[28] though not yet in global business.

Most books on business ethics tend to deal with issues like questionable accounting practices, misleading advertising and marketing, workers' rights, consumer privacy, corruption, sustainability, corporate social responsibility and the like. Academic textbooks in particular tend to address ethical theory and moral decision-making in some detail, while practitioner guidebooks simply focus on those ethical issues that arise within the various functional areas of business and how these can be avoided or overcome. Arguably, school-leaver undergraduates might lack sufficient maturity to grapple with business ethics, while post-experience graduate students could have pragmatic perspectives on how it applies to their industry and profession. In most cases, courses and workshops on ethics address issues of acting immorally within legitimate firms, government and non-government organisations, but seldom address indirect involvement with illicit operations run by criminal organisations, officials, clans, armies, militia, rebel groups and so on. Much of the business literature is preoccupied with corporate social responsibility in support of investment returns without examining any tacit or inadvertent complicity in shadow trades. By contrast, there has been scant attempt to document shadow trades and analyse their socio-economic impact on individual victims, vulnerable groups, social structures, government policy and the rule of law, let alone undermine their viability.

The interminable debate in global ethics between the three main approaches of universalism, pluralism and relativism may arguably be due to the polarisations of systems based on values/ideals versus traditions/practices. Appeals by those in the western world to human rights and economic justice as axiomatic principles in a universalist framework tend to be resisted by those of other worlds that appeal to cultural heritage, resulting in an untenable situation for global ethics. Essentially this is also a conflict between philosophy and the social science perspectives of ethics, based on differing methodologies, with the latter adopted more by an increasingly assertive post-colonial world in the context of a no longer ascendant western world.

Hellsten argues that no single ethical framework can apply worldwide and transnational understandings are imperative if the various stakeholders are to balance their responsibilities at the local, national, regional and international levels.[29] Nonetheless the study of global ethics, influenced by the discipline of international relations, is about moral responsibilities of citizens, corporations, governments, inter-government organisations and other entities involved in issues with global dimensions. While commendable, interdisciplinary approaches risk being ethno-ethics that are no more suitable for world issues than rationalistic ones that, could be argued, result from and apply to a western context. Although he does not propose any synthesis of ethical frameworks, Hellsten cautions against unwittingly having a neo-colonialist or almost imperialistic attitude in surveying alternative ethical frameworks in the so-called east, to benchmark against western ones.

Delinquency Delineated

Various terms have been used to classify business that operates outside the law or at the edge of morality, like illicit trade, illegitimate firms, shadow economy, deviant firms, grey trade, black markets and the like. Often used inter-changeably, such terms enjoy little consensus in both academic publications or popular media on the definition of each or whether and how they overlap or intersect. In their book on the subject, Gilman, Goldhammer and Weber conceptualise deviant globalisation as encompassing the 'cross-border economic networks that produce, move and consume things as various as narcotics and rare wildlife, loot antiquities and counterfeit goods, dirty money and toxic waste, as well as human beings in search of undocumented work and unorthodox sexual activities'.[30] Adopting a more legalistic tone, Naim defines illicit trade as 'trade that breaks the rules – the laws, regulations, licenses, embargoes, and all the procedures that nation-states employ to organise commerce, protect their citizens, raise revenues, and enforce moral codes'.[31] Taking a political science perspective in her edited book on transnational threats, Thachuk considers these to range 'from terrorism, to widespread international crime, to the rapid transfer of privately held armaments technologies, to international narcotics trafficking, to money laundering and corruption, to cyberwar and cybercrimes, to mass migration and human trafficking' and much more.[32]

The legitimate entities and illicit operations are interlinked, and often these shadow activities contribute to the financial profit of legitimate businesses, regardless of legality and morality. It is hard to separate legitimate from illegitimate players for as Naylor et al. had argued, the former can and do transact with the latter deliberately, with the latter catering to the business supply-chain demands, such as labour, resources and finance for the former.[33] Since legitimate entities engage in illicit activities and illegitimate entities engage in licit activities for mutual benefit, Içduygu and Toktas illustrate that, particularly in the developing/emergent world, differentiating them is difficult for national criminal justice systems.[34] Likewise, activists against sweatshops, unfair trade and conflict resources claim to be able to identify illicit and licit activities in global business, and yet states struggle to differentiate these consistently.[35] More crucially, despite their aspirations and claims to be ethical, consumers fuel the shadow trades by typically choosing to remain ignorant of unethical practices in complex supply chains of products. Instead they may rationalise their purchases as being economical, though this could be on account of the producer using exploited labour, conflict resources, polluting processes and tax evasion.

In this book, shadow trade is characterised as any business practice or operation that contravenes or circumvents national, regional and/or international laws, regulations and policies, which nonetheless gets integrated into legitimate global business, constituting its dark side. The illegitimate entities involved are not always transnational criminal syndicates but also *ad hoc* borderless networks of opportunistic agents from the informal economy and thus pose a challenge to law enforcement. Regardless, such trades are of a morally objectionable nature in exploiting and/or causing harm to individuals, societies, animals and eco-systems whether in the short term or longer term. This conceptualisation recognises that there are shades of legitimacy within each shadow trade and across all, and that these could be substantially integrated into legitimate, legal and morally acceptable businesses, tainting or camouflaging them to the benefit of some. It also implies that these trades are typically opaque in that aspects are not fully accessible to all but those operating such businesses, while other aspects are dismal in that the outcomes of their operations are incorporated surreptitiously into the world economy.

Depth Soundings

Research is certainly critical for determining the hazard, causality and compensation of worldwide problems created in all their distinct complexities, be these climate change, terrorism, nuclear plant leakage, financial crises or dangerous viruses. Quite perceptively does Beck note that such global risks are intrinsically asymmetrical, with the differential of power between nation-state allowing problems to be exported.[36] Such analyses would find resonance with the notion of shadow trades in that these risks cross national borders from the industrialised to the developing-emergent world. While some trades have long gestation, as in the cases of toxic wastes and organ harvesting, others involve complex chains of cause-and-effect, as in the cases of money laundering and conflict minerals. In keeping with post-modern and post-colonial stances, Rehbein argues that research subjects are capable of reflexivity in the social sciences, even if it be in resistance against the dominant culture, and so proposes a kaleidoscopic dialectic in which seemingly incommensurable disciplines interact to foster new perspectives.[37] Besides, critical ideas must be interpreted in every particular context, thereby encompassing knowledge and practice, theory and ethics.

This would certainly be essential to critically analysing the shadow trades, especially as the unintended or overlooked consequences of world economic policies and global business practices.

Revisiting Responsibility

Socio-economic Justice

The field of international relations, which had been traditionally statist and rationalist in its focus, has come to recognise multinational corporations (MNCs) as major actors in society and the economy that ought to be regulated. Nonetheless there is the constructivist view that governments need to go beyond regulating MNCs to collaborating with them in social and economic responsibilities. The argument of Hofferberth et al. is that MNCs are increasingly able to go beyond economic rationalism and be motivated instead by social norms and logics of appropriate behaviours as corporate citizens.[38] While this perspective might help remove the notion of a zero-sum game between nation-state versus corporation on socio-ethical issues, it is debatable whether the corporate actions remain largely driven by economic self-interest, including reputational risk aversion. These actions are now tempered by new norms promoted by various civil societies, with non-government organisations (NGOs) serving as catalysts to bring about change in MNCs, which then get enunciated as their own corporate social responsibility (CSR) commitments. However, these might be simply a corporate co-optation of the rhetoric of social responsibility evidenced in its speeches, publicity and reporting all duly observed, with no substantive change in business strategy occurring since there is little holding to account, except when a scandal or crisis breaks.

On the question of how the economic goals of corporations are to be reconciled with the social goals of polities, there are two extreme views. One is that the hidden hand of the market operates in capitalism to rein in the excesses of corporations on risk of failure, so as to promote the greater social good, as propagated by Adam Smith. The other is the conviction that the government on behalf of its citizens needs to intervene in the economy to constrain corporations if social good is to be optimised, as held by John Maynard Keynes. In between these views, Sandoval argues that there are four approaches to corporate social responsibility.[39] Reductionism seeks to capitalise on social problems as business opportunities and a means to achieve competitive advantage and pre-empt regulation by government. Projectionism idealises businesses as accepting their obligation to meet all stakeholder expectations, thus addressing social issues without foregoing profitability. Dualism differentiates the corporate role to achieve private profit from its role to benefit society, seeing the former as enabling the latter and often at a later stage. Dialectics acknowledges the inherent conflict between achieving profit through the exploitation of labour and addressing the social issues it causes, thus perceiving all corporate social responsibility discourse as dishonest. Commendably, Gollnhofer and Schouten urge a transformative shift towards being about 'responsibility to socialise corporations' (RSC) or the recognition of 'common-wealth' and democratisation of the economy, including the workplace.[40]

Corporate Citizenship

The corporation's right to participate in the political life of the nation-states in which it operates, and commensurate obligation to accept its responsibilities to that society, is affirmed in the notion of corporate citizenship. With corporations growing increasingly influential in capitalist economies, they need to act also as quasi-societal organisations in collaboration with inter-government organisations.[41] This would represent a shift from a legal notion of citizenship as about rights and duties, to a moral notion in which its values call for legitimate and sustainable profits rather than profit maximisation for short-term financial reporting. As corporations move from causality-based to capability-based responsibilities, social justice becomes not a matter of voluntary charity contributions but of ethical imperative to advocate against the wrongs of the various economies and societies they operate in. In terms of Carroll's long-standing conceptualisation of corporate social responsibility, corporations have been better at fulfilling their economic responsibility to be profitable, their legal responsibility to abide by laws, their philanthropic responsibilities to support socio-cultural endeavours, but less so their ethical responsibilities to do what is fair and just, especially at some cost to themselves.[42] In arguing for an extension of the notion of corporate citizenship, instead of its conflation with corporate social responsibility, Matten and colleagues argue that corporations as drivers of globalisation have to take on roles previously held by the now-disempowered nation-states.[43] However, business ethics seems to largely remain reduced to the minimalist ethos of corporate social responsibility (CSR) and organisational ethical codes.

As the shadow trades comprise business operations across far-flung borders that are difficult for national governments to monitor and regulate, multinational corporations can have a significant role to play in tackling their growth. In as much as such corporations are represented in multiple countries, these are often in a stronger position than many national governments to advance social change worldwide, in contrast to simply exempting itself from national sovereignty over its operations in the name of economic globalisation. If any multinational corporation is to establish its legitimacy as a global corporate citizen, it needs to act morally, collaborating with national and regional governments, inter-government organisations and non-government organisations in incremental efforts to bring about socio-economic justice. According to Sen, any social institution's value rests in its contribution to true human freedom, defined as removing the shackles of illiteracy, hunger, poor health, lack of civil rights and the like.[44] Instead of simply addressing the demands of selective stakeholders and seeking its own citizenship rights in various countries of operation, MNCs need to respect if not defend the civil, social and political rights of all fellow citizens. Some MNCs may reactively improve slums, providing healthcare, sponsoring schools, monitoring working conditions, recognising property rights and the like, often in token fashion to further their own public and government relations agenda. Quite apart from such efforts, corporations have arguably a moral responsibility to address the causes and consequences of shadow trades impinging their business operations and respective industries worldwide.

Legislative Mandate

In industrialised countries, political lobbying by top executives and professional lobbyists has been instrumental for the enactment and content of specific laws, and on public policy issues critically important to corporations, but of marginal interest to citizens and society. In the context of the US, constituency-building by corporations was found to be generally more effective than exercising economic muscle in motivating the support for social issues by politicians given their self-interest for re-election.[45] In developing countries where poverty levels are high, corporations and industries that provide employment and export revenue tend to gain considerable political clout with their host-country governments to avoid regulation. Yet MNCs are still susceptible to moral pressure via inter-government and non-government organisations, often at the behest of other governments and more ethically compliant competitor corporations from the industrialised world. Thus, CSR needs to aim not just at avoidance of negative perceptions of firms' impact on a society towards proactive work on economic development. Alleviation of poverty lies at the root of most shadow trades (Table 2.1), whether human, resource, product or financial, and multinational corporations particularly have shared responsibility for any exploitation within the ambit of their industry.

Table 2.1 Forms of shadow trades

HUMAN TRADES	RESOURCE TRADES	PRODUCT TRADES	SERVICES TRADES
People Smuggling	**Conflict Mining**	**Arms Transfers**	**Money Laundering**
Human Trafficking	**Wildlife Poaching**	**Waste Transhipment**	**Tax Evasion**
Indentured Work	**Illegal Logging**	**E-waste Recycling**	**Transplant Tourism**
Coerced Labour	**Heritage Theft**	**Organs Acquisition**	**Military Contracting**
Mail-Order Brides	Oil Smuggling	Fake Pharmaceuticals	Lobbying & Corruption
Birth Surrogacy	Unregulated Fishing	Fertiliser & Pesticides	Crypto-Commerce
International Adoptions	Water Siphoning	Narcotics Smuggling	Piracy & Ransom

Note: Trades in bold are covered in the specific trade chapters; most others via case studies and/or in the penultimate chapter.

The willingness of the garment industry in Bangladesh to allow monitoring of its labour practices, particularly concerning child labour by IGOs and NGOs, was a landmark event and template for use elsewhere.[46] However, there are unrelenting misgivings that it was disguised protectionism by the industrialised world of their own garment industries or related unionised workers, if not well-meaning but misguided *vis-à-vis* the social and economic realities in the developing world. Arguably, the much-lauded Kimberley Diamonds Process is flawed and a broader scope for diamonds monitoring is needed if the social threats that the process was meant to address are to be effectively addressed.[47] Similarly, a more flexible approach to tobacco control policy than provided within the WTO could prove more effective in overcoming the inducement to tobacco smuggling. Otherwise, tobacco firms may well find it in their self-interest to participate in the illicit trade in cigarettes rather than cooperate with governments against it, thus undermining health policies in affected countries.[48] Till now most accounts of North Korean economic relations highlight its government's involvement in illicit trade, while despite sanctions there has been greater trade and investment there by China and South Korea.[49] All these examples demonstrate how international regulations do not necessarily mean resultant decline in shadow trades.

Discerning Shadows

Comparative Ethics

As most countries are in essence multicultural, managers of multinational corporations, inter-government agencies and non-government organisations need to be made sensitive to variations in ethical perception differences and especially not to make assumptions from general religious or moral orientations. In developing countries such as Indonesia, perceptions of ethical problems have been found to differ among three micro-cultural groups, in large part explained by their varying religious, political and economic values.[50] On the other hand, despite their apparent diversity, the world's religions can achieve consensus in business ethics on themes such as sustainability, distributive justice and human rights.[51] Yet much academic research on comparative practice in business ethics continues to define culture myopically at best in stereotypical national terms, and at worst as relatively irrelevant. Notably, memoranda of understanding about universally acceptable ethical business practices have been devised, such as the UN Global Compact. Nonetheless these constitute a shift of responsibility from the nation-state in enforcing laws to IGOs and NGOs in monitoring compliance, if not also to industries themselves, though allowed to be done controversially via self-reporting.

Having historically attracted criticism as having negative impact on the economies and societies of their host-countries, multinational corporations may now have a special role to play through CSR. There has been growing convergence on analysing global business multidimensionally, in industrialised, emergent and developing economies, about labour exploitation, consumerism, pollution, resource depletion, corruption and human rights. Yet to date it is questionable whether CSR efforts of multinational corporations make up sufficiently for their adverse impacts on countries and societies around the world. Since these ethical issues have been first raised in the wider society and then addressed by business, academic research has tended to be reactive rather than proactive. As reflected by the two leading academic journals in the field, there may be two distinct perspectives on global business: one broader and inter-disciplinary, seeing it as a force for peace, and the other narrower and focused managerially on firm-level activities that simply cross borders.[52] In the interim, a more realistic approach might be to complement the dominant paradigm of the capitalist world economy through interventions that channel social activism into working collaboratively with corporations and governments to balance the contradictions of market demands and public ethics.

Managerial Scruples

Most models about business morality tend to be framed with the corporation at the centre with its stakeholder responsibilities defined mostly by rhetoric about corporate social responsibility. Of the approaches to business ethics systematised by Rossouw, which are not mutually exclusive but complementary, the 'social scientific' approach is concerned with arriving at objective knowledge. The 'managerial' one seeks to assist managers to cope with practical ethical issues, while the 'organisation interest' approach sees ethics as instrumental to economic success. The 'ethical guidance' approach aims to define ethical standards at the macro-economic level of policy, meso-economic level of moral obligations of firms and micro-economic level of intra-organisational behaviour. The 'ethical control' one is concerned rather with controls, both internal and external to the organisation, which prevent ethical failures and/or rectify those that take place. Finally, the 'ethical development' approach locates ethical behaviour in the characters of business leaders and hence focuses on their development of a moral vision. It would seem that most business ethics publications aim to be of managerial guidance or organisational interest, with little emphasis on ethical development. What has been rightly called for instead is moral imagination, or the ability to think and act independently of dominant mindsets, coupled with a systemic approach that links individual to organisational and societal levels of analysis.[53]

Pertinent to tackling the shadow trades is the distinction Jacques and Wright draw between violent and non-violent resource exchanges. They argue for peaceable behaviour as a counterfoil to understanding violence in any criminal activity.[54] Such is the radical re-evaluation of the status quo imperative for countering the shadow trades alongside global business because the boundaries between illicit operations and legitimate corporations are considerably blurred in our capitalist world system. The concept of there being a dark side of management has grown in acceptance over the last decade. As elaborated by Hanlon, it originates in the early 20th century when the ability of the working class to resist capitalist production in its drive to reduce dependence on skilled labour was undermined through the increasing division of labour, organisational design and technology development. Addressing the issue of motivating workers, management academics and consultants called for the selection and training of malleable workers with suitable personalities and attitudes to be persuaded via superficially favourable work environments to create and capture value. Particularly in post-industrial service-dominant economies, employee presentation, empathy and personality traits are prioritised in working with clients and colleagues. Thus, the worker becomes a neo-liberal subject dependent on the employment market for selling one's pseudo-personality rather than professional expertise.[55] The dark side of management then is this process by which human capital is manipulated to higher productivity for greater corporate profit by managers who seem instead to benignly empower workers. It warrants addressing in relation to the differences and similarities with the newer concept of shadow trades introduced in this book and this is done in the dim arena section at the end of this chapter.

Commentary in Conclusion

Periodic moral outrage over a specific shadow trade and drastic measures hastily taken are not necessarily productive in identifying the deeper issues and addressing the longer-term consequences of questionable cross-border businesses. Historically, major changes in society, whether on slavery past or climate change present, have been spearheaded by champions or a small cohort who have made aware a sizeable majority and galvanised a dedicated minority to be vocal advocates of the voiceless victims. In as much as corporate leadership is sensitive to consumer boycotts and shareholder queries resulting in share price and profitability falls, political leaders are highly motivated by re-electability, by opinion polls and by electoral votes. Enquiry by scholars, governments and non-profit organisations should rather be thought of as 're-searching' or looking at current knowledge and available information with new eyes. More ambitiously academia might aim at shedding new light on global business, just as this book endeavours to do in laying a foundation for research on the shadow trades and a roadmap for intervention. Both corporate and governmental leadership groups are also sensitive to media exposés which translate to dire consequences for them, and hence there is a crying need for independent media, editorial autonomy, journalist freedoms and whistle-blower protections to be guaranteed in law, highly regulated and strictly enforced.

If its major books are any guide, business ethics seems to be preoccupied with a narrow range of issues and keeps harking back to classical philosophies while ignoring moral debates over the past century, as well as the social context and political structures such as neo-colonialism and globalisation. Without any overarching goal challenging us to think and act differently, *ad hoc* reactions to scandalous practices uncovered, such as instituting legislation and enforcement, can often prove counter-productive eventually. What needs to be recognised is that shadow trades are sizeable business networks in their own right and need to be systematically scrutinised within national social and world economic contexts, regardless of how abhorrent what is traded in and how. Academics have largely neglected the pertinent issue of the shadow trades accompanying global business as a dark side, even as political engagement through such research represents an opportunity to go beyond their oft-criticised ivory tower orientation and the disciplinary silos periodically lamented, yet enduring. Hence this book advocates in-depth action research on shadow trades and models an inter-disciplinary endeavour to further moral knowledge, to propose ethical standards at various levels of the world economy, and to aid in the development of responsible business, societal and government leadership.

DIM DOMAIN

MANAGEMENT DARK SIDES *VIS-À-VIS* SHADOW TRADES

The coinage of the catchy term 'dark side' to highlight the unfortunate aspects of management has led to a spate of research and writing highlighting various forms and business functions of their application, not all of it of the same academic critical pedigree. Researchers in the organisational dark side began with an exploration of issues of workplace violence and aggression, but have broadened it to include stress, sexual harassment, pursuit of power and impression management, among others. Such behaviours can be injurious not just to the individual workers but to the organisation as a whole. Some have measurable costs, such as absenteeism, workplace deviance, turnover, fraud, destruction of property and theft of assets. Others, such as breach of confidentiality, stress, lowered productivity, organised resistance, corporate irresponsibility and violations of laws, may be less quantifiable in organisational cost. Relentless pursuit of competitive success can foster links to organised crime, state capture and support of authoritarian regimes.

Administrative Violence

One extension is exploration of the dark side of leadership or how so-called transformational, instructional, distributed and turnaround leadership forms may not always result in organisational good. The less acknowledged counter-productive forms of leadership characterised by controlling behaviours, abusive actions, toxic relationships and harassment tend to cause stress, particularly on the most vulnerable

(Continued)

employees, even in educational institutions.[56] Entrepreneurship represents a special form of leadership that enables success of new enterprises but can be problematic in collaborative roles as managers, colleagues and clients of investors. Given their need for control and recognition, they can stifle others' insights, ascribe blame and cause financial loss.[57] It has also been pointed out that leadership practices from the private sector are increasingly imposed on public sector managers. Given differences in organisational ethos and employee motivations, such practices are harmful in the public sector, thus representing another facet of a dark side to management concepts.[58] Another dark side of public management is said to be the co-optation of their networks, which is meant to improve performance but leads to favouring the politically powerful and causing greater social inequity. Others who have similarly adopted a psychological perspective to a dark side in leadership have covered the areas of executive styles, gender at work and team behaviour.

Yet to mask illegality within organisations, such dark side activities tend to be communicated as legitimate and consensus-building, and challenging to research except perhaps by ethnography, narrative analysis and covert methodologies.[59] Status-seeking behaviour in organisations can result in the sabotage of the work of colleagues and the artificial boosting of one's own performance. Related to this is the behaviour of organisational psychopaths who rise up the hierarchy through charm, manipulation and misrepresentation in their pursuit of power, status and wealth. Yet their amoral, highly political and short-term decisions display a proneness to accounting fraud, investor disregard, unwise acquisitions, stock market manipulation, workplace bullying and corporate social irresponsibility.[60] Yet others writing on the dark side of management have specialised on human resource management, consulting careers and entrepreneurship.

Market Misbehaviours

Applied to marketing, discussions of its dark side encompass a range of aspects and their resolution, largely to the benefit of marketer corporations, explored in a special issue: the questionable practice of ambush marketing, where brands associate themselves with an event, such as in sports or music, without being the official sponsor. Using theoretical concepts, academic researchers have argued that this dark side to marketing is actually beneficial to the official sponsors if they are able to use the presence of ambush marketers to highlight their own brand distinctiveness. Consumers who resist the power of marketing through their everyday actions often go unnoticed by marketers. Thus, research uncovered the beating, ditching and hiding aspects of consumer resistance, supposedly for further investigation by academics without reference to insights for marketers. Likewise, an article on materialism and compulsive buying, considered a form of the dark side in consumer behaviour, offers new insights to researchers without addressing how these marketers may capitalise on the propensity.[61]

Research on newer electronic technologies contributes to what they term as consumer 'misbehaviour' by understanding the technology–consumer relationship that leads to this purported dark side of consumer behaviour. Content marketing purports to convert potential customers into loyal clients by giving out relevant but non-product information. The dark side to this involves misinformation through crafting contradictory content for different target audiences. As the internet enables infinite content variations to various segments without competition, the target audiences unwittingly work to extend social media reach for the business. On the other side of the equation, consumer trolling of marketer websites characterised by mischief, entertainment and deception is meant to spur social media responses, often without malicious intent. Still, it is problematic for marketers to police online, as they cannot count on legal remedies nor on social media sites to censor, thus it is said to be a dark side. Though social media platforms offer tools to combat this phenomenon, such as banning trolls from the brand community or warning consumers, marketers may counter-productively increase the very attention much sought-after by them.[62]

Other related subfields of marketing to which dark side arguments have been applied include retailing, which has been accused of corporate social irresponsibility by consumer advocacy groups. Instead of addressing the retailing practices *per se*, academic researchers devised a scale that identified 14 factors of such irresponsibility in the perception of consumers for retailers to use in measuring and presumably to manage.[63] In contrast, a research article on the dark side of customer relationship marketing identifies 10 forms of practices that marketing services use as means and targets. Instead it suggests that these are widespread, dysfunctional and damaging forms of an otherwise beneficial process towards sustained customer loyalty.[64] Business-to-business relationship strategies are noted for reciprocity-enabling value creation through mutual learning leading to success. But the dark side here is said to be the under-researched structural issues with the relationship, such as size differences, capacity development, creativity and market dynamics changing over time.[65] Likewise, the short-term success of knowledge management initiatives can concurrently create a dark side of diminished problem-solving competence, dogmatism and social alienation that surfaces only later with remarkable regularity.[66] Supply chain management is relevant to marketing in that disruption as a result of trimming inventory does lead to discontented customers, but this is misrepresented as a dark side which can be remedied by the supply continuity model advocated.[67]

Crucial Queries

Are there more similarities than differences between the various business and management dark sides? Are shadow trades their equivalent as a dark side of global business, or are they quite different by definition and characteristics?

Can the concept of the dark side of management apply to any of the shadow trades, and if so which? Is labour exploitation an extreme form of management since it seeks to maximise profit through workers? Or is this stretching that dark side concept of management too far?

(Continued)

Why do research articles on the dark side of marketing consistently recommend even further investigation? Or do these already provide insights into how questionable practices can be managed and adverse perceptions be overcome?

Do content marketing and influencing constitute the dark side of social media and brand community websites? Or is there a more insidious practice of surreptitious online collection and monetising of private data for the manipulation of consumer behaviour?

FURTHER RESOURCES

Research Works

Albanese, J. S. (2011). *Transnational Crime and the 21st Century: Criminal Enterprise, Corruption, and Opportunity*. New York: Oxford University Press.

Efrat, A. (2012). *Governing Guns, Preventing Plunder: International Cooperation against Illicit Trade*. New York: Oxford University Press.

Shelley, L. I. (2018). *Dark Commerce: How a New Illicit Economy is Threatening our Future*. Princeton, NJ and Oxford: Princeton University Press.

Varese, F. (2011). *Mafias on the Move: How Organized Crime Conquers New Territories*. Princeton, NJ and London: Princeton University Press.

Informational Websites

Global Financial Integrity [https://gfintegrity.org]
Havoscope Black Market [www.havocscope.com/]
Illicit Trade [https://illicittrade.com/]
Interpol [https://www.interpol.int/Crime-areas]
OECD Directorate for Public Governance [www.oecd.org/gov/risk/illicit-trade.htm]
United Nations Office on Drugs and Crime [www.unodc.org/]

Annotated Documentaries

National Geographic (2010-2016). *Border Wars* [55:00 min. each]. Multiple episodes on the work of the US customs and border agents.

National Geographic (2008). *Illicit: The Dark Trade* [55:00 min.]. Television documentary based on the book by Moises Naím of the same name.

A&E Television Networks (2006). *The Russian Mafia* [44:00 min.]. Part of the series, The World History of Organised Crime.

IWMVienna (2018). *McMafia and the Geopolitics of Crime* [1 h. 26 min.]. Talk by Misha Glenny on the growth of global organised crime.

General Reading

Phillips, T. (2007). *Knockoff: The Deadly Trade in Counterfeit Goods*. London: Kogan Page.

Glenny, M. (2008). *McMafia: A Journey through the Global Underworld*. London: Bodley Head.

Saviano, R. (2008). *Gomorrah: A Personal Journey into the Violent International Empire of Naples' Organized Crime System*. London: Pan Books/Macmillan.

Endnotes

1. Michalos, Alex C. (1997). Issues for business ethics in the nineties and beyond. *Journal of Business Ethics, 16*(3), 219–230.
2. Tenbrunsel, Ann E. (2008). Ethics in today's business world: reflections for business scholars. *Journal of Business Ethics, 80*(1), 1–4.
3. Waters, M. (1995). *Globalization*. London and New York: Routledge, pp. 158–164.
4. Sen, A. (2017). *The State, Industrialization and Class Formations in India: A Neo-Marxist Perspective on Colonialism, Underdevelopment and Development*. London: Routledge.
5. Berger, P. L. (1987). *The Capitalist Revolution*. Aldershot, UK: Gower, p. 166.
6. Bockman, J. (2015). Socialist globalization against capitalist neocolonialism: the economic ideas behind the New International Economic Order. *Humanity: An International Journal of Human Rights, Humanitarianism, and Development, 6*(1), 109–128.
7. Raghavan, C. (1993). The new world order: a view from the south. *Beyond National Sovereignty: International Communication in the 1990s*. Norwood, NJ: Ablex Publishing Corporation.
8. Wallerstein, I. M. (1991). *Geopolitics and Geoculture: Essays on the Changing World-System*. New York: Cambridge University Press.
9. Shannon, T. R. (1989). *World System Perspective*. San Francisco, CA: Westview Press.
10. Lash, S., & Urry, J. (1987). *The End of Organized Capitalism*. Cambridge: Polity Press.
11. Huggan, G. (1997). The neocolonialism of postcolonialism: a cautionary note. *Links and Letters, 4*, 19–24.
12. Ogar, J. N., Nwoye, L., & Bassey, S. A. (2019). Archetype of globalization: illusory comfort of neo-colonialism in Africa. *International Journal of Humanities and Innovation (IJHI), 2*(3), 90–95.
13. Sartre, J. P. (2001). Colonialism is a system. *Interventions, 3*(1), 127–140.
14. Athow, B., & Blanton, R. G. (2002). Colonial style and colonial legacies: trade patterns in British and French Africa. *Journal of Global South Studies, 19*(2), 219.
15. De Maria, B. (2008). Neo-colonialism through measurement: a critique of the corruption perception index. *Critical Perspectives on International Business, 4*(2/3), 184–202.
16. McKenna, S. (2011). A critical analysis of North American business leaders' Neocolonial discourse: global fears and local consequences. *Organization, 18*(3), 387–406.
17. Balasubramanyam, V. N. (2015). China and India's economic relations with African countries: neo-colonialism eastern style? *Journal of Chinese Economic and Business Studies, 13*(1), 17–31.
18. Dicken, P. (2007). *Global Shift: The Internationalization of Economic Activity*. Thousand Oaks, CA: Sage Publications.

19. Robertson, R. (1992). *Globalization: Social Theory and Global Culture* (Vol. 16). Thousand Oaks, CA: Sage Publications.
20. Harvey, D. (2005). *The New Imperialism*. Oxford: Oxford University Press.
21. Peacock, W. G., Hoover, G. A., & Killian, C. D. (1988). Divergence and convergence in international development: a decomposition analysis of inequality in the world system. *American Sociological Review, 53*(6): 838–852.
22. Robertson, B., & Pinstrup-Andersen, P. (2010). Global land acquisition: neo-colonialism or development opportunity? *Food Security, 2*(3), 271–283.
23. Hussey, I., & Curnow, J. (2013). Fair Trade, neocolonial developmentalism and racialized power relations. *Interface: A Journal for and about Social Movements, 5*(1), 40–68.
24. Freidberg, S. (2003). Cleaning up down South: supermarkets, ethical trade and African horticulture. *Social & Cultural Geography, 4*(1), 27–43.
25. Magala, S. (2006). Critical theory: 15 years later. *Critical Perspectives on International Business, 2*(3), 183–194.
26. Honneth, A. (2009). *Pathologies of Reason: On the Legacy of Critical Theory* (Vol. 23). New York: Columbia University Press.
27. Linklater, Andrew. (2007). *Critical Theory and World Politics: Citizenship, Sovereignty and Humanity*. London and New York: Routledge, pp. 149–155.
28. Andreas, P. (2004). Illicit international political economy: the clandestine side of globalization. *Review of International Political Economy, 11*(3), 641–652.
29. Hellsten, S. K. (2015). Ethics: universal or global? The trends in studies of ethics in the context of globalization. *Journal of Global Ethics, 11*(1), 80–89.
30. Gilman, N., Goldhammer, J., & Weber, S. (eds.). (2011). *Deviant Globalization: Black Market Economy in the 21st Century*. New York: Continuum. p. 1.
31. Naim, Moises (2010). *Illicit: How Smugglers, Traffickers and Copycats are Hijacking the Global Economy*. New York: Random House. p. 2.
32. Thachuk, K. L. (ed.). (2007). *Transnational Threats: Smuggling and Trafficking in Arms, Drugs, and Human Life*. London: Greenwood/Praeger. p. 8.
33. Naylor, R. T., Taylor, D., & Bahramitah, R. (2002). *A Typology of Profit-Driven Crimes*. Ottawa: Research and Statistics Division, Department of Justice Canada.
34. Içduygu, A., & Toktas, S. (2002). How do smuggling and trafficking operate via irregular border crossings in the Middle East? Evidence from fieldwork in Turkey. *International Migration, 40*(6), 25–54.
35. Dillman, B. (2007). Introduction: shining light on the shadows: the political economy of illicit transactions in the Mediterranean. *Mediterranean Politics, 12*(2), 123–139.
36. Beck, U. (2008). World at risk: the new task of Critical Theory. *Development and Society, 37*(1), 1–21.
37. Rehbein, B. (2010). Critical Theory and the rise of the Global South. *Transcience Journal, 1*(2).

38. Hofferberth, M., Brühl, T., Burkart, E., Fey, M., & Peltner, A. (2011). Multinational enterprises as 'social actors': constructivist explanations for corporate social responsibility. *Global Society, 25*(2), 205–226.

39. Sandoval, M. (2015). From CSR to RSC: A contribution to the critique of the political economy of corporate social responsibility. *Review of Radical Political Economics, 47*(4), 608–624.

40. Gollnhofer, J. F., & Schouten, J. W. (2017). Complementing the dominant social paradigm with sustainability. *Journal of Macromarketing, 37*(2), 143–152, 0276146717696892.

41. Wettstein, F. (2005). From causality to capability. *Journal of Corporate Citizenship*, (19).

42. Carroll, A. B. (1999). Corporate social responsibility: evolution of a definitional construct. *Business & Society, 38*(3), 268–295.

43. Matten, D., Crane, A., & Chapple, W. (2003). Behind the mask: revealing the true face of corporate citizenship. *Journal of Business Ethics, 45*(1–2), 109–120. doi: https://doi.org/10.1080/09614520050010340

44. Development in Practice (2000). Book review: *Development as Freedom* by Amartya Sen. *Development in Practice, 10*(2), 258.

45. Lord, M. D. (2000). Constituency-based lobbying as corporate political strategy: testing an agency theory perspective. *Business and Politics, 2*(3), 289–308.

46. Nielsen, M. E. (2005). The politics of corporate responsibility and child labour in the Bangladeshi garment industry. *International Affairs, 81*(3), 559–580.

47. Gooch, T. M. (2008). Conflict diamonds or illicit diamonds: should the difference matter to the Kimberley Process certification scheme. *Natural Resources Journal, 48*, 189.

48. Lin, T. Y. (2014). The status of FCTC in the interpretation of compensable indirect expropriation and the right to adopt stricter tobacco control measures under Bits. *Asian Journal of WTO & International Health Law & Policy, 9*, 123.

49. Haggard, S., & Noland, M. (2008). North Korea's foreign economic relations. *International Relations of the Asia-Pacific, 8*(2), 219–246.

50. Sarwono, S. S., & Armstrong, R. W. (2001). Micro-cultural differences and perceived ethical problems: an international business perspective. *Journal of Business Ethics, 30*(1), 41–56.

51. Enderle, G. (2011). Three major challenges for business and economic ethics in the next ten years: wealth creation, human rights, and active involvement of the world's religions. *Business and Professional Ethics Journal, 30*(3/4), 231–252.

52. Kolk, A. (2016). The social responsibility of international business: from ethics and the environment to CSR and sustainable development. *Journal of World Business, 51*(1), 23–34.

53. Werhane, P. H. (2008). Mental models, moral imagination and system thinking in the age of globalization. *Journal of Business Ethics, 78*(3), 463–474.

54. Jacques, S., & Wright, R. (2008). The relevance of peace to studies of drug market violence. *Criminology, 46*(1), 221–254.

55. Hanlon, G. (2015). *The Dark Side of Management: A Secret History of Management Theory*. London: Routledge.

56. Harris, A., & Jones, M. (2018). The dark side of leadership and management. *School Leadership & Management, 38*(5), 475–477.

57. Kets de Vries, M. F. (1985). The dark side of entrepreneurship. *Harvard Business Review, 63*(6), 160–167.

58. Vogel, R., & Masal, D. (2012). Publicness, motivation, and leadership: the dark side of private management concepts in the public sector. *Administrative Si Management Public*, (19), 6.

59. Linstead, S., Maréchal, G., & Griffin, R. W. (2014). Theorizing and researching the dark side of organization. *Organization Studies, 35*(2), 165–188.

60. Boddy, C. R. (2006). The dark side of management decisions: organisational psychopaths. *Management Decision, 44*(10), 1461–1475.

61. Daunt, K. L., Greer, D. A., Pancer, E., McShane, L., & Poole, M. (2017). The dark side of marketing. *Journal of Marketing Management, 33*(15–16).

62. Daunt, K. L., Greer, D. A., Pancer, E., McShane, L., & Poole, M. (2017). The dark side of marketing. *Journal of Marketing Management, 33*(15–16).

63. Wagner, T., Bicen, P., & Hall, Z. R. (2008). The dark side of retailing: towards a scale of corporate social irresponsibility. *International Journal of Retail & Distribution Management, 36*(2), 124–142.

64. Frow, P., Payne, A., Wilkinson, I. F., & Young, L. (2011). Customer management and CRM: Addressing the dark side. *Journal of Services Marketing, 25*(2), 79–89.

65. Abosag, I., Yen, D. A., & Barnes, B. R. (2016). What is dark about the dark-side of business relationships? *Industrial Marketing Management, 55*, 5–9.

66. Chua, A. Y. (2009). The dark side of successful knowledge management initiatives. *Journal of Knowledge Management, 13*(4), 32–40.

67. Zsidisin, G. A., Ragatz, G. L., & Melnyk, S. A. (2005). The dark side of supply chain management. *Transportation Research Board Annual Meeting*, Washington, DC, 12–16 January.

CHAPTER 3

IRREGULAR MIGRATION & LABOUR EXPLOITATION

Credit: Vijay Putra/Pexels

Overview in Introduction

So long as migration in search of livelihood has been an intrinsic part of the world economy, various forms of exploitation have tended to co-exist, particularly in the developing-emergent world but also in the industrialised one. Supplementing reliable estimates from reports by international organisations with information from media and academic sources, this chapter outlines the extent, locations and profitability of trafficking, smuggling, bondage and coercion worldwide. It endeavours to model the antecedent push-pull factors, such as civil strife, trade policies, climate change and poverty, and consequent links to specific types of work in selected industries. Tentative proposals are made in this chapter for tackling the issues through worker empowerment, decriminalising victims, consumer sensitisation and sourcing de-marketing. Since labour exploitation is associated with employee relations, occupational stress, industrial sociology, workplace health and safety, public policy and human rights, among others, practitioners and researchers in those fields have a role in addressing the plight for these hidden migrant workers. Hence this chapter will endeavour to address people smuggling, coerced labour, indentured work, sex work, child labour, the informal economy, capitalist economics, poverty, developing countries, global supply chains and worker empowerment.

Trading People

Historical Precedence

The enslavement and trafficking of humans has been an intrinsic part of conflict and conquests throughout history, whether by empires that made our history books or by one tribe versus another in remote parts of continents which were never adequately documented in ages past. It has also been a violent accompaniment to mainstream trade in commodities and goods, as with the trans-Atlantic slavery from Africa, which involved Europe and North America, even while a similar trade existed less obtrusively in the western Indian Ocean and across the Sahara. Peasants in many lands worldwide have been serfs to feudal landowners and nobility, not just in medieval times but right through to the present. Other peoples faced with famine or war at home, notably from China and India in recent centuries, decided to migrate as low-paid and bonded workers to distant lands in pursuit of economic opportunity, political refuge or both. Furthermore, indentured labour was the chief means for European colonists to move peoples from one territory in their control to another within their global empires, often across oceans, to serve their corporations or the wealthy. Such migrants became indispensable to harvest plantations, mine minerals, build railways and the like, unavoidable essentially after slavery was abolished.

Contemporary Manifestations

As abhorrent as trading in human beings is considered in contemporary mores, it none-theless continues to exist today side-by-side with global business in legitimate goods and services, albeit unobtrusively. Given that migration from developing and emer-gent economies is in response to the demand for cheap labour in industrialised ones, trafficking, bondage, coercion, smuggling and other forms of human exploitation will co-exist. Though the variegated nature of such exploited labour makes for difficulty of clear definition and thus of addressing the problem, especially the emancipation of vic-tims. Despite the extant laws prohibiting these practices worldwide, there is mounting evidence that the situation is patently otherwise, and this ought not to be the purview solely for sociologists, geographers, social workers and criminologists. The fact that traf-ficked, bonded and coerced labour appears intractable is due to market demand for their low-cost service, which makes it an issue worthy of business research (Table 3.1). Yet the contemporary deficit in such investigation and intervention by economics and manage-ment scholars and practitioners would seem to imply that such shadow trades in people are deemed either relatively insignificant or irrelevant within capitalist world economy.

Table 3.1   Regional distribution of modern slavery[1]

REGION	COERCED LABOUR	FORCED MARRIAGE	TOTAL SLAVERY	PREVALENCE (%)
Asia-Pacific	16,550,000	8,440,000	24,990,000	0.61
Africa	3,420,000	5,820,000	9,240,000	0.76
Europe	3,250,000	340,000	3,590,000	0.39
Americas	1,280,000	670,000	1,950,000	0.19
Arab States	350,000	170,000	520,000	0.33
World	24,850,000	15,442,000	40,293,000	0.54

Demarcating the Abuse

Human Trafficking

Considerable diversity of definition, research methodology, even political agenda, exists in compiling statistics on human trafficking, not to mention difficulty of access to this highly sensitive shadow trade. The United Nations defines human traffick-ing as comprising three important elements: 'acts of recruiting, transferring and receiving people; by the means of threat, force or deception; and for the purpose of exploitation', but offers no definitive statistics.[2] Over a decade ago the International Organisation for Migration (IOM) put the number trafficked across borders at 4 mil-lion persons and the total revenues of this trade at USD 7 billion.[3] Yet the US State

Department identifies rather conservatively around 100,000 victims of trafficking globally per year, and records only about 15,000 prosecutions and 9,000 convictions of the perpetrators.[4] The International Labor Organisation (ILO) has estimated human trafficking to be a business worth at least USD 32 billion, which approximates to 3.2 percent of the global trade in fuels or 5.1 percent of the global trade in travel services.[5] Thus, untold millions are trafficked surreptitiously across as well as within continents, typically via remote regions with ill-defined and unmonitored borders.

The growth of interest in human trafficking within the industrialised world itself seems to have coincided with the rise of victims from Europe in need of protection.[6] Still numerous other Asian, African, Latin American as well as former Eastern Bloc and Soviet countries have been identified by the United Nations Office for Drugs and Crime (UNODC) as sources or transit points for trafficked person within their region or beyond, as well as destination countries which also include the industrialised world (Figure 3.1). In both source and transit countries, travel agencies are often the intermediaries for stolen passports and fake visas supplied by specialist criminal groups. As egregious as the trafficking of women into sex work may be, this is far from the only form deserving attention. Belatedly acknowledged have been links to mainstream global sport, as in the trafficking of promising young players from Africa to Europe with the promise of training, who then face fees and repayment of costs to agents on selection by any team, or abandonment upon non-selection.[7] An oft-neglected area, one which is much harder to keep track of, is the trafficking of persons across regional economic groupings and with larger countries, including big emergent markets such as Brazil, Russia, India and China, invariably from their poorer, rural areas to wealthier, urban ones.

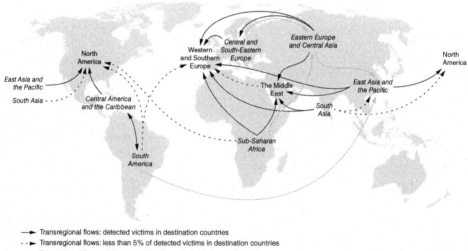

→ Transregional flows: detected victims in destination countries
-- ► Transregional flows: less than 5% of detected victims in destination countries
···▻ Transregional flows: victims repatriated from destination countries

Note: The boundaries and names shown and the designations used on the map do not imply official endorsement or acceptance by the United Nations.

Figure 3.1   Major global human trafficking routes[8]

Copyright © UNODC, Global Report on Trafficking in Persons 2018 (United Nations Publication, Sales No. E.19. IV.2.), Map 6: Main detected transregional trafficking flows, 2014-2017. Used with permission.

People Smuggling

In the case of people smuggling, the victims are often independent economic migrants or political refugees who pay their own way, but who might nonetheless end up in exploitative employment at their destination. It is strictly defined in the UN Migrant Smuggling Protocol as 'procurement, in order to obtain, directly or indirectly, a financial or other material benefit, of the illegal entry of a person into a nation-state of which the person is not a national or a permanent resident'.[9] People smuggling on a larger scale globally tends to be undertaken by traditional criminal gangs such as mafias and triad societies, although it can and is be done by small-scale operators like the coyotes along the Mexico–US border. By far the largest group from sub-Saharan Africa comes from Nigeria, where smuggling is closely linked with migrant communities already established in Europe as well as traditional authorities such as religious leaders back home.[10]

In the Asian context, people smuggling from China is said to be done by small family businesses often in legitimate travel and the export–import industry, who see this trade as a lucrative side-line.[11] More sinister are the links alleged between the Taiwanese government and business groups in the smuggling of people via developing countries in Latin America into the industrialised world.[12] Smuggled women and children are utilised especially in sex work for the tourism industry and as low-wage workers in sweatshops for producing goods of every description, often in and/or for the industrialised world. When they end up in domestic work, cottage industry, migratory farm labour, isolated small businesses or even illicit trades, the victims of people smuggling are often invisible to social researchers, economists, policy-makers and law enforcers.

Debt Bondage

Despite its criminalisation under the Palermo Protocol, debt bondage constitutes about half of all coerced labour worldwide.[13] Many legitimate migratory workers worldwide end up as bonded labour in domestic work, child-minding, drug couriering, armed robbery, street hawking and begging.[14] Debt leading to bonded labour is conventionally defined as occurring when a person offers his or her services or that of a family member under his control as security or repayment for a loan or an advance on recruitment and expatriation expenses. Feudalism that characterised the Medieval Age in Europe continues to be common practice in farming in many developing and emergent economies today. The International Labor Organisation (ILO) estimates that there are 8.1 million global victims of bonded labour mid-decade in the 2000s, deeming it the single most common form of human enslavement.[15] The non-government organisation, Free the Slaves, has placed the number of slaves globally much higher at 27 million instead, and virtually unchanged over the last decade, with between 15–20 million of these being in debt bondage on the Indian subcontinent alone.[16]

In West Africa lies Mauritania, with a long tradition of slavery, where due to weak legislation and poor enforcement about 43,000 of its population remain enslaved well into the 21st century through debt bondage, among other means.[17] Presently there have been allegations of bonded labour in the Middle East, including in the construction of the Olympic stadia in Qatar.[18] Many more migrant workers in the region work in retail, domestic, cleaning and other lowly jobs on sponsorship visas that allow their employers full control over employee lives, free of local labour laws. Largely unreported in the media as a form of bonded labour is the option for professional sports teams to trade players without the latter's consent, reminiscent of the ownership of prize gladiators in ancient times, even if contemporary sportspeople bonded by contracts earn millions of dollars. Reflecting just a part of complex social systems of enslavement, statistics on bonded labour are compelling, regardless of how they may have been estimated. It might also count as slavery particularly where the services are not valued fairly, mobility is severely restricted, there is no time limit and/or the debtor is placed in a perpetually servile position.

Coerced Labour

The ILO estimates that 40.3 million people have been victims of modern-day slavery, 24.9 million of these in coerced labour and the remainder through forced marriages, with women and girls constituting 71 percent of the total.[19] Profits from their labour are estimated to be worth USD 150 billion, most of it, or USD 99 billion, generated in sex work.[20] Hence statistics and profit figures provided by the ILO, the most authoritative source available, can and ought to be used for lobbying governments to act immediately, despite not being able to document the multidimensional nature of the problem for more effective policy interventions longer term (Figure 3.2). Notably these demonstrate that the greatest profits are wrung from such labour in the industrialised world, likely that of newer migrants from the developing world. Thus, the issue of coerced labour may not be adequately addressed nationally but regionally, if not internationally with all its attendant challenges of differing laws, enforcement and even values.

When classifying irregular migration in half a dozen forms, political and economic motivations are often merged for refugees, asylum-seekers and other coerced migrants because violence, catastrophes and development projects could well have undermined their usual means of livelihood.[21] In many countries, coerced labour is closely tied in legislation with trafficking for that purpose, while in some other countries it can be a stand-alone offence without any trafficking involved. Nonetheless there are governments themselves in East Asia that export their prisoners and other citizens as cheap or unpaid labourers to other developing and emergent countries, as documented in the case study accompanying this chapter. All of this calls for criminal law interventions where trafficking is involved, for labour law interventions where trafficking is not involved but employment standards are nonetheless violated, and for mixed legal interventions when coerced labour is involved, regardless of whether there was trafficking.[22] In the interest of fairness, it must be recognised that coerced employment does also occur in the industrialised world as well, as exemplified by the US, which require that inmates work in commercial enterprises, with little or no remuneration, to subsidise the prison industry.

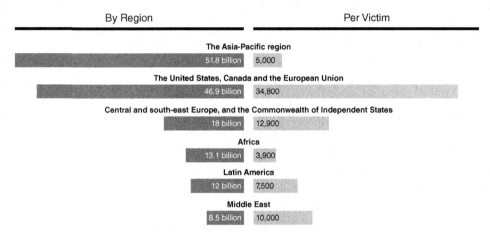

By Region		Per Victim
The Asia-Pacific region		
51.8 billion		5,000
The United States, Canada and the European Union		
46.9 billion		34,800
Central and south-east Europe, and the Commonwealth of Independent States		
18 billion		12,900
Africa		
13.1 billion		3,900
Latin America		
12 billion		7,500
Middle East		
8.5 billion		10,000

Figure 3.2   Estimated annual profits of coerced labour (in USD) [23]

Migration Explicated

Although neo-classical economics posits that migration is largely caused by income differentials, according to advocates of labour economics the phenomenon is more multifarious, encompassing perceptions of opportunities for employment, capital and risk reduction. Migrations systems theory emphasises instead the political, economic and cultural ties often spawned by past colonisation between sending and receiving countries which constitute the system.[24] Thus, the inauguration of any transnational labour migration can be understood by synthesising insights from world-systems theory on how the penetration of capitalism from the core countries into periphery societies disrupts customary livelihoods.[25] This migration is then sustained by subsequent developments of inequitable distribution of wealth, changed cultural values, diasporic networks, and commercial agents, among other socio-economic factors. The consequence is a combination of push and pull factors that could help explain the different forms of exploited labour in diverse industries.

Push Factors

Poverty and destitution

The primary motivation among those undertaking the risks of migration via trafficking or smuggling is typically economic, namely the prospect of abject poverty or even death at home versus the potential of survival and prosperity abroad. The push is particularly urgent at times of conflict, famine and natural disasters, including those associated with climate change. What is seldom acknowledged is that some governments are sympathetic towards labour out-migration, at least by default in not stemming the outflow. Given their own inability to provide employment or other economic opportunities or to address political or environmental calamities, these governments thus avoid social upheaval by a restive, often youthful, populace. Governments in certain developing countries even have a formal policy of facilitating the export of labour, which functions as a safety valve for local unemployment and a source of foreign income.[26] Those home-country governments subsequently become dependent on remittances from their migrant workers abroad as invaluable foreign currency for national reserves and for offsetting trade imbalances to the extent of promoting their citizens as a form of service export to emergent and industrialised countries.

Export barriers

Overly high tariff barriers and generous farming subsidies in the industrialised world, such as the US, Japan and European Union (EU) are the indirect cause of unemployment and under-employment in Africa, Latin America and Asia. Lack of export access by developing countries of their legitimate agriculture products and other commodities to industrialised countries can be an impetus to migration. The developing-world farmers are driven to abandon their own fields and seek to be smuggled into industrialised countries to work on their state-subsidised agricultural sector which may lack local labour willing to plant, tend and harvest under harsh conditions and at low wages. Furthermore, low or declining commodity prices set largely by institutional buyers in the industrialised world threaten the livelihoods of millions in the agricultural sectors of the developing world. This may leave the citizens of the latter countries with little recourse but to grow other crops, such as coca and poppy plants, which can be converted into illicit drugs to be smuggled for lucrative sale into the former countries. Yet it has been demonstrated that as small as a 1 percent increase in the commodity prices paid to the developing countries of Africa could virtually eliminate their dependence on aid funding.[27] The minimal amounts of foreign aid and development funding to developing countries, often coming with stipulations about non-subsidy by their governments, in comparison with generous subsidies to domestic agriculture and industry in the industrialised world is another contentious issue.

Conflict and war

The onset of violent civil conflict is usually the culmination of an extended political struggle in which the rights of one or more of that society's constituent groups have been denied full fruition. Inter-state wars may be justified on political grounds, though invariably there is an underlying economic agenda. The arms industry is also culpable for its role in fuelling or prolonging such wars, as sometimes are their home-country governments which might have political or economic agendas for fostering proxy wars. The resultant state of war between countries or rival claimants to civil authority is a prescription for lawlessness and provides the necessary ingredients for a shadow or dark economy. Certainly, the social dislocation contingent on war is a trigger for human trafficking or smuggling both within and across borders, if not also into coerced or bonded labour subsequently. Potential for family break-up and the loosening of community ties caused by the dislocation by war and civil strife is a contributory factor to forced migration. The trafficking of women even in post-conflict situations has been thoroughly researched in the context of the Bosnian war where it grew to a multi-million dollar 'industry' even though no organised crime participation had existed previously and against which counter-efforts proved inadequate.[28] Given the turmoil in their home countries, such irregular migrants are seldom able to access legitimate channels for asylum seeking or labour migration.

Marginality and displacement

Discrimination on ethnicity, language, religion, gender and politics, through which individuals and even whole communities are made unwelcome in their home regions, is another factor in emigration, legal or otherwise. Further denied access to education, jobs and housing, while feeling generally insecure remaining, such persons are motivated to explore ways to relocate, including via seeking asylum. Consequent extreme inability to support families financially, famine and disease are further catalysts of transnational migration. Thus, some who utilise people smugglers or who consent to traffickers would in fact qualify as asylum-seekers fleeing political and economic crises. Paradoxically, pre-migration trauma is found to be closely related to post-migration difficulties with social integration, employment and stress.[29] Indigenous rights, which should include both occupation of native lands as well as the resources beneath the surface, tend to be side-lined in government negotiations with multinational corporations. Furthermore, rapid transformation of the environment within or close by indigenous communities tends to disrupt cultures and lifestyles, seldom in a neutral or positive way.

Climate and calamities

The rapid change in weather patterns is increasingly becoming a trigger of forced-migration as habitations, particularly those of the poor, become unviable due to drought, sea-level rise, flooding, desertification of farmland, depletion of fish-stocks and the like. Climate refugees may presently be a remote problem affecting primarily low-lying coral atolls of the South Pacific and island countries in the Indian Ocean. New Zealand is commendable for pioneering annual quotas of refugee intakes from those areas affected. However, projections of sea-level rise caused by greenhouse gases will see more of continents, major parts of some countries and many significant cities permanently flooded, causing catastrophic levels of climate migration, with all its attendant socio-economic consequences.[30] Though not always related to climate change, disasters such as floods, forest fires, earthquakes, droughts, tsunamis and such are further push-factors for migration, especially from developing and emergent countries where infrastructure is weak, emergency services limited and social security nets lacking for those thus affected.

Pull Factors

Economic liberalisation

Contrary to neo-classical economics, liberalisation of foreign trade and investment has not reduced but actually increased labour migration, yet the latter phenomenon is under-researched because of its mistaken association with criminality in government policies.[31] The self-same lowering of trade barriers that is driving economic globalisation has also been fostering the growth of people smuggling and human trafficking, among other shadow trades. In fact, when governments tighten immigration policies, transnational crime syndicates become greater beneficiaries of higher demand for their services in people smuggling and human trafficking. Dominance by organised crime of formerly planned economies such as in the former Eastern Bloc and the former Soviet Union are exemplars of the consequences of rapid economic liberalisation without commensurate institutions for corporate governance, rule of law, an independent media and the establishment of civil society groups. In an integrated world economy, measures by nation-states taken autonomously of each other have limited effectiveness in protecting the human rights of workers, undermining exploiters' profitability, reducing social conflicts and enhancing economic opportunities.

Media propaganda

Persuading consumers via the media of the desirability of the goods and services produced by multinational corporations is imperative for sustaining the free-market economy. Indiscriminate advertising, editorial content and television programming, often sourced from emergent and industrialised countries, must then share some responsibility for fostering dissatisfaction among citizens of developing countries with their lower standard of living in comparison. In addition, the growth of the internet has been responsible for peer-to-peer networks for sharing of experiences and images, chat-rooms for stalking, mail-order bride services, advertisement of sex tourism and more, which has facilitated the trafficking of persons, particularly into sex work.[32] Ease of telecommunications is also capitalised on by traffickers and smugglers in coordinating the movement of people across vast geographic distances. Typically, people are persuaded to migrate while ignorant of the attendant risks and hardships, and thus become vulnerable to exploitation. Subject to selective media promotion of capitalist consumerism, economic migrants and trafficked workers realise rather belatedly that the grass is seldom greener on the other side of the border in the industrialised world. Even when remaining at home, workers get drawn into extensive supply chains and manufacturing outsourcing operations of multinational corporations which cannot always ensure their end-products are not tarnished by exploitative labour input.

Officialdom complicity

In many developing and emergent economies, where law enforcement is under-resourced, underpaid lowly officials are easily tempted to overlook illicit operations. Together with higher levels of the government in the police, border control and the military, this can include facilitating the transnational trafficking or smuggling of people for a profitable fee. Hence most transnational threats from the black or grey economy come from corrupt individuals and criminal groups, not from the governments of nation-states *per se*.[33] There have been periodic allegations that inter-government peace-keeping forces, even under UN auspices, have been involved in human trafficking, including for sex work.[34] The undergirding push-factors of poverty, unemployment and famine make potential migrants amenable to traffickers and smugglers, who in turn are facilitated by corrupt officials in both home and transit countries. Understandably then, bilateral agreements between these countries and stricter laws within each country prove quite ineffective, even futile, at stemming the shadow trade comprising illicit human trafficking, people smuggling and coerced labour to serve the labour markets abroad, legitimate or otherwise. So exploitative migration for work globally needs to be addressed by more than legislation, but by law enforcement of anti-corruption measures, if there is to be sustainable tackling of its dynamics.

Criminal networks

Moving persons across borders and countries is carried out by different types of criminals, all drawn by the high profits that can be earned. The presence of agents locally and their promotion of opportunities abroad are influential in the recruitment of victims. Cooperatively, they work to move their victims or clients over vast distances from poorer to more affluent regions, though this invariably increases costs and the risks of detection. The endurance of cross-border trafficking flows involving large numbers is testament to the flexible nature of the criminal enterprise comprising different levels from small local operators to medium regional groups to global syndicates.[35] Trafficking networks may also incorporate legitimate organisations like labour brokers, freight-forwarders and travel agencies, not to mention ethnic clan members and diasporic community leaders. Developing typologies of trafficking/ smuggling entities and identifying the financial interests underlying them will eventually prove invaluable for implementing proactive measures against these shadow trades, and these measures could prove more appropriate than criminal prosecution in retrospect.

Familial obligations

Illegal immigrants who form the bulk of those smuggled across borders trade-off the relatively higher wages to support family back home against the likelihood of being caught and deported, as well as the odd chance of there being an amnesty. From an economics perspective, that policy ambiguity characterises the issue of migrant labour, legal and illegal, in most industrialised countries on account of political expedience in balancing competing economic interests within.[36] It is judicious to realise that Enlightenment notions of inalienable rights undergirding laws against labour exploitation in the West may actually be at odds with the Confucian culture of victims from East Asia which emphasises obligations to the family, social networks and the state.[37] Thus, the motivations of people to migrate abroad for work, and their willingness to endure oppression in order to support their kin, may simply be an extension of their cultural propensity to do the same within their own countries. Just as the precipitating factors of the human trade are not unidimensional, nor are their facilitating processes fully independent from one another; they are delicately interwoven.

Tackling the Interplay

Examining the innovations of these shadow traders may well serve all concerned stakeholders of the legitimate economy in retaliating with similar creativity to addressing the problem.[38] Business research ought to focus on the pursuit of strategies and policies to undermine them rather than result in the shadow trades becoming another specialisation for academic publishing within extant social sciences disciplines. Tapping into interdisciplinary findings on the phenomena should aim instead to equip citizens, consumers, workers, union officials, government policy-makers and administrators, business executives and civil society groups alike to work better at addressing the plight of these trades' victims. Incapacity in the interim to arrive at solutions for eradicating human trafficking and other forms of labour exploitation ought to be no constraint on generating possible alternative interventions to explore.

Macro-level Policies

Formalised entry

Regular migration from the developing world to the industrialised, while occasionally available in principle, is in practice limited, tainted with corruption that preys on the desperation of the aspiring migrant. In some situations, irregular migrants are tolerated, as when there are waiting low-skilled jobs that they can readily fill. Still they are confined to certain sectors, denied other rights, such as health and family reunion, and easily dismissed once no longer needed.[39] If there were a cost-based legitimate channel for labour migration, then the exploitative businesses, from illegitimate or quasi-legal agencies to smugglers and traffickers, might be seriously undermined. Once the informal migrant trade is decriminalised, labour economists might explore the feasibility of host-governments imposing employment permits pegged around the cost of illegal entry and/or expatriation priced slightly above people smugglers' charges.[40] Finite employment contracts, without right of permanent residence but other employment rights, could mean countries and their industries have access to much needed labour at times of economic boom that traffickers seek illegally to provide. Similarly, a government levy or higher payroll tax may be imposed to cover migrant workers' health and other social costs, including premature repatriation. Social protection agencies could institute a gratuity payment or lump-sum which migrant workers receive on leaving at contract-end.[41] This could form the basis of sustainable micro-enterprise, community development, further education, skilled employment or pensioned retirement once back in their home countries.

Migrant protections

Trafficked or smuggled people are seldom able to seek protection in the countries to which they are transported because on being rescued they are routinely deported to their countries-of-origin. Once home they could be subject to retribution from all parties complicit in their trafficking and smuggling, including corrupt police and other government departments.[42] Sensitivity in the treatment of irregular migrant workers and effective rehabilitation of livelihood in their home countries are among areas to which academic and practitioner minds might be applied. Even in a free-market economy there could be innovations to regulate protection for migrant labourers, even if originally trafficked or smuggled in. Application of all the employment laws pertaining to wage, occupational health, hours of work, etc. without exemptions, unlike in export processing zones (EPZs) even for local citizens, could be a solution to labour exploitation of trafficked, smuggled and bonded workers.

It is noteworthy that while the majority of countries have signed the ILO Convention on Forced Labour, 1930, relatively few have signed four subsequent conventions over the next seven decades designed to punish traffickers and to protect their victims.[43] The fining not just of traffickers, smugglers and workers, but also of employers and employment agencies, whether complicit or deceived, might be a deterrent worth devising by legislators. Yet there could easily be recidivism among rescued illegal migrant workers with forced repatriation home just being a paid-for sabbatical between stints abroad, necessitated by continued poverty at home. Labour economists might help us understand whether it would be highly exploitative or else overly generous if the migrants were paid the same low wage as citizens, presuming the latter consent to the arrangement. It is worth noting that often conditions that illegal migrants face in the host-country, while abhorrent to concerned parties there, might be better than what was left at home.

Victim decriminalisation

Despite the illicit nature of their operations, traffickers, smugglers and exploitative employers could be charged under existing and enhanced employment laws in industrialised countries. Since the latter typically require contracts, reasonable hours of work, workplace health and safety, training and development, minimum wage, medical and annual leave, and superannuation, many illicit operations might be rendered economically unviable. Pragmatically, there could be a case for legalising brothels and regulating sweatshops, thus enabling the registration of their workers to ensure their safety, working conditions, health and non-exploitation, including foreign workers on short-term work permits. However, there appears to be much policy ambiguity that only serves to aid the exploiters and harm the victims, such as the US government's misguided notion that adult prostitutes in particular do not always fit the legal definition of victim. There have also been objections from embassies as well as bureaus within its State Department which did not want certain countries criticised for labour exploitation for strategic diplomatic reasons.[44] Hence, despite its vaunted determination to address human trafficking, the US government has refused to countenance any legislation that would expand anti-trafficking efforts or the sharing of information by its own government departments in order to devise effective strategies to combat this shadow trade.

Meso-level Mediations

Investigatory research

The dearth of information on trafficking and coerced labour, both quantitative and qualitative, is even more acute in source and transit countries than in destination countries. The call by Salt and Stein to treat human trafficking as a form of business migration with both illegal and legal modes, demonstrably having profit-loss accounting, information-gathering, agents, recruitment, operations management, integration into host societies and so on, seems to have gone generally unheeded by academics and practitioners in the decades since.[45] Pointing out that control measures and legal-punitive approaches do not suffice to control the trafficking, especially of women, Van Impe called for a multidisciplinary approach which addresses both the push and pull factors, such as of historic waves of labour migration and trafficking from the Philippines, Latin America, Africa and Eastern Europe.[46] The Global Programme Against Trafficking (GPAT) is a worthy attempt by the United Nations to redress this situation, allowing for contributions from a variety of sources on all aspects of trafficking,[47] although presently its data highlight the interventions of criminal justice systems rather than the full extent of the problem.

Civic consciousness

Discrimination invariably undergirds the exploitation of fellow human beings from abroad or from within their own country who are seen as less deserving than those of their own ethnicity, social class and religion. It can only be perceived as morally acceptable to enslave, exhaust and discard without any regard if these outsiders are defined not as fellow humans with equal rights but as somehow inferior beings. It is thus imperative that civic education, political communications and social marketing needs to be directed at changing perceptions, however challenging the process of eradicating long-held and institutionalised prejudice. More than all those efforts, the rights and privileges of all residents in a society, not just citizens, need to be enshrined in national constitutions and supported by laws against discrimination, perhaps policies for affirmative action too. One alternative for managers and entrepreneurs, were it available, may be to contract migrant labour for specific needful projects rather than indefinite employment periods.[48] This practice could be instrumental in avoiding the social cohesion problems of sizeable migrant communities living in ghettos characterised by high unemployment and crime in subsequent periods of economic decline. Although there are many challenges to obtaining accurate data on so-called hidden populations as those trafficked, exploited or even just involved independently in clandestine trades, these are not insurmountable because these populations seldom remain invisible.[49]

Stakeholder sensitisation

Awareness-raising efforts ought to be directed to highlighting the ethical issues of all forms of irregular migration, whether illegal, trafficked or coerced for both sending and receiving countries. Exploitation of their labour is possible even in artificially constituted economic processing zones (EPZs) where the laws of neither the host country nor the home country apply to the corporations operating there.[50] Political leaders might also be beneficiaries financially from such free trade zones at the expense of citizens, either through their own business interests sited there or through political donations from owners of those supply-chain enterprises. Multinational corporations that outsource production routinely protest that they impose an ethical code on their suppliers and audit compliance. But this seldom extends beyond the first level of agents and contractors in a multi-level supply chain of subcontractors, sub-subcontractors and informal sweatshop workers. It ought to be noted that similar exploitative practices attend software programming, medical record transcribing and call centres outsourced abroad by multinational corporations, even governments.

Hence the mass media have a moral responsibility to investigate and report on the realities of irregular migration and labour exploitation in the supply chains of corporations, even at the risk of alienating their advertising sponsors. Consumers are relatively unaware of the source of their products and, if sensitised to the issue, will seek to discriminate in their purchases, thus affecting the complicit manufacturers and marketers. Researchers in marketing are particularly well positioned to gather relevant data and lobby corporations and consumers to support the fight against these shadow trades. In addition, academics in business sub-disciplines such as human resources, operations and marketing, not to mention those in law, social work, public administration and political science, have roles to play in advocacy, research, policy and education on related aspects of these shadow trades.

Liberating Humanity

Myopia to Exodus

The poorest of the poor worldwide, the lower socio-economic strata of populations in developing, emergent and industrialised economies, are by far the most vulnerable to irregular migration and labour exploitation. While their oppressors might be motivated by financial greed, the victims are driven by sheer economic desperation, with many consumers and businesses being the unwitting beneficiaries. The undergirding push-factors of poverty, unemployment and possibly famine in their home countries, and equally the pull-factors of jobs, income and better living standards in their destination countries must be radically addressed. Without this, stricter laws and enforcement within and between countries could prove futile in stemming the tide of human trafficking, people smuggling and coerced labour, and consequent labour exploitation. These are not just ethical issues for sociologists, political scientists, geographers, and lawyers alone to concern themselves with, but for management and business academics to proffer their expertise on undermining the economics of these trades. Yet because slavery in the US was managed according to the classical management principles then prevalent, there seems to be collective amnesia about this shadow trade currently within the discipline, lest it acknowledge the taint of participation in human oppression.[51]

Invisibility of Toil

Even if it can be argued that such shadow trades are small relative to legitimate trade in goods and services, the truth remains that much of the latter is tarnished by such labour procured unethically and treated exploitatively, possibly criminally. It is quite evident that the efforts of policy-makers, social workers and law enforcement, among others, commendable as these might be, have been insufficient to address the inroads of these trades. Smuggled and trafficked women and children are commonly utilised in sex work for the tourism industry, but also as low-wage workers in sweat-shops for producing goods of every description sometimes in, if not often for, the industrialised world. Once channelled into domestic work, cottage industry, migratory farm labour, isolated micro-enterprise or the informal economy, the victims of people smuggling become ever more hidden to social researchers, policy-makers and law enforcers.[52] Consequently, the interrelated areas of people trafficking, human smuggling and coerced labour feed into the labour supply of many legitimate businesses in the world economy with which innumerable goods and services are created (Figure 3.3). From retail products and agricultural produce to industrial machinery and hospitality services, these are likely more pervasive than consumers are led to believe and businesses are prepared to acknowledge as symbolic stealing from poorly-paid workers. What these stages represent nonetheless are the myriad points at which interventions to alleviate the scourge of irregular migration and labour exploitation may be made, from the precipitating conditions and migration modes through the labour forms to the job types and industry sectors in which these are prevalent.

Commentary in Conclusion

All interventions to eradicate or ameliorate irregular migration and labour exploitation must have as their higher goal that of enabling freedom from servitude by any individual or group of people to another. Social psychologists might aid us in understanding the mindset of the victims of trafficking, smuggling and bonded labour in making the desperate life-altering decisions – between staying home and dying slowly but surely, or taking the risk of non-survival to a possibly better life abroad. Communications campaigns in the source countries, especially of women and children, are imperative to warn them and their families about unscrupulous agents, dangers *en route* and exploitative employment abroad, as well as to promote sympathetic social reintegration of repatriated victims. Via social marketing on the mass media, the potential illegal migrant needs to be persuaded to comprehend the slim chance of high-income employment abroad and the greater certainty of irreparable loss of personal resources, health and life. Moreover, the challenges of social integration into their countries of emigration, as well as cultural alienation from their countries of origin need to be confronted realistically.

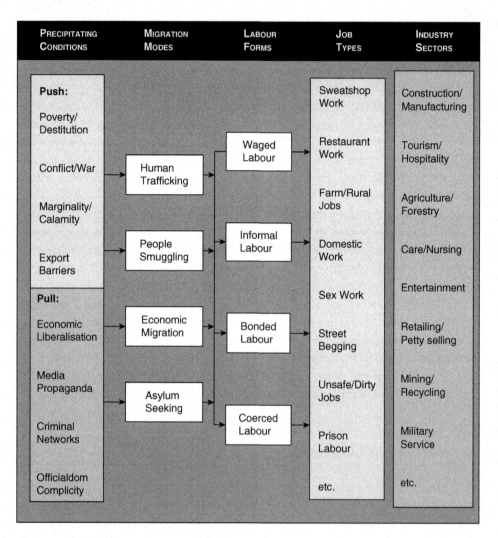

Figure 3.3 Tracing labour source-contexts to end-business deployment[53]

It will take the creation of employment opportunity, political stability, ethnic non-discrimination and other forms of socio-economic justice to render irregular migration unnecessary and labour exploitation irrelevant. The demand yet exploitation for low-skilled labour from developing countries can be seen as related to the relentless mechanisation and digitisation of production and services in emergent and industrialised countries, against which they compete on cost. Global economies-of-scale as the central driver of capitalist production and marketing are anathema to grass-roots entrepreneurship, small-to-medium enterprise and community economy in countries of all developmental levels. It is noteworthy that those developing countries that are more successful at economic growth, such as the Newly Industrialising Countries (NICs) and Middle-Income Countries (MICs), are among those worldwide whose citizens are least vulnerable to being thus exploited by traffickers and smugglers. However, unfortunately the economic success of these countries has resulted in them attracting and exploiting less fortunate citizens of their respective geographical regions. Ultimately universal education, with its eventual effect on employability, as well as sustainable economic development, are the key antidotes to human trafficking, smuggling, bondage and exploitative migrant labour.

DIM DOMAIN

GLOBAL SERFDOM VIGNETTES

Given the intrinsic function of keeping costs down in the capitalist world economy, exploited migrant labour clearly cannot be ignored indefinitely by corporations and governments, or by consumers and civil society. Corporations ought to address the issue as part of employee relations, occupational stress, labour outsourcing, and workplace health and safety. Furthermore, investigation by inter-disciplinary academics of the abuses of migrant labour, human trafficking and bonded labour should analyse their dynamics as well as their consequences. Business academics especially need to cease ignoring these trades, thus unwittingly condoning their socio-economic injustice in many developing and emergent economies, but work instead for the protection of victims and the prosecution of their oppressors. More detailed case studies on slave, child, sexual and prison labour worldwide are certainly needed to document and demonstrate inroads into the global supply chains of legitimate industry.[54] Advocacy and activism are imperative, not just in uncovering the existence of these shadow trades, but indubitably in working to render them uneconomic.

Slave Labour in West Africa

The cocoa industry in countries like Cote d'Ivoire, Liberia, Cameroon, and São Tomé and Principe has had a long history of utilising trafficked, smuggled and coerced labour dating back to the 19th century. It was accepted practice by local landowners and ignored by European colonists till the 1950s, despite boycotts dating from four decades earlier adopted by some chocolate manufacturers abroad. Not all the exploited labour results from trafficking but is due to a complex pattern of economic migration driven by the relative wealth or poverty of countries, and

(Continued)

even incidences of civil war and periodic famine in West Africa.[55] Market pressure to reduce prices invariably results in family members helping, and hence child labour for a start, and when this is insufficient, in trafficked and exploited labour being used. Serious decline in prices for cocoa on the world markets, the vicissitudes of currency exchange rates and the speculative nature of global liberalised commodity markets could well be linked to farmers resorting to exploitative labour practices in their local contexts.

Addressing the place of coerced labour in this industry requires an understanding of the different systems of growing, processing and trading cocoa, within the countries as well as globally, which is already well documented. There have been successful initiatives with cooperatives of farmers to negotiate better prices and improve production and to promote the marketing of 'fair-trade' cocoa-based products. While their impact can be significant for some growers, these have been limited for the majority of them who are sharecroppers. Lack of education and knowledge of the world outside their villages makes even the economic migrants vulnerable to subsequent trafficking and long-term labour exploitation overseas. As a consequence, much of the cocoa-based products consumed in markets worldwide appear to be tainted by exploitative labour practices in the developing world. The products in which cocoa is used are far-reaching in the culinary heritage of the industrialised world, such as in confectionaries and beverages. Yet boycotting chocolates, as was done as recently as 2000 in Europe when news broke of exploitative practices in cocoa farming, can be counter-productive to the eradication of trafficking and slavery for it only diverts workers into other industries under the same conditions.[56]

Child Labour in South America

Although there are reports on the existence of child labour in Paraguay, statistics on the extent of it bordering on slavery are somewhat incomplete. Despite its ratifications of all UN and ILO conventions about exploitative labour, an estimated 25 percent of the children working as domestic help in the country were under 10 years of age, whereas the legal minimum is 15 years. Living with their employers and without contact with family, they are particularly vulnerable to exploitation and abuse. Likewise, since the mid-1990s there have been government and non-government organisation reports of child prostitution in the tourist industry of coastal towns and of child pornography, although there are no statistics apart from the numbers of children reported missing and the children brought into the care of the authorities after arrest. There has also been evidence of the trafficking of children into Paraguay from Ecuador and Columbia for coerced begging and selling of textiles.[57] Over a third of the 300,000 domestic workers in Peru are under 18 years of age and there is ample evidence of trafficking of girls for sex work domestically and regionally. Further, there are an estimated 50,000 children in the mining industry, working alongside their families in artisanal mines abandoned by industrial producers. These child labourers carry heavy loads, dive in flooded shafts, handle mercury, are exposed to toxic chemicals and gases, suffer damaged hearing from explosions, among other dangers and health risks faced, not to mention being subject to physical abuse, domestic violence and sexual exploitation.[58]

Quite apart from the well-documented practice of coerced labour of men in clearing the Amazon forest in Brazil,[59] there is the less publicised but no less prevalent phenomenon of child domestic workers. Interviews with over 1,000 of these children and their parents established that most were female, very poor, with little formal education and of African descent. Their average wage was half the official minimum wage but up to 22 percent did not receive any wages at all, with the majority not receiving a day off periodically or any vacations.[60] In the 1990s, some 500 children were found to be working crushing rocks in a part of Guatemala, often suffering illness due to the dust, heat and effort, although these children were later rehabilitated. Over the past decade women and girls have been trafficked from Brazil, Paraguay and Dominican Republic into Argentina, while Argentinean women are trafficked nationally as well as internationally to Brazil and Spain. While most Bolivian women and girls were trafficked into the sex industry, often catering to tourists, the men together with their families were trafficked into exploitative labour in the textile industry within Argentina.[61] A study of Latin American children working in street situations, while retaining family links, found that 15 percent survived on prostitution, while a further 50 percent engaged in it irregularly. In 2001, over 50 Bolivian children and teens were found working under armed guard in four sweatshops, after having been kidnapped and sedated while being trafficked. It is relevant that cases against textile factory owners for exploitative labour of Bolivian adults were dismissed, raising suspicions of police and judicial collusion with the political-economic elite, including the use of threats and bribes to intimidate the witnesses.[62] Although their domestic work may not enter the global supply chain directly, with children labouring in the mining, textile and tourism industries, broadly defined, this certainly does constitute a shadow trade.

Prison Labour in East Asia

Quite routinely authoritarian regimes in East Asia face allegations in various media of prison labour. The issue is particularly pertinent in the case of China, which manufactures numerous products at low-cost for multinational corporations that are then marketed worldwide. The US China Commission has criticised the refusal of the authorities to permit inspections of its prison camps in defiance of agreements signed previously. In particular, China argues that political dissenters in its 'reform-by-labour' camps, which lie outside its judicial system, are not classified as prisoners and thus exempt from inspection. Across all the other prisons, less than one inspection visit per year was permitted between 1996 and 2005. None of these was within 60 days of the request, as specified in the agreement, and none has happened since 2005. The size of the prison labour force and quantum of its economic production has been difficult to establish, although a figure of 10 million prisoners has been mooted in the past based in part on the addresses of firms that are identical

(Continued)

to or in close proximity with prisons.[63] Nonetheless, increased pressures on Chinese state institutions to be financially self-funding and the collusion of corrupt politicians with commercial ventures have meant that increased profitability via prison labour has gained pre-eminence. Despite a number of cases cited about products of prison labour being imported, this is generally believed to constitute only a small percentage of all China-made goods imported into the US and Europe. Although not strictly trafficked, the prison workers are unquestionably enslaved and their outputs enter the global marketplace in one form or another.

There appears to be ample evidence from interviews with former prisoners in North Korea of coerced labour in the various institutions for incarceration variously termed political detention camps, labour training camps and re-education camps. Again, definitive numbers on prisoners and their economic contribution is impossible to obtain from that repressive totalitarian state. Many of these were refugees to China, repatriated against international conventions to North Korea, and there imprisoned under very severe living and work conditions.[64] While their labour has been largely in agriculture, brick-making or stone-carting for local consumption, one economic activity is the growing of poppies for heroin production and export to the global market, another shadow trade. Up to 100,000 workers have been dispatched to some 30 countries worldwide to earn foreign revenue for the state, while being subjected to movement restrictions, low or no wages, debt bondage, poor living conditions, intimidation and violence.[65] Similar allegations of coerced labour are commonplace with the military junta-controlled state of Myanmar, often after destroying their livelihoods in agriculture. While often this labour has been on military farms, as porters for soldiers and on road construction, it may include work on plantations which cater to the world market for rubber and teak.[66] There has been precedence for a legal case to be brought against a multinational for complicity, namely the use of coerced labour by the Burmese army while guarding a gas pipeline of Unocal, now owned by Chevron.[67] While it may not constitute trafficking in the strictest sense, the victims are invariably from minority ethnic groups in conflict with the central government and who are coerced to labour in other parts of the country than their own homelands.

Sexual Labour in Western Europe

In the late 1990s it was discovered that only 12 out of 25 European countries had produced data on the trafficking of women and only seven could do so for the trafficking of children. Despite some 120,000 women and children being trafficked into Western Europe per year, there were less than 100 convictions recorded in a single year. Although few countries are able to provide data across the years, sources on trafficking into the sex trade in Germany and the Netherlands confirm year-on-year increases, even if in single-digit percentages. However, the growth rate within Central and Eastern Europe, the prime source of women trafficked into the rest of Europe, has been extraordinary, at between 44 percent and 78 percent over the decade of the 1990s.[68] Estimates of the number of women and child trafficked or smuggled into Europe in the mid-1990s range widely from 50,000 to 300,000 per year, depending on the methodologies used and the levels within the various organisations doing the estimates, illustrating that such data collection is a matter of much conjecture, political sensitivity and anecdotal evidence.[69]

A sizeable number of women trafficked or smuggled into sex work in Western Europe are from outside the continent, namely from the developing regions of Africa, Asia and Latin America, and notably their poorer countries, constituting a major border-less business. A number of Central European countries, such as Bosnia-Herzegovina, Moldova and Croatia, plus Turkey, act as gateways for trafficking and smuggling people from Asia and Africa into the European Union.[70] The largest contingent from Africa originates in Nigeria, since trafficking there is closely related with their diasporic com-munities in Europe. Influential local leaders, such as priests and tribal chiefs, medi-ate binding financial pacts between the trafficked and the traffickers.[71] In the UK, a church-based initiative estimated that there were 4,000 women trafficked into pros-titution annually, the majority from Eastern Europe, the Baltic states, the Balkans, China, Malaysia and Thailand, with 60 percent of them entering the country illegally. This is far in excess of the figure that the UK government publishes and whose efforts seem focused on finding and deporting illegal immigrants rather than prosecution of the traffickers, criminalisation of punters or care of the victims.[72] However, it needs to be acknowledged that trafficking also happens within the industrial world, with the business and political elite involved in the exploitation of their own young and vulnerable with impunity.[73]

By no means are any type of inhumane management of human resources con-fined only to the countries and regions highlighted in statistics and case histories, for the phenomenon is quite global in extent. According to the UN, 161 countries are affected by human trafficking, 127 of these as countries-of-origin, 98 as tran-sit countries and 137 as destination countries.[74] While sexual labour forced on traf-ficked or smuggled women is the most egregious and child bonded labour comes a close second, these are by no means the only forms of exploitation in any region. Others invariably include sweatshops, contract cleaning, domestic and care-giving work under wages, conditions and terms that no enlightened society should con-done wherever in the world it is conducted. Needless to say, there is bonded labour in Latin America and Asia, sexual exploitation outside Europe, child labour in the Middle East and Asia as well, prison or coerced labour beyond Asia, and so on. It might be argued that such cases have been extensively researched and published previously, even if largely in non-academic arenas. However, this actually reinforces a central tenet of this book that such labour exploitation is not only the domain of government, inter-government and non-government organisations, but has as much to do with businesses and consumers that benefit from it.

Crucial Queries

Do fair-trade products which purport to guarantee adequate remuneration for the producers necessarily mean that marketers mark up prices for consumers

(Continued)

proportionately? How can timber manufactured into paper products or furniture be readily identified as being from unlicensed forest clearance and/or harvested using exploitative labour practices?

Why would women rescued from trafficking into the sex industry in high-income countries sometimes prefer not to be repatriated to their home countries? Could it be argued that those women who pay to be smuggled into higher-income countries in order to undertake sex work by choice – perhaps because it is the best-paying short-term income – are not strictly victims?

Should children be removed from labour for others' and the family enterprise when their parents cannot afford to educate them but are dependent on their earnings? How acceptable is the risk that they are then vulnerable to becoming beggars, out-of-sight domestic workers or even sexually exploited by paedophiles?

To what extent are countries-of-origin complicit in exporting their youthful citizens to reduce social agitation over employment opportunities and poverty? Should these governments be held accountable for irregular migration, and if so how?

Can prison labour actually be deemed reformative and ensure training for gainful employment upon release? How legitimate is the use of prisoners in factories driven by marketer and retailer requirements for competitive lower-cost products to harness greater sales worldwide and better profit margins?

FURTHER RESOURCES

Research Works

Clark, J. B., & Poucki, S. (eds.). (2018). *The Sage Handbook of Human Trafficking and Modern-Day Slavery*. London: Sage Publications.

Elliott, J. (2014). *The Role of Consent in Human Trafficking*. London: Routledge.

Kara, S. (2014). *Bonded Labor: Tackling the System of Slavery in South Asia*. New York: Columbia University Press.

Milivojevic, S., Pickering, S., & Segrave, M. (2017). *Sex Trafficking and Modern Slavery: The Absence of Evidence*. London: Routledge.

Sanchez, G. (2014). *Human Smuggling and Border Crossings*. London: Routledge.

Shelley, L. (2010). *Human Trafficking: A Global Perspective*. Cambridge: Cambridge University Press.

Tiano, S., & Murphy-Aguilar, M. (eds.). (2016). *Borderline Slavery: Mexico, United States, and The Human Trade*. London and New York: Routledge.

Informational Websites

AntiSlavery International [www.antislavery.org/slavery-today/human-trafficking/]

End Slavery Now [www.endslaverynow.org/learn/books-films]

Freedom Fund [https://freedomfund.org/]

Global Slavery Index [www.globalslaveryindex.org/2018/findings/highlights/]

UN Office for Drugs and Crime [www.unodc.org/unodc/en/human-trafficking/ index.html?ref= menuside]

Coalition to Abolish Slavery & Trafficking [www.castla.org/training-resources/]

Annotated Documentaries

CNN (2014). *Children for Sale: The Fight to End Trafficking* [42:00 min.]. Part of the CNN Freedom Project series of documentaries.

Al Jazeera (2016). *Borderless: Undercover with the People Smugglers* [25:00 min.]. On the factors driving people to seek safety in Europe. Broadcast on the 'People and Power' weekly programme.

Kobes Media (2017). *Invisible Chains: Bonded Labour in India's Brick Kilns* [12:00 min.]. On debt bondage linked with other slavery, such as forced labour and trafficking around South Asia.

The Why Foundation (2016). *Secret Slaves of the Middle East* [44:11 min.]. On the plight of women from developing countries deceived into domestic work from which they cannot leave.

Al Jazeera (2020). *Chocolate's Heart of Darkness* [47:48 min.]. On trafficking of child labour across West African borders into work on cocoa plantations despite laws forbidding this.

General Reading

Batstone, D. B. (2007). *Not for Sale: The Return of the Global Slave Trade – and How We Can Fight It*. New York: Harper San Fancisco.

Brown, T. L. (2000). *Sex Slaves: The Trafficking of Women in Asia*. London: Virago Press.

McDonald-Gibson, C. (2016). *Cast Away: True Stories of Survival from Europe's Refugee Crisis*. London: Portobello Books.

Cox, B. (2013). *This Immoral Trade: Slavery in the 21st Century* (updated and extended edition). Derby, CT: Monarch Books.

Gupta, R. (2013). *Enslaved: The New British Slavery*. London: Portobello Books.

Segal, R. (2002). *Islam's Black Slaves: The Other Black Diaspora*. London: Atlantic Books/ Macmillan.

Endnotes

1. International Labor Organisation (ILO) (2017). *Global Estimates of Modern Slavery*. Geneva: International Labor Organisation.

2. United Nations (2000). *Convention against Transnational Organized Crime and its Protocol to Prevent, Suppress and Punish Trafficking in Persons, especially Women and Children*. New York: United Nations.

3. International Organisation for Migration (IOM) (2005). *Data and Research on Human Trafficking: A Global Survey*. Geneva: International Organisation for Migration.

4. US State Department (2018). *Trafficking in Persons Report*. Washington, DC: US Department of State.

5. ILO (2005). *A Global Alliance Against Forced Labour*. Geneva: International Labor Organisation.

6. Jadic, G., & Finckenauer, J. O. (2005). Representations and misrepresentations of human trafficking. *Trends in Organized Crime, 8*(3), Spring.

7. Montesh, M. (2011). Football trafficking: a new African slave trade. *Commonwealth Youth and Development, 9*(1), 4–17.

8. United National Office for Drugs and Crime (UNODC) (2018). Map 6. *Global Report on Human Trafficking 2018*. Geneva: United National Office for Drugs and Crime.

9. UNODC (2003). *Protocol against the Smuggling of Migrants by Land, Sea and Air*. New York: United Nations Office for Drugs and Crime. p. 2.

10. Carling J. (2005). *Trafficking in Women from Nigeria to Europe*. Washington, DC: Migration Policy Institute. [www.migrationinformation.org/ Feature/ display.cfm? ID=318 – accessed 04 November 2014].

11. Zhang, S. X., & Gaylord, M. (1996). Bound for Golden Mountain: the social organisation of Chinese alien smuggling. *Crime, Law & Social Change, 25*, 1–16.

12. Myers, W. H. (ed.). (1995). Orb weavers – the global webs: the structure and activities of transnational ethnic Chinese criminal groups. *Transnational Organized Crime, 1*(4), 1–36.

13. End Slavery Now (2016). *Bonded Labor*. [www.endslaverynow.org/learn/slavery-to day/bonded-labor – accessed 20 April 2017].

14. Olujuwon, T. (2008). Combating trafficking in persons: a case study of Nigeria. *European Journal of Scientific Research, 24*(1), 23–32.

15. ILO (2005). Global Report on Forced Labour in Asia: Debt Bondage, Trafficking and State-Imposed Forced Labour – Promoting Jobs, Protecting People. Geneva: International Labor Organisation.

16. Free the Slaves (2007). *Modern slavery*. [www.freetheslaves.net – accessed 09 March 2018].

17. Global Slavery Index (2016). Mauritania. [https://downloads.globalslaveryindex. org/ ephemeral/GSI-2016-Full-Report-1538511531.pdf – accessed 10 October 2017].

18. Millward, P. (2017). World Cup 2022 and Qatar's construction projects: relational power in networks and relational responsibilities to migrant workers. *Current Sociology, 65*(5), 756–776.

19. Extracted from ILO (2017). *Global Estimates of Modern Slavery*. Geneva: International Labor Organisation & Walk Free Foundation.

20. ILO (2014). *Profits and Poverty: The Economics of Forced Labour*. Geneva: International Labor Organisation.

21. Castles, S. (2000). International migration at the beginning of the twenty-first century: global trends and issues. *International Social Science Journal, 52*(165).

22. Skrivankova, K. (2010). *Between Decent Work and Forced Labour: Examining the Continuum of Exploitation* [JRF Programme Paper: Forced Labour]. York, UK: Joseph Rowntree Foundation.

23. ILO (2014). *Profits and Poverty: The Economics of Forced Labour*. Geneva: International Labor Organisation. [Cited at https://msw.usc.edu/freedoms-journey-understand ing-human-trafficking/ – accessed 17 May 2017].

24. Kritz, M. M., Lin, L. L., & Zlotnik, H. (eds.). (1992). *International Migration Systems*. Oxford: Clarendon Press.

25. Massey, D. S. (1999). International migration at the dawn of the twenty-first century: the role of the state. *Population and Development Review, 25*(2), 303–322.

26. Athukorala, P. (2006). International labour migration in East Asia: trends, patterns and policy issues. *Asian-Pacific Economic Literature* [compilation].

27. Sachs, J. (2005). *The End of Poverty: Economic Possibilities for Our Time*. New York: Penguin Press.

28. Rathgerber, C. (2002). The victimization of women through human trafficking – an aftermath of war? *European Journal of Crime, Criminal Law and Criminal Justice, 10*(2–3), 152–163.

29. Li, Miao (2016). Pre-migration trauma and post-migration stressors for Asian and Latino American immigrants: transnational stress proliferation. *Social Indicators Research, 129*(1), 47–59.

30. Biermann, F., & Boas, I. (2010). Preparing for a warmer world: towards a global governance system to protect climate refugees. *Global Environmental Politics, 10*(1), 60–88.

31. Koslowski, R. (2001). Economic globalization, human smuggling and global governance. In D. Kyle & R. Koslowski (eds.), *Global Human Smuggling*. Baltimore, MD: Johns Hopkins University Press.

32. Chawki, M., & Wahab, M. (2004). Technology is a double-edged sword: illegal human trafficking in the information age. *Fourth Annual Conference of the European Society of Criminology*, 25–28 August, Amsterdam, the Netherlands.

33. Thachuk, K. L. (ed.). (2007). *Transnational Threats: Smuggling and Trafficking in Arms, Drugs and Human Life*. Westport, CT: Praeger/Greenwood Publishing.

34. Lendman, S. (2010). UN peacekeepers complicit in sex trade. *Baltimore Chronicle*, 23 October.

35. UNODC (2014). *Global Report on Trafficking in Persons*. New York: United Nations Office on Drugs and Crime.

36. Gang I. N., & Yun, M. S. (2007). Immigration amnesty and immigrant's earnings. *Immigration: Trends, Consequences and Prospects for the United States, Research in Labor Economics, 27*, 273–309.

37. Olsen, H. H. (2008). The snake from Fujian Province to Morecombe Bay: an analysis of the problem of human trafficking in sweated labour. *European Journal of Crime, Criminal Law and Criminal Justice, 16*, 1–35.

38. Naim, M. (2005). *Illicit: How Smugglers, Traffickers and Copycats are Hijacking the Global Economy*. London: Random House.

39. Epstein, G. S., & Weiss, A. (2001). A theory of immigration amnesties. *IZA Discussion Paper No. 302*. Bonn: Institute for the Study of Labour.

40. Athukorala, P. (2006). International labour migration in East Asia: trends, patterns and policy issues. *Asian-Pacific Economic Literature* [compilation].

41. Rodrik, D. (2002). *Feasible Globalization*. NBER Working Paper No. 9129. Cambridge, MA: National Bureau of Economic Research.

42. Miko, F. T. (2007). International human trafficking [Chapter 3]. In K. L. Thachuk (ed.), *Transnational Threats: Smuggling and Trafficking in Arms, Drugs and Human Life*. Westport, CT: Praeger/Greenwood Publishing.

43. Kaye, M. (2003). The migration-trafficking nexus: combating trafficking by protecting migrants' human rights. [Available at: www.antislavery.org]

44. Miller, J. R. (2008). US Justice Dept blind to slavery. *International Herald Tribune*, 12–13 July, page 4.

45. Salt, J., & Stein, J. (1997). Migration as business: the case of trafficking. *International Migration, 35*(4), 467–494.

46. Van Impe, K. (2000). People for sale: the need for a multidisciplinary approach towards human trafficking. *International Migration, 38*(3), 113–191.

47. Kangaspunta, K. (2003). Mapping the inhuman trade: preliminary finds of the human trafficking database. Paper presented at the *UN Division for the Advancement of Women Consultative Meeting*, 2–4 December, Malmo, Sweden.

48. Winters, L. A., Walmsley, T. L., Wang, Z. K., & Grynberg, R. (2003). Liberalising temporary movement of natural persons: an agenda for the development round. *World Economy, 26*(8), 1137–1161.

49. Tyldum, G., & Brunovskis, A. (2005). Describing the unobserved: methodological challenges in empirical studies on human trafficking. *International Migration, 43*(1/2), 17–34.

50. Naomi, K. (2001). *No Logo*. London: Flamingo.

51. Cooke, B. (2003). The denial of slavery in management studies. *Journal of Management Studies, 40*(8).

52. Laczko, F., & Gramegna, M. A. (2003). Developing better indicators of human trafficking. *Brown Journal of World Affairs, 10*(1), 179–194.

53. Thomas, A. O. (2009). Migrant, trafficked and bonded workers: human rights abuse or resources mismanagement. *Proceedings of the International Academy for African Business & Development Conference*, 19–23 May, Kampala, Uganda.

54. Barham, J. (2008). Slaves in the global supply chain. *Security Management, 52*(3), 44.

55. Ould, D. (2004). *The Cocoa Industry in West Africa: A History of Exploitation*. London: Anti-Slavery International.

56. Ould, D. (2004). *The Cocoa Industry in West Africa: A History of Exploitation*. London: Anti-Slavery International.

57. Kaye, M. (2006). *Contemporary Forms of Slavery in Paraguay*. [www.antislavery.org – accessed 14 November 2012].

58. Sharma, B. (2006). *Contemporary Forms of Slavery in Peru*. [www.antislavery.org – accessed 26 June 2010].

59. Hall, K. (2004). Slavery exists out of sight in Brazil. [www.mongabay.com/external/slavery_in_brazil.htm – accessed 12 January 2009].

60. Sharma, B. (2006). *Contemporary Forms of Slavery in Peru*. [www.antislavery.org – accessed 26 June 2010].

61. Brown, P. (2001). *Do You Know about the New ILO Worst Forms of Child Labour Convention 1999*. Geneva: NGO Group for the Convention on the Rights of the Child.

62. Kaye, M. (2006). *Contemporary Forms of Slavery in Argentina*. [Available at: www.antislavery.org – accessed 14 November 2012].

63. US–China Commission (2008). *2008 Report to Congress of the US–China Economic and Security Review Commission*. Washington, DC: US Government Printing Office, pp. 317–326.

64. Lee, H. (2014). A call for aggressive media campaign regarding DPRK prison camps. *Northwestern University Journal of International Human Rights, 12,* 213.

65. Gyupchanova, T. (2018). Labor and human rights conditions of North Korean workers dispatched overseas: a look at the DPRK's exploitative practices in Russia, Poland, and Mongolia. *Cornell International Law Journal, 51,* 183.

66. Amnesty International (2005). Myanmar: tens of thousands facing forced labour, beatings and theft. [http://web.amnesty.org/library/index/engasa160232005 – accessed 17 December 2008].

67. Economist (2008). Test case: companies and human rights. *The Economist,* 1 November, page 77.

68. Laczko, F., & Gramegna, M. A. (2003). Developing better indicators of human trafficking. *Brown Journal of World Affairs, 10*(1), 179–194.

69. Salt, J. (2002). *European International Migration: Evaluation of the Current Situation*. European Population Papers Series No. 5. Strasbourg: Council of Europe.

70. Väyrynen, R. (2003). *Illegal Immigration, Human Trafficking, and Organized Crime*. Discussion Paper No. 2003/72. World Institute for Developing Economics Research, United Nations University.

71. Carling J. (2005). Trafficking in women from Nigeria to Europe. Washington, DC: Migration Policy Institute. [www.migrationinformation.org/ Feature/ display.cfm? ID=318].

72. Gupta, R. (2007). *Enslaved: The New British Savery*. London: Portobello Books, pp. 247–252.

73. Raymond, J. G. (2019). Immunity Incorporated: all the injustice that Jeffrey Epstein can buy. *Dignity: A Journal on Sexual Exploitation and Violence, 4*(1), 1.

74. UNODC (2010). *Trafficking of Persons into Europe for Sexual Exploitation*. New York: United Nations Organisation for Drugs and Crime/Global Initiative to Fight Trafficking (GIFT).

CHAPTER 4

TRANSPLANT TOURISM & ORGANS ACQUISITION

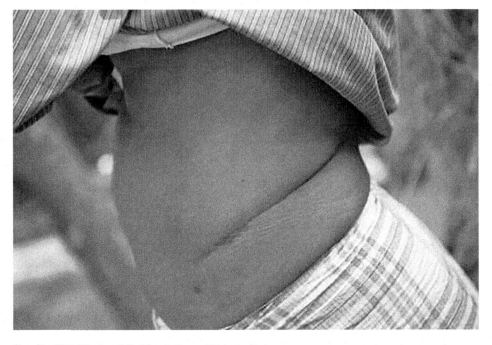

Credit: *MSU Today*, Michigan State University

Overview in Introduction

The harvesting of human body parts for transplant remains largely the purview of investigative journalism, a concern to the medical fraternity, and the source for the occasional legal scandal. Given that there has been relatively little research on the size of this shadow trade, estimates have been the result of considerable conjecture, even though the sale of body parts tends to be advertised online and in the media of certain developing countries. Despite periodic public outrage over their acquisition from the underprivileged, worldwide demand is increasing. This leads to longer lifespans, greater affluence as well as advances in transplant surgery in industrialised and even emergent countries. Meanwhile the connection of global diaspora with the sources of body parts and the location of surgery goes generally unnoticed. This chapter illustrates that, more than just an economic or technological phenomenon, the practice of organs acquisition has political, cultural and ideological dimensions. It concludes by evaluating the means of raising local supply and dampening global demand for human organs as strategic responses to this shadow trade. Among the intersecting subjects addressed in this chapter are: organs procurement, transplant tourism, altruistic donation, paid donors, brokers, diasporic markets, opt-in/opt-out systems, regulated reimbursement, pricing body parts, cultural taboos and health promotion.

Plight versus Rights

Growth of the Therapy

As far back as the 18th century, organ transplants have been experimented on animals and humans, most resulting in failure. In the mid-20th century the first human organ to be transplanted successfully was the kidney, followed by liver, heart and pancreas transplants by the late 1960s. Medical breakthroughs such as tissue-typing and immune-suppressant drugs in the mid-1970s enabled a higher survival rate for recipients.[1] Transplant surgery has become relatively commonplace as a beneficial therapy worldwide, especially in the industrialised world. In recent decades it is increasingly adopted in emergent economies, at least among their rising upper-middle class. Consequently, the demand for organs in transplant surgery persistently far exceeds their supply, leading to the questionable purchase of these from developing countries. Thus far the size of the global market has had to be the result of some conjecture even by inter-government agencies and non-government organisations. Nonetheless the retail value has been estimated reliably at the start of the 2010s as between USD600 million to USD1.2 billion, arguably making it among the top ten shadow trades.[2] Scarce business research seems to have delved into the trade in human body parts, even in the sub-discipline of healthcare management, and so it remains largely the concern of the medical fraternity and public policy-makers. Consequently, this dismal, if lucrative, global business has been the source of the occasional legal scandal, the purview of investigative journalism, dispassionate economic modelling of future prices, or the ethnographic study of critical anthropology.

Spreading the Pain

Organ transplants are an affordable means of surviving organ failure for the affluent and donations from living donors are deemed preferable over cadaveric organs, the latter typically donated by the aged and terminally ill. So long as there is a scarcity of organs available for transplant in the country of the patient, there will invariably be a global market for human organs harvested largely from the indigent poor in the developing world. The World Health Organisation (WHO), in collaboration with the Global Observatory on Donation and Transplantation, remains one of the better and more reliable sources of information on the incidence of transplant surgery worldwide. Their decade-old statistics, which numbers traded organs in the hundreds and thousands, may appear rather insignificant, but these are only of those that are declared (Figure 4.1). Its synthesis from different data sources does not cover the actual situation in each and every country for a variety of political, regulatory, infrastructural and methodological reasons.[3]

The semi-official sale of body parts has been reported on periodically in a number of developing/emergent countries, notably India, Bangladesh, Turkey, Brazil and the Philippines, as well as in some post-transitional economies within Eastern and Central Europe. Being characteristically secretive, China is periodically implicated in this shadow trade, particularly because its high rate of judicial executions raises speculation. From time to time there has been furore also over sales of cadaver parts both to and even within the industrialised world itself, implicating hospitals, laboratories, pharmaceutical firms, research institutes and universities alike. Certainly, those transplants that are conducted clandestinely will never be reported, regardless of locality, besides data on transplantations being neither widely available nor readily accessible in many developing and emergent economies. More recent data on the origins and destinations of organs in the global trade comes from activist groups but remains more contested.

Curative Contagion

Transplant on Demand

The preference for living over cadaveric organs and consequent need for concurrent surgery to preserve the quality of the transplanted organ have spawned the trend towards medical-surgical tourism. In this case, the developing-country donor

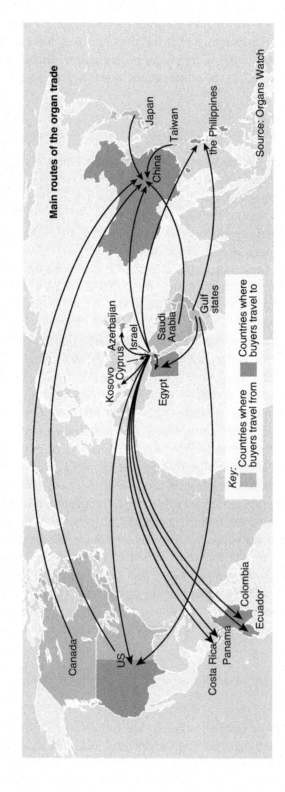

Figure 4.1 Global organ transplants: the main trade routes[4]

Reprinted by kind permission of New Internationalist. Copyright New Internationalist. www.newint.org.

is flown either to the industrialised country of the recipient, and vice versa, or to a third country, for the duration of the surgery and recuperation. Initially reported in countries like India, Pakistan, China and the Philippines, this phenomenon has spread in recent decades to a number of other developing, emergent and transitional economies in Asia, the Middle East, Latin America, Eastern Europe and South Africa. By the late 2000s, some of those countries had taken legislative steps to control the neo-colonialist trade in organs via transplant tourism, although it is unclear whether enforcement is sufficiently rigorous. Despite a law in India permitting only relatives to donate kidneys, the practice of acquiring kidneys through fraudulent documentation remains prevalent, exemplified with a case of some 500 persons in poor villages allegedly forcibly operated on by one surgeon alone.[5]

On the surface, such medical-surgical tourism may seem benign and ethically-neutral in merely providing services of global quality at a fraction of their cost in the industrialised world. Presumably it enables healthcare to be affordable to more people, such as in the middle classes in the developing and emergent world, thus being more socially equitable.[6] It is sometimes argued that such paid-for surgery by those patients coming from the industrialised world enables hospitals in the developing world to provide free or highly subsidised healthcare to their local poor, including transplant surgery itself. Arguably, the concerns expressed about risks to foreign patients may largely reflect societal prejudice against medical practitioners in the developing world as well as disguised fear by surgeons in the industrialised world of competition for their lucrative medical custom. Medical-surgical tourism may also be a way of circumventing legal strictures, religious sanctions and cultural taboos in their home countries, such as fertility treatment, abortions and sex-change, and so may be seen as a valid option by citizens thus discriminated and disadvantaged.[7] Given the wide range of medical-surgical tourism, from dentistry and cosmetic surgery to birth surrogacy, neurosurgery and organ transplantation, it is highly debatable whether public policies and international regulations can cover all categories.

Pricing Spare-parts

Although the opacity of the black market trade in human body parts makes estimates of its size challenging, indicative prices for every kind of transplant package globally are readily accessible online. While acknowledging that there are no reliable data on organ trafficking, the WHO reports that brokers charge wealthy patients between USD100,000 and USD200,000 for a transplant package, while paying between USD1,000 and USD5,000 to the impoverished donor.[8] For the purposes of transplant, the kidney is the organ of choice since one may be donated by a living person who can survive on the retained kidney. The price for a kidney is said to range from USD500 in Iraq to USD5,000 in Turkey.[9] Nonetheless quotes on online websites for transplant surgery, including organ acquisition, demonstrate the considerable differential in price between that in an industrialised country and that promoted as being available in a developing country (Table 4.1). Indicatively, the cost for a kidney transplant in a country like Pakistan or China could be less than a tenth of what it would cost in the US, and no more than a third of what it would cost in another country, such as Israel or the Philippines. This represents a boon for privatised healthcare in a capitalist economy.

Table 4.1   Comparative prices for transplant tourism packages[10] [11]

LOCATION	RECIPIENT ORIGIN	ORGAN	OFF-SHORE PACKAGE (USD)	EQUIVALENT USA PACKAGE (USD)	PRICE RATIO: OFF-SHORE/ USA (%)
China		Kidney	42,000-63,000	414,800	10.2–15.2
		Liver	40,000-75,000	812,500	4.9–9.2
		Lung	150,000	861,700	17.4
		Heart	130,000	1,382,400	9.4
Pakistan	Local	Kidney	6,000-10,000	414,800	1.5–2.4
	Foreign	Kidney	20,000-30,000	414,800	4.8–7.2
Philippines		Kidney	65,000-100,000	414,800	15.6–24.0
Israel	Local	Kidney	100,000-120,000	414,800	24.0–28.9
	Foreign	Kidney	125,000-135,000	414,800	30.1–32.5

Note: Data extracted and analysed from multiple online and offline sources, including those cited in chapter text.

As per the Istanbul Declaration, doctors were advised to counsel patients against going abroad to procure an organ for transplant, given the ethical issues. However, a study of nephrologists, transplant surgeons, coordinators and patients found that, as healthcare professionals, they did not wish to question their patients about either their intentions or past actions. This study in the Netherlands also found it difficult to ascertain the extent of transplant tourism, even though there was knowledge that patients had travelled to China, Iran, India and Pakistan, often countries of their ethnic origins, on account of being familiar in those environments. Many such countries are known for involvement in the trafficking of persons for the purposes of kidney harvesting. This poses ethical challenges which call for international regulation and enforcement. Yet, despite the close links, some advocate differentiating between transplant tourism, transplant commercialism and trafficking persons for organ harvesting. No presumptions seem to be made that the last form is implicit in the former two, in addressing the unmet demand for organs within nation-states and geo-political groupings and providing resources for enforcement against trafficking.[12]

Desperate Patients

Any move to prohibit body-part sales would undoubtedly mean longer waiting lists for a suitable donor to be found, and for the potential recipients this portends the risk of death in the interim.[13] An estimated 100,000 patients in the USA remain on waiting lists for years, despite transplants being done at the rate of nearly 30,000 each year.[14] Meanwhile these patients are subjected to a regime of long hours spent almost daily tethered to a dialysis machine, at significant cost to the patient, their private insurer and/or the government. Nonetheless, paying handsomely for a transplant abroad is no guarantee of survival and improved health, a fact frequently concealed by parties to this shadow trade. On the whole, those who receive organs from unrelated living donors do significantly worse in terms of graft failure, viral infections, needing greater immuno-suppression medication, complications such as diabetes as well as patient non-survival.[15] In fact, the outcome for child patients of transplant tourism is particularly unfortunate. Quite apart from the relatively unpredictable problem of organ rejection, there are the risks of incompetent surgery, infection through poor medical care, and other complications occurring both immediately in the transplant destination and in the longer term in the usually more expensive home country of the patient-tourist.

Vulnerable Donors

Underpaid donors

Poverty, unemployment, personal crises and debt are primary drivers of donors selling their organs or tissue in developing countries. They are regularly paid much less than promised after various deductions, medical and non-medical, are made *post-hoc*. The price mark-up then runs into hundreds and thousands of percent on the organs harvested from paid donors (Table 4.2). Illiteracy seems a contributory factor because the indigent poor are consequently more prone to such deception and exploitation. Academic research in India has confirmed media reports elsewhere in the developing world that the donors continue to live in dire poverty, suffer ill-health and personally would not recommend that others follow suit.[16] The implications of poor health for future wage earnings and the subsequent cost of medical care, the latter typically underwritten by the developing-country government, are almost never factored into the pricing of the donated organ by the commercial providers. Meanwhile the recipients are charged a significant premium for the organ within the transplant package, with most of the income and profit being shared among the brokers, doctors, hospitals, travel agents, hotels and other ancillary services.

Surreptitious harvesting

Not all donors or sellers of body parts may be voluntary for in some countries there have been numerous news stories of people who have been persuaded into surgery for some unspecified ailment, only to later discover a kidney has been removed. In other cases, people have been lured abroad by the promise of better-paying jobs and then discovered that the real purpose was the harvesting of their body parts or bonded labour to pay for repatriation. Every now and then 'urban myths' surface about persons finding themselves waking up from being drugged only to find that one of their kidneys has been surgically removed. Such tales cannot be totally discounted. Disappearances of street children or inmates from orphanages have also been suspected to be linked to this shadow trade.[17] It is debatable whether the harvesting of stem cells for research and of foetuses aborted naturally or surgically for therapeutic purposes could fit into this category of involuntary donation.

Coerced contribution

The practice of harvesting body parts from live or executed prisoners or war captives has been established as having taken place in countries under various dictatorships in the past. In spite of official policy changes in China, the increase in capital punishments for commercial offences and political dissent continue to be linked to the profitability of the trade in human body parts, even including execution-on-demand for needy foreign patients visiting.[18] There is the questionable practice of death-row prisoners donating their organs as a 'gift-to-society' in recompense for their offences, and even the allusion to the body of every citizen being in principle owned by the state under strict communist interpretation. There have also been documented allegations in other poor countries, such as India and Pakistan, of the vulnerable being forced, under threat of violence, to donate a kidney, perhaps for debt default or a change of mind over an earlier consent to the surgery.

Table 4.2 Price escalation for transplant organs[19]

DONOR/ SURGERY LOCATIONS	HUMAN ORGAN	PAYMENT PROMISED TO DONOR (USD)	PAYMENT RECEIVED BY DONOR (USD)	BROKER/ DONOR DEDUCTION (%)	PACKAGE COST TO RECIPIENT (USD)	RECIPIENT/ DONOR PREMIUM (%)
Brazil/Israel	Kidney	> 10,000	3,000–6,000	–40–70	20,000	+33–66
Israel/Israel	Kidney		10,000–20,000		100,000–160,000	+500–1,600
India/India	Kidney	1,410	1,070	–25	20,000	+1,400
Pakistan/ Pakistan	Kidney	1,737–2,400	1,377–1,600	–20	7,271	+300
Turkey/Egypt	Kidney	30,000	10,000	–67	35,000–40,000	+35–40
Philippines	Kidney	2,750	2,133	–22	65,000–85,000	+2,360–4,000

Note: Data extracted and analysed from multiple online and offline sources including those cited.

Diagnosing the Malaise

Incidence and Growth

Lucrative therapy, needful research

With the progressive privatisation of healthcare worldwide, governments have a diminishing role as the traditional arbiter between altruistic donors and recipients on prioritised national waiting lists. Organ transplant surgery might be among the most well-paid specialisations in medicine, rivalling cosmetic surgery,[20] and thus attracting a dubious global supply chain cashing-in on the need for its most critical element, namely the body parts themselves. Blood plasma sold by the poor to medical laboratories, clinics and pharmaceutical firms, even in industrial countries, are used in transfusion therapies. Skin and tissue extraction from cadavers is becoming routine in some countries, with or without the consent of the deceased and/or their family. Yet another and more recent area of growth is in the transplantation of others' human embryos in fertility treatment, commercial birthing surrogacy and stem cell therapies. Moreover, the transplant medical industry is not the sole destination since all forms of body parts or whole bodies are used in pharmaceutical and medical research, as well as in practitioner training.

Increased demand, decreased supply

With affluent lifestyles being common in the industrialised world and becoming so in emergent economies, so has the incidence of kidney failure increased, precipitated by the consequent health issues of obesity, hypertension and diabetes.[21] On the other hand, the decline of strokes, heart attacks and even fatal accidents through public health-and-safety campaigns as well as better medical care have inadvertently caused a decline in the number of cadaveric donors of organs for transplant available locally in industrialised countries. Complicating factors include compatibility between donor and recipient, surgery prioritisation by the youthfulness of the potential recipient, the quality of the donor's organ, and the transmission of other diseases including hepatitis, cancer and HIV/AIDS, among others. Together with the urgency of the patient's medical condition and the proximity of the donor to the patient for rapid transport, these factors make transplant surgery as a medical remedy particularly challenging.

Worldwide Marketplace

Politics and economics

The trade in human organs may be symptomatic of economic globalisation as much as of medical progress in transplant surgery over the last century. While deploring the fact that it was relatively under-researched despite periodic scandals over coercive sourcing from the underprivileged of the developing world, Harrison points out that this is not just an economic phenomenon.[22] Among other things, it is a political one in terms of the diminished role of government in social services, a cultural one in the diffusion of Western notions of modernisation, and an ideological phenomenon in favouring capitalist forms of exchange. All these contexts and factors do contribute to this particular shadow trade in human organs thriving, which, together with exploring the alternative modes of exchange worldwide involving donors and recipients, is crucial to surmounting most ethical reservations. Furthermore, there are various sectors and players, both legal and illegitimate, involved in a complex borderless network for organs acquisition for transplantation (Figure 4.2) which needs regulation and monitoring.

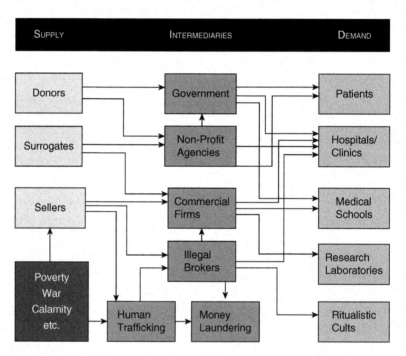

Figure 4.2 Web of organs acquisition

Digital arbitrage

The advent of the internet and momentous growth of e-commerce have given new impetus to the trade in human body parts as people in need of transplant surgery gain ready access to donors, doctors, hospitals and packages on a global scale. As in the global market for any goods and services, there is price arbitrage in transplant surgery and other medical services as people discover them to be affordable abroad, as travel becomes less expensive, as immigration barriers decline, as language barriers lessen and as standards of healthcare rise abroad. Hence the shadow trade in human body parts is both a beneficiary of and a contributor to these globalisation trends in transplant tourism, but is also linked to money laundering and other illicit activities.[23] In this context, the argument about whether to enforce regulation or to impose a ban on the trade in human body parts in any single legal jurisdiction may possibly be counter-productive as both measures risk pushing this already partially concealed global business further underground.

Cultural affinity

Social support that is important to recuperation does seem to dictate surgery nearer the home country, culture or region of the patient. In a globalised world, this could be extended to include countries that share a world-language connection, such as among developing countries formerly colonised by the same European country. Thus, a transplant patient from a country once colonised by the British Empire, such as Kenya, may feel more comfortable having surgery conducted in an Asian country that was similarly colonised, like Singapore. From the statistics available, there is an apparent preference of wealthy Arabs in the Gulf States to seek out other countries with predominantly Muslim populations, such as Pakistan.[24] This apparent prejudice towards donors because of dietary and religious sensibilities, in addition to the apparent economic disparity, is seldom addressed explicitly. Regardless, these patterns betray a preference for cultural links, whether largely colonial or religious, which override other considerations for the location of transplant surgery.

Diasporic markets

Somewhat neglected in discussions of the shadow trade in organ transplantation is mention of the connection of global diasporas from the developing world with both the sources of body parts and the location of surgery. For while people of other nationalities and ethnicities might also be tapping into this trade, the connection of global diaspora of the country of ethnic origin plays a significant part.[25] Limited statistics and anecdotal accounts give reason to believe that it is largely wealthier Overseas Chinese with citizenships elsewhere in Asia who seek out human organs and the accompanying transplant surgery in China and Taiwan. Likewise, those Non-Resident Indians (NRIs) living in Europe and North America seem to prefer having transplant surgery in India and Mauritius, the latter having an ethnic Indian majority. Even though these choices reflect cultural affinity, it still remains a form of neo-colonial exploitation by these diaspora from wealthier countries of peoples in poorer ones, even when they are of similar ethnic heritage.

Third-country providers

In South Africa, which has an advanced medical system for the Africa continent, between 2001 and 2003, donors were recruited from Brazil and Romania, among other countries, for transplant patients arriving mainly from Israel, possibly recruited from the occupied Palestinian Territories.[26] It may be argued that these healthcare providers are from the semi-periphery countries that serve as intermediaries between core and periphery ones in the unequal world capitalist system. There is little reason to doubt that similar practices take place in other regions in the world, possibly with both donors and recipients moving smaller distances to a third country within their geographic region. This is especially so in economically integrated regions that no longer require visas to cross borders or have rather porous borders, and where the medico-legal environment might be less stringent than in the so-called industrialised world. Growing trust in the medical facilities and expertise in emerging economies is a further compelling consideration in the choice of treatment location outside industrialised countries.

Enabling Sectors

Hospitals and clinics

While hospitals are most often implicated in the global trade in human body parts, what constitutes an institution providing surgical services may vary from country to country. Often a relatively well-equipped private clinic and an unscrupulous surgeon might suffice for transplant surgery and might be clandestine so as to not attract regulation by the medical profession or government.[27] Where the patient and/or the donor, even the surgeon and assisting staff, are from abroad or from a long distance away within the country, it is unlikely that there could be a future formal complaint of professional malpractice or/and prosecution for criminal negligence. Though not strictly involving a human organ, another legitimate medical field is that of fertility treatment, which involves egg donation and artificial insemination of surrogates, in the latter case often drawn from the poor in developing or emergent economies.[28]

Travel services

Discreet participants in and beneficiaries of the human organs trade are the commercial providers of air-tickets, visas and hotel accommodation for both donors and recipients alike. In some cases, they might also be brokers of organs, or at least promoters of both medical tourism destinations and providers of transplantation services, although this has not always been optimised, as in Thailand, despite being a noted destination.[29] It is quite challenging to differentiate travellers who might have legitimate grounds to visit another country for tourism, business, family reunion and other medical treatment, from those who do so solely for transplant surgery involving the purchase of human organs harvested from donors, living or dead, local or from a third country. A related tourism field is the role of adoption and birth-surrogacy agencies which purport to assist childless couples, offering the latter a complete package, including travel to the country of the child.

Peasant-labourers

Studies in a number of developing countries have demonstrated that commercial living organ donors are consistently drawn from the most vulnerable segment of their societies, namely unskilled workers and peasants. Being poorly educated, under-employed and living below the poverty line, they come under pressure to donate organs as a consequence of the slightest personal financial crisis.[30] An illustration of the shadow trade link between organs harvesting with bonded labour or modern-day slavery is labourers doing so to free themselves from debt servitude. A majority of organ sellers can also be bonded labourers, as was noteworthy with 66 percent of those studied in Pakistan.[31] Sadly, the organ removal has been demonstrated to cause a deterioration of health in the vast majority of labourer-donors, resulting in a decline in their ability to work and thus a further worsened financial situation.

Religion and ritual

While the mainstream health and related sectors may be amenable to regulation and monitoring, the harvesting of organs and other body parts for cultural or religious practices are archetypally not. All body parts, including bones and hair, or even whole bodies, can be used by traditional healers for medical potions and by priests in religious rituals.[32] Especially troubling is the use of the body parts of children, especially those who are albino, as has been the case in many parts of Africa, an indictment of the failure of the education system in past colonial and present post-colonial eras. Typically conducted in remote regions in developing countries or among migrant minorities, such customary practices are especially difficult to eradicate among adherents, even where there are national laws forbidding them, because these are unenforceable except in more affluent urban areas.

Prognosis for Intervention

Ethical Quandaries

Altruism versus sale

The critical ethical dilemma in organ transplantation must surely be what criteria to use in deciding between recipients. In managed systems for altruistic donations, this can be a moral minefield. Should a life-saving organ be given to a younger person rather than an older one, a parent rather than a single person, a brilliant professional or scientist over an unskilled worker? To some extent this conundrum is circumvented by a market-based system, but the moral debate consequent to establishing this system turns on the question of whether human organs ought to be marketed and sold for a price, as any other commodity. An additional ethical issue in this global trade is whether the rich patients, however desperate, ought to be able to buy organs from the poor, however destitute, and thus by-pass all societal constraints of a waiting list for transplant surgery through a market-based system.

One perspective is that even in our era of medical advances and global free markets, organ acquisition is still a form of exploitation of the poor of the developing world by the affluent of the industrialised world. The socio-economic injustice and human rights abuse involved are akin to the colonialism, even slavery, of past eras. Notable among proponents of this critical view of the surgeons, hospitals, laboratories and bioethicists is Scheper-Hughes, whose landmark ethnographic study of the global trade encompassed comprehensively a number of sources, intermediary and recipient groups, institutions, cities and countries.[33] The opposing view is that prohibition against the commercialisation of organ donation denies the poor of one more economic opportunity for improving their lot. It argues that opponents of organs acquisition from the poor have not proven that it violates their human rights, while criminalisation possibly exacerbates the trafficking of such donors and their lack of long-term care.[34]

Establishing death

Although live donors are considered preferable, for cadaveric organs acquisition for transplantation the critical ethical issue concerns deciding the point of death, because organs deteriorate upon heart-death. The middle road is brain-death, which allows the person to be pronounced dead with the cessation of brain activity while the body continues to live, especially when the heart and lungs are aided mechanically. However, this acceptance of brain-death is far from universal, even in industrialised societies, and besides, there remains a distinct preference for live donors in many developing and emergent societies.[35] Then there is the vexing issue of determining death for donation given the possibility of controlled cardiac death, which can be induced on the basis of prognosis of non-survivable neurological injuries.[36] A further controversy concerns the administration of medications for preserving the organs rather than for benefiting the dying patient. Demand by a foreign-tourist patient awaiting a donated organ could subtly raise the risk of both induced death and organ preservation in contravention of universal human rights.

Anonymity versus disclosure

An as yet unresolved issue is whether the family of a dead donor ought to be allowed to know or even encouraged to have contact with the recipient. It raises the real possibility of establishing pseudo-kinship networks between the most unlikely of candidates, with parallels with child adoption. More communitarian societies would seem to be better candidates for such new social networks, except that more traditional cultures in those societies mitigate against organ donation at all, or at least to strangers. Where the sale of organs is forbidden, as with kidneys in the USA, fictionalised emotional ties have been used to give the semblance of altruistic donation by a paid donor.[37] The maintenance of pseudo-kinship between donor and recipient is particularly impractical in cross-border organ transplants and the risks involved would seem to tilt the balance towards maintaining the anonymity of donor and recipient.

Engendering Supply

Opt-in or opt-out systems

Virtually all countries, including in the industrialised world, have faced an uphill battle to achieve sufficient assent to the donating of organs to meet their transplant needs. Some countries have chosen to adopt opt-in policies in which potential donors are persuaded to permit the harvesting of various organs and body parts upon their death. However, grieving families have commonly refused to comply with these wishes of the deceased. Other countries have chosen to adopt opt-out policies, compelling individuals to deliberately refuse to permit the harvesting of their organs upon death. While this has been touted as being more successful in raising the pool of available organs for transplant, opt-out raises larger issues of the role of the state and the rights of the individuals, lessening the importance of the family in any decision to donate or not.[38] Appeals to the grieving family could be phrased in terms of his or her death being made meaningful by their donation of an organ to a needy dying person who also has a family. In communitarian cultures the imperative would be to have the donor's wish to opt-in be counter-signed by close family members in order to pre-empt reservations or objections by the latter if expressed upon death of the former.[39]

Regulated reimbursements

Although at odds with the Istanbul Declaration and WHO Guiding Principles, any scheme for living donations that provides fair compensation with proper pre- and post-operative care would undercut the exploitative practices of the black market in human organs. Worthy of emulation internationally is the system pioneered in Iran for the compensation and healthcare of live donors by the government that has resulted in the elimination of waiting lists.[40] It seeks to compensate the organ donors legitimately with safeguards such as that both parties must be of the same nationality, which may seem discriminatory, but helps in overcoming any stigma of mercenary motivation. Where the donor and recipient might be from different countries, a legalised compensation scheme cannot eliminate the black market without a regional cooperative network in which medical professionals are sanctioned if and when they engage beyond it. All that being said, it is unlikely that many industrialised countries would be inclined to adopt a system pioneered by a developing-emergent one, however innovative and viable.

Hybrid systems

While acknowledging their respective controversies, four typical solutions to raising organ availability are presumed consent, directed donation, commodification and cloning. But another is a hybrid system of commodification and altruistic donation, in other words a public-private and legal system, which Goodwin is at pains to debunk as a form of slavery in appealing to the African-American population that she focuses on for having a high rate of organ failure.[41] Attempts to curb the black market in human body parts appear destined to fail if not accompanied by the creation of a legitimate means of bridging the gap between supply and demand. Examples of programmes in Scandinavia that procure and exchange organs and tissue regionally could also provide the basis for instituting a similar system in developing and emergent economies in Asia.[42] The more that donations are made reliably available upon the death of a donor, the less the pressure for transplants from paid live donors, especially from among the vulnerable poor, particularly from developing countries. Thus, there exist a variety of alternatives for managing the supply and demand for transplant organs involving governments, healthcare institutions, markets and non-profit agencies, which may be scrutinised for adoption or adaptation in various political, economic, cultural and technological contexts (Figure 4.3).

Full-cost pricing

Using late-1990s data, economists have sought to establish an equilibrium price for organ donations that would increase supply, reduce queues, eliminate the black market, and generally reduce misery at the marginal raising of costs overall[43]. While a commendable attempt, there is something dehumanising about estimating the value of statistical life, quality of life and risk of death for donors within the US that results in a broad range of prices for kidneys from about USD 7,000 to USD 28,000. In the development of comprehensive costing incorporating post-donation healthcare, civil society and non-profit organisations involved in the health sector ought to be appealed to for assistance[44]. For until provision is made for the long-term healthcare of both donors and recipients, the true societal cost of the organs exchange will be loaded on the inevitably poorer individual donor in an inequitable economic system.

Genetic modification

In the near future genetically engineered animal parts could present a viable alternative to human body parts and undermine the trade, though there remains cultural or religious resistance especially to those from pigs[45]. Animal rights activists would doubtless raise the ethical issue of breeding, testing and killing animals for human medical purposes. Given a choice, people generally tend to favour an artificial part over an animal or even human part under the perception that it is healthier and safer, though this again could be subject to cultural differences between ethnic groups within a society[46]. The prospect of using stem cells to create human body parts to order would seem to be a welcome alternative, were it not for the ethical controversy of harvesting stem cells from cultivated or aborted embryos in the first place that usually invites religious prohibition. What is yet to be contemplated are the implications of such acquisition of stem cells from developing-emergent countries with a lack of relevant laws or lax ones, for various therapeutic and research purposes in the industrial world. Who should bear the cost of research and development in these alternatives to human organs for transplant is another issue.

Dampening Demand

Demography planning

Very little is said in the literature and media about reducing the demand for human organs, or at least arresting the high growth rate of that demand. It is understandable problematic to have to suggest that the demand is largely due to increasing life expectancy in countries that are developing economically.[47] Nevertheless this disproportionate demand, due in large part to the ageing of populations, may be caused by draconian family planning in emergent economies such as China, and declining child-bearing in much of the industrialised world, particularly in Europe, which may need to be addressed as it is in Sweden with family-friendly policies. The other option of increasing migration from developing countries with growing populations, such as in Africa, Latin America and Asia, is controversial given the political, economic and cultural issues arising, not to mention growing xenophobia tapped into by right-wing leaders.

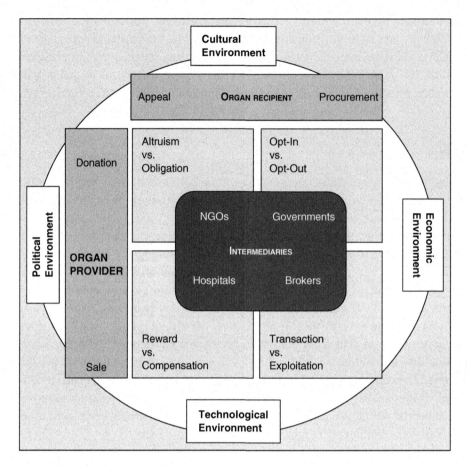

Figure 4.3   Contexts and modes for organs exchange

Health promotion

As many of the medical conditions leading to the need for organ transplants can be linked to unhealthy diets, there has been social activism against aggressive marketing by the fast-food and packaged food industries. While such campaigns have occurred and continue to grow in the industrialised world, these are less likely to be initiated or find much traction in the developing world, even though the rising middle classes in many of these countries are increasingly consumers of those unhealthy processed foods.[48] Governments in developing and emergent economies could also be disinclined to discourage investment by multinational firms in their packaged-food industries, let alone constrain their operations and exporting. The other contributor to medical conditions necessitating transplants is the lack of exercise and the increase of sedentary lifestyles in industrialised countries or among the affluent in emergent economies, which may be overcome through the promotion of sports and regular exercise. This is often sponsored by governments and private health insurance firms in industrialised countries, but few developing countries, apart from those with a social-ist leaning, have adopted comprehensive national sports and exercise programmes.

Universalising healthcare

Earlier diagnosis of serious medical conditions may ameliorate the need for organ transplant as therapy. Concurrently, genetic testing to discern a predisposition to significant illness could reduce the demand for transplants through early detection and treatment as well as prescribed dietary or lifestyle changes. Better and affordable healthcare systems are imperative, but this is sorely lacking in developing countries due to economic constraints and/or government mismanagement. Despite evidence that countries with largely publicly funded healthcare systems have demonstrably healthier populations, even there the trend for years now has been towards semi-privatised healthcare.[49] Unfortunately the neo-liberal agenda of user-pays medicine recommended to developing countries facing national debt by the IMF and the World Bank shifts the costs of healthcare to patients, raising the risk of insurance denials of treatment and job-loss upon serious illness such as those involving organ failure.

Treating the Malpractice

People before Profit

The spread of capitalism worldwide in recent decades may be responsible for the pre-sent commodification of organs donation as well as demand for transplant expertise, raising of healthcare expectations and choice for longer lifespans. Healthcare is no longer a matter of government provision but of individual responsibility for patients to fend for themselves in search of medical services, if not locally then internationally. The profit motive of medical insurers, which is typical in the industrialised countries, seeking to reduce the costs of long-term alternative treatment or transplant costs in the home country might be a contributor to the growth of the transplant industry in the developing-emergent world. Transparency is essential by all parties, such as pharmaceu-tical and insurance companies that profit from organ transplantation for the rich at the expense of social justice to the poor.[50] To that list might be added medical practitioners, hospitals, travel agencies, hoteliers and other intermediaries in this shadow trade cater-ing to the donors and recipients, both of which are vulnerable to exploitation.

Granting Oversight

The commercial recruitment of donors among the poor is unethical exploitation for profit of the intermediaries with the culpable non-intervention by their gov-ernments and the negligent unawareness by civil society. While most industrialised countries have laws against human organ sales, most developing countries lack such laws, have weak laws, or neglect to enforce their pertinent laws. The outcome could be said to constitute medical apartheid, by which organs are harvested from the poor, with minimal compensation, to be used by the affluent worldwide. In a capitalist world economy, the question might be not whether human organs will be traded commercially, but whether such trade is regulated or not, with due protection for both donors and recipients from exploitation. That regulatory oversight holds the potential to narrow the spread between the cost of procurement from the donor and the price to the recipient, thus driving out the profiteering players in this dubious global business. Thus, it is imperative that parallel systems of altruistic versus paid donations ought to be explored in the context of each country in which organs acquisition and transplantation occurs, with some worldwide guidelines adopted upon their provision.

Commentary in Conclusion

Organs acquisition and transplant tourism may be symptomatic of an abdication by the healthcare profession, both public and private, from developing the more resource-intensive cadaveric organ allocation systems and to provide post-surgical care for live donors within the same socio-medical system as the recipient. Recognition is needed that many countries in the developing and emergent world have dual-economies – one for the masses who live below internationally-defined poverty levels and another for the middle to upper classes. While the latter in Asia, Africa, the Middle East and Latin America may not have incomes that match those in the industrialised world, they may nonetheless demand better standards of healthcare than are provided by the public health system, thus spawning a private transplant industry at or nearer home. Therefore, any discussion of the issue of this business of organ transplant surgery ought to differentiate between those countries which are legitimately promoting healthcare as an economic sector attracting clients regionally, and those countries which through policy neglect encourage opportunistic entrepreneurs into a so-called transplant-tourism industry, exploiting desperate patients and donors alike. What is pivotal to addressing this shadow trade of transplant tourism and organs procurement is legal provision against the exploitation of poorer peoples, often alleged of past colonial regimes, which ought not to be acceptable in the present age.

──────────────── DIM DOMAIN ────────────────

KIDNEY SUPPLY REMEDIES

The professional accreditation of transplant surgeons may be one answer to concerns about the quality of and ethics in transplant surgery. However, there would need to be multi-country licensing of specialists as they could be trained elsewhere from where they practise. But what legal recourse would there be for both donors and recipients for botched procedures conducted in transnational settings? The resistance of doctors in the home country of the patient to provide post-surgical care may be the greatest barrier to growth of this global industry. What if there could be international collaboration on organ transplantation with agreement pre-procedure for post-transplant aftercare for both recipient and donor alike? A key issue is whether transplant recipients ought to be legitimately penalised for doing what they deem is in their best interests at the time, namely having surgery available elsewhere at an affordable cost borne privately. The examples of some countries for the oversight and underwriting of the transaction between parties might be worthy of investigation, emulation and adaptation elsewhere in the world.

China

Based largely on journalistic and civil society sources, there has been a sharp rise in executions of youthful persons for relatively minor crimes in China. This is said to be to supply fresh organs for transplantation, mainly for senior party officials and wealthy foreigners. The prisoners are said to have been condemned and selected for execution depending on blood type, scheduled for death according to the convenience of the recipient, said to have consented to donation, been drugged, shot, occasionally respired and kept alive until the transplant. While the costs of such transplants are a fraction of what they would cost outside China, within the country they are a valuable source of revenue to the hospitals in an era of limited public funding. In 2006, a US Congressional investigation claimed to have found increasing evidence of the systematic matching and preparation of condemned prisoners, particularly from the Falun Gong sect which had been banned for political dissent, for organ transplantation on execution to order.[51]

Japan

In nearby Japan, rated as an industrialised country, a law was passed in 1997 which defined brain-death primarily in terms of the potential of organ transplantation such that two humans in identical clinical condition could be diagnosed differently. Consequently, relatives may not choose to have their family member die a natural death, except if they consent to subsequent transplantation, which turns out to be more lucrative than life-support systems, both publicly funded, raising concerns about unethical practice. That the motivation is the surgical fees is confirmed by the fact that many surgeries done with contaminated organs have limited hope of success.[52] Likewise, the success of the organs procurement system in Spain is attributed to its dependence on cadaveric donations, enabled by trained professionals working in hospitals who more than doubled organ procurements from 14 per million in 1989 to 34 per million in 2002.[53]

(Continued)

Pakistan

Although, in 1991, 75 percent of kidneys transplanted in Pakistan were from family members, by 2003 about 80 percent were coming from unrelated donors, with half of the over 2,000 transplants being done on foreign citizens. In contrast to neighbouring India and other Islamic countries, Pakistan lacks legislation governing transplants, thus aiding its development into a major regional centre for transplant tourism.[54] This may in part be due to its geographical proximity to the affluent Gulf region in the Middle East, where the patients might have a decided preference for organ donation from a fellow Muslim who keeps the same dietary taboos. In the Middle East generally, the Muslim acceptance of cadaveric donation has had to be boosted by the state rewarding the living donor or family of the deceased, which has worked successfully to eliminate waiting lists. A survey among medical students in Turkey reported that while 84.9 percent of them had knowledge of organ transplantation, by far their primary source was the mass media.[55] While 58.4 percent appeared willing to donate their own organs, the fact that only 1.2 percent held a donation card does not augur well for their influence on encouraging altruistic donation.

India

Increasingly a destination for medical tourism, India offers excellent medical and surgical services with lower cost of procedure than in higher income countries. In recent years it can provide hospitals with advanced technology, no waiting time and professional surgeons. Medical India Tourism offers packages for organ transplants of kidney, liver, lung, cornea, bone marrow, and other body parts. These packages include air travel, hotel stay, surgery cost, specialist consultation, medication, and the services of professional staff at affordable prices. Although their preference is for patients to provide a living donor who is a relative, such as a sibling, parent or spouse, transplants of unrelated donors are accepted at a higher cost. Kidney transplant packages for related donor and recipient costs USD7,207, while for the unrelated donor and recipient it costs USD10,052, which implies a payment to the donor. Liver transplant surgery is priced even higher at USD50,000 to USD60,000.[56]

South Africa

Despite the sale of human organs being illegal in South Africa, transplantation services have been advertised at traffic intersections to car drivers, who tend to be the affluent in the country. According to the pamphlets distributed by a woman disguised in a surgical mask and latex gloves, body parts could be supplied within a week, and transplants would be done at a world-class medical facility. Organs for purchase reportedly included hearts, costing South African Rand (ZAR) 1.5 million (USD116,000); and kidneys for just over ZAR 3.5 million (USD270,000); spleens for just ZAR 7,000 (USD540); and eyes for ZAR 2,000 (USD160) each. The pamphlet was said to have read:

Need organs? We can source organs within 168 hours; healthy, reliable and fully tested.... So why languish in poor health when the poor could be used to help you live long and prosper? Our buildings, doctors and equipment are all top of the line.

A website address, but no physical address for the clinic was listed – the contact number provided was in use by a man who trades in these human organs.[57]

Brazil

The sale of organs by the poor in Brazil is so prevalent that parts of its cities are noted for being where organ brokers recruit most of their paid donors. One instance is the slums or *favelas* in Salvador da Bahia, where 2.6 million or 60 percent of the city's residents dwell in desperate living conditions. Furthermore, there is evidence that organ theft exists in Brazil, but with a different type of victim: the deceased poor. While Brazil has 'presumed consent' donation laws, only the wealthy are able to persuade doctors against considering a brain-dead relative as a donor, because the poor find their brain-dead relative removed without consultation for organ acquisition. But focusing on poor donors and corruption locally, as in Brazil, ignores what has caused their underlying dire economic straits. Some argue that paid donation is not just a means to provide needful income, and that legalisation of the practice may be a way of relieving poverty. While organ sales are typically perceived as a national issue, the globalisation of the market cannot be discounted. First, the marketplace for organs now spans the world, created by national regulations elsewhere that restrict the supply of live or cadaveric organs. Secondly, technological developments have enabled not only transplantation techniques, but also transportation and information. For example, donors from Brazil can find themselves having surgery done in Israel to benefit a recipient from South Africa. Thus, paid poor donors can be sourced from anywhere in the world since together with affluent recipients they can travel to a reputable medical facility for the transplant surgery.[58]

USA

In the USA, families can donate a close relative's organs or tissues upon death, unless the deceased relative effectively prohibited it beforehand. Were an individual able to sell a cadaveric organ before death, more people may do so, increasing the organs supply overall. While this may increase the donations by those declared brain-dead on life-support, opportunities to sell organs would mostly happen after actual death ensues. Whether an organ can be retrieved after death depends on factors such as length of time after death, cause of death and the health problems of the deceased. So, the programme would rather increase the supply of tissue, corneas, valves and bone, which can be retrieved from cadaveric donors with fewer restrictions on health and longer times for retrieval. Any market in organ acquisition

(Continued)

will only arise if current laws are repealed, allowing living donors to sell their organs for profit, but this raises numerous social issues. Opponents argue that the poor will seek to sell organs to the affluent for the sole purpose of alleviating their economic situation. Proponents for legalising organs sale argue instead that these poor living donors would benefit financially through selling. Meanwhile potential donors among the financially stable are unlikely to be persuaded to sell organs, unless the profit is sufficient to cover the perceived medical risk.[59]

Crucial Queries

Is organ acquisition more an issue of cultural and social mores than of political and economic measures? Would encouragement of donation upon death or even legislation presuming consent for the removal of organs then be a way of reducing the demand for living donations?

Which of the national models of practice regarding organs exchange are more equitable and commendable for gradual implementation by more countries? Can and should the regulations, practices and models in one country be applicable to and adopted by others?

Are some types of organ more of a concern ethically than others and worthy of greater regulation? Should organ donation always be altruistic and restricted to the blood relatives of the recipient, thus diminishing the market for paid sourcing?

Is sourcing organs from the poor, whether locally or from abroad, a form of enslavement and exploitation by the wealthier? Which is greater: the desperation of the terminally ill recipient or that of the paid donor for relief from crushing poverty?

Can poor donors be viably paid higher prices for their harvested organs and guaranteed long-term post-surgery medical care for any complications? Is it possible to ensure that medical tourism by wealthy foreigners subsidises healthcare for the citizens of developing-emergent countries?

FURTHER RESOURCES

Research Works

Cherry, M. J. (2015). *Kidney for Sale by Owner: Human Organs, Transplantation, and the Market*. Washington, DC: Georgetown University Press.

Parry, B., Greenhough, B., & Dyck, I. (2016). *Bodies across Borders: The Global Circulation of Body Parts, Medical Tourists and Professionals*. London: Routledge.

Richards, J. R. (2012). *The Ethics of Transplants: Why Careless Thought Costs Lives*. Oxford: Oxford University Press.

Scheper-Hughes, N., & Wacquant, L. (eds.). (2002). *Commodifying Bodies* (Vol. 7, No. 2-3). London: Sage Publishing.

Sharp, L. A. (2013). *The Transplant Imaginary: Mechanical Hearts, Animal Parts, and Moral Thinking in Highly Experimental Science*. Berkeley, CA: University of California Press.

Territo, L., & Matteson, R. (eds.). (2011). *The International Trafficking of Human Organs: A Multidisciplinary Perspective*. Boca Raton, FL: CRC Press.

Veatch, R. M., & Ross, L. F. (2015). *Transplantation Ethics*. Washington, DC: Georgetown University Press.

Informational Websites

Global Observatory on Donation and Transplantation [www.transplant-observatory.org/]

National Kidney Foundation [www.kidney.org/news/newsroom/factsheets/Organ-Donation-and-Transplantation-Stats]

UK National Health Service [www.odt.nhs.uk/statistics-and-reports/]

United Network for Organ Sharing [transplantliving.org/]

US Department of Health and Human Services [www.organdonor.gov/statistics-stories/statistics.html]

World Health Organisation [www.who.int/transplantation/organ/en/]

Annotated Documentaries

Al Jazeera (2016) *Asia's Kidney Black Market* [25:31 min.]. This '101 East' programme follows the kidney trafficking route, interviewing donors, police, brokers and doctors.

Journeyman Pictures (2014). *Exposing Mexico's Surrogacy Industry* [25:54 min.]. It uncovers transnational surrogacy, which is booming in countries where regulatory frameworks are near to non-existent.

PBS (2017). *Organs on Demand* [11:13 min.]. This public news broadcast explores whether China has really stopped obtaining organs from executed prisoners.

Channel 17/Grom TV (2013). *Unnatural Selection* [58:05 min.]. A two-part film by a journalist posing as a donor, showing how the black market operates in the former Soviet Union.

True Vision (2004). *The Transplant Trade* [1 h. 17 min.]. This documentary evaluates the moral debate on the global *trade* in body parts.

General Reading

Carney, S. (2011). *The Red Market: On the Trail of the World's Organ Brokers, Bone Thieves, Blood Farmers, and Child Traffickers*. New York: William Morrow, pp. 68–70.

Purkayastha, B., & Yousaf, F. N. (2018). *Human Trafficking: Trade for Sex, Labor, and Organs*. Cambridge: Polity Press.

Teresi, D. (2012). *The Undead: Organ Harvesting, The Ice-Water Test, Beating Heart Cadavers*. New York: Pantheon.

Endnotes

1. DuBray, B. J., & Busuttil, R. W. (2017). Historical review of solid organ transplantation. In S. Nadig & J. Wertheim (eds.), *Technological Advances in Organ Transplantation*. Cham, Switzerland: Springer International.

2. Haken, J. (2011). Transnational crime in the developing world. *Global Financial Integrity, 12*(11).

3. Shimazono, Y. (2007). The state of the international organ trade: a provisional picture based on integration of available information. *Bulletin of the World Health Organization, 85*(12), 955–962.

4. Scheper-Hughes, N. (2014). Human traffic: exposing the brutal organ trade. *New Internationalist, 1*.

5. Chopra, A. (2008). Harvesting kidneys from the poor for rich patients. *US News & World Report, 144*(5), 18 February.

6. Rai, A. (2019). Medical tourism: an introduction. In *Medical Tourism in Kolkata, Eastern India*. Cham, Switzerland: Springer International, pp. 1–41.

7. Connell, J. (2016). Reducing the scale? From global images to border crossings in medical tourism. *Global Networks, 16*(4), 531–550.

8. World Health Organisation (WHO) (2004). Organ trafficking and transplantation pose new challenges. *In Focus*, 1 September.

9. NaturalNews.com (2007). Organ transplant industry pushes for legal right to buy and sell body parts on the global market. *NaturalNews.com* [www.naturalnews. com/ z020581.html].

10. Bos, Michael (2015) *Trafficking in Human Organs*. Brussels: European Parliament.

11. Statista (2019) Organ transplantation costs in the U.S. 2017. [www.statista.com/ statistics/ 808471/organ-transplantation-costs-us/ – accessed 11 January 2019].

12. Ambagtsheer, F., Zaitch, D., & Weimar, W. (2013). The battle for human organs: organ trafficking and transplant tourism in a global context. *Global Crime, 14*(1), 1–26.

13. NaturalNews.com (2007). Organ transplant industry pushes for legal right to buy and sell body parts on the global market. *NaturalNews.com* [www.naturalnews. com/ z020581.html].

14. Economist (2008). Organ transplants: the gap between supply and demand. *The Economist*, 9 October.

15. Majid, A., Al-Khalidi, L., Bushra, A., Opelz, G., & Shaefer, F. (2010). Outcomes of kidney transplant tourism in children: a single center experience. *Pediatric Nephrology, 25*, 155–159.

16. Goyal, M., Mehta, R. L., Schneiderman, L. J., & Sehgal, A. R. (2002). Economic and health consequences of selling a kidney in India. *Journal of the American Medical Association, 288*(13), October.

17. Dubinsky, K. (2007). Babies without borders: rescue, kidnap, and the symbolic child. *Journal of Women's History, 19*(1), 142–150.

18. Trey, T., Sharif, A., Schwarz, A., Fiatarone Singh, M., & Lavee, J. (2016). Transplant medicine in China: need for transparency and international scrutiny remains. *American Journal of Transplantation, 16*(11), 3115–3120.

19. Extracted from data tables and anecdotal text cited in Ambagtsheer, F., & Weimar, W. (eds.). (2016). *Trafficking in Human Beings for the Purpose of Organ Removal: Results and Recommendations* [HOTT Project]. Lengerich: Pabst, pp. 50–52.

20. Baimas-George, M., Fleischer, B., Slakey, D., Kandil, E., Korndorffer Jr, J. R., & DuCoin, C. (2017). Is it all about the money? Not all surgical subspecialization leads to higher lifetime revenue when compared to general surgery. *Journal of Surgical Education, 74*(6), e62–e66.

21. Van Assche, K. (2018). *Organ Transplant Tourism: Expert Memorandum prepared for Parliamentary Assembly, Council of Europe*. Brussels: Council of Europe.

22. Harrison, T. (1999). Globalisation and the trade in human body parts. *The Canadian Review of Sociology and Anthropology, 36*(1), 21–35.

23. Heinl, M. P., Yu, B., & Wijesekera, D. (2019). A framework to reveal clandestine organ trafficking in the dark web and beyond. *Journal of Digital Forensics, Security and Law, 14*(1), 2.

24. Siddiqui, S. (2012). Untapped market: can Pakistan become a hub for medical tourism? Express Tribune, 17 April. [https://tribune.com.pk/story/365757/untapped-market-can-pakistan-become-a-hub-for-medical-tourism/ – retrieved 26 June 2020].

25. Connell, J. (2019). Medical mobility and tourism. In *Handbook of Globalisation and Tourism*. Cheltenham: Edward Elgar Publishing.

26. Smith, D. (2010). South African hospital firm admits 'cash for kidney' transplants. *The Guardian*, 10 November.

27. Lunt, N., Horsfall, D., & Hanefeld, J. (2016). Medical tourism: a snapshot of evidence on treatment abroad. *Maturitas, 88*, 37–44.

28. Ikemoto, L. C. (2018). 37. Reproductive tourism. In O. K. Obasogie & M. Darnovsky (eds.), *Beyond Bioethics: Toward a New Biopolitics*. Berkeley, CA: University of California Press.

29. Kaewkitipong, L. (2018). The Thai medical tourism supply chain: its stakeholders, their collaboration and information exchange. *Thammasat Review, 21*(2), 60–90.

30. Budiani-Saberi, D. A., & Karim, K. A. (2009). The social determinants of organ trafficking: a reflection of social equity. *Social Medicine, 4*(1) March, 48–51.

31. Naqvi, S. A. A., Ali, B., Mazhar, F., Zafar, M. N., & Rizvi, S. A. H. (2007). A socioeconomic survey of kidney vendors in Pakistan. *Transplant International, 20*(11), 934–939.

32. Naim, M. (2005). *Illicit: How Smugglers, Traffickers and Copycats are Hijacking the Global Economy*. London: Random House.

33. Scheper-Hughes, N. (2004). Parts unknown: undercover ethnography of the organs-trafficking underworld. *Ethnography, 5*(1), 29–73.

34. Matas, A. J. (2004). The case for living kidney sales: rationale, objections and concerns. *American Journal of Transplantation, 4*(12), 2007–2017.

35. Sharp, L. (2006). *Strange Harvest: Organ Transplants, Denatured Bodies and the Transformed Self*. Berkeley, CA: University of California Press.

36. Voo, T., Campbell, A. V., & de Castro, L. D. (2009). The ethics of organ transplantation: shortages and strategies. *Annals Academy of Medicine, 38*(4), April, 359–364.

37. Demme, R. A. (2010). Ethical concerns about an organ market. *Journal of the National Medical Association, 102*(1), 46–50.

38. Dalal, A. R. (2015). Philosophy of organ donation: review of ethical facets. *World Journal of Transplantation, 5*(2), 44.

39. Voo, T., Campbell, A. V., & de Castro, L. D. (2009). The ethics of organ transplantation: shortages and strategies. *Annals Academy of Medicine, 38*(4), April, 359–364.

40. Voo, T., Campbell, A. V., and de Castro, L. D. (2009). The ethics of organ transplantation: shortages and strategies. *Annals Academy of Medicine, 38*(4), April, 359–364.

41. Goodwin, M. (2006). *Black Markets: The Supply and Demand for Body Parts.* New York: Cambridge University Press, pp. 21–24.

42. Bagheri, A. (2007). Asia in the spotlight of the international organ trade: time to take action. *Asian Journal of WTO and International Health, 2*(1), March, 11–24.

43. Becker, G. S., & Ellias, J. J. (2003). Introducing incentives in the market for live and cadaveric organ donations. Paper presented at the *Organ Transplantation: Economic, Ethical and Policy Issues Conference,* 16 May, University of Chicago.

44. Budiani-Saberi, D. A., & Karim, K. A. (2009). The social determinants of organ trafficking: a reflection of social equity. *Social Medicine, 4*(1), March, 48–51.

45. Hryhorowicz, M., Zeyland, J., Słomski, R., & Lipiński, D. (2017). Genetically modified pigs as organ donors for xenotransplantation. *Molecular Biotechnology, 59*(9–10), 435–444.

46. Hasan, A. (ed.). (2017). *Tissue Engineering for Artificial Organs: Regenerative Medicine, Smart Diagnostics and Personalized Medicine.* Hoboken, NJ: John Wiley & Sons.

47. Roh, Y. N. (2018). Organ donation. In G. Tsoulfas (ed.), *Organ Donation and Transplantation: Current Status and Future Challenges.* San Francisco, CA: BOD – Books-on-Demand.

48. Monteiro, C. A., Moubarac, J. C., Cannon, G., Ng, S. W., & Popkin, B. (2013). Ultra-processed products are becoming dominant in the global food system. *Obesity Reviews, 14,* 21–28.

49. Bradley, E. H. et al. (2016). Variation in health outcomes: the role of spending on social services, public health, and health care, 2000–09. *Health Affairs, 35*(5), 760–768.

50. Budiani-Saberi, D. A., & Karim, K. A. (2009). The social determinants of organ trafficking: a reflection of social equity. *Social Medicine, 4*(1), March, 48–51.

51. Committee on International Relations (2006). Falun Gong: organ harvesting and China's ongoing war on human rights. Hearing before the *Subcommittee on Oversight and Investigations,* Serial no. 109-239, 29 September.

52. Becker, C. (1999). Money talks, money kills – the economics of transplantation in Japan and China. *Bioethics, 13*(3/4), 236–243.

53. Baghieri, A. (2007). Asia in the spotlight of the international organ trade: time to take action. *Asian Journal of WTO and International Health, 2*(1), March, 11–24.

54. Moazam, F. (2005). Kidney trade and transplant tourism: Pakistan, the emerging leader. *Bioethics Links, 3*(3).

55. Bilgel, H., Sadikoglu, G., & Bilgel, N. (2006). Knowledge and attitudes about organ donation among medical students. *Transplantationmedizin, 18,* 91–96.

56. Medical Tourism India (2018) Organ transplant packages in India. [www.medicalindiatourism.com/treatment-packages/organ-transplant – accessed 25 December 2018].

57. Francke, R. L. (2017). Organs for sale: a heart costs R1.5 million. *Daily Voice*, 3 April.

58. Gresham, P. (2010). Selling life: the global organs trade and the part played by Brazilian slum-dwellers. [www.philgresham.com/docs/selling-life.pdf – accessed 14 August 2018].

59. Kolnsberg, H. R. (2003). An economic study: should we sell human organs? *International Journal of Social Economics, 30*(10), 1049–1069.

CHAPTER 5

RESOURCE PILFERAGE & ENVIRONMENT DEGRADATION

Credit: Pedro Henrique Santos/Unsplash

Overview in Introduction

Control over resources invaluable to the world economy tends to precipitate or at least contribute to a significant proportion of international, regional and intra-state conflicts worldwide. Typically, such resources include metals, precious stones, rare earths and timber, as well as wildlife, cultural heritage and other valuable national assets, typically extracted from developing countries and destined for emergent and industrialised economies. Most notably, the oil industry has spurred major wars, while precious metal mining remains tainted by involvement in civil conflicts. Invariably this shadow trade in conflict resources is accompanied by human rights breaches, including violence by insurgent groups, terrorists, local militias, government troops as well as other armed combatants. This chapter uncovers how, despite embargoes and boycotts, such resources enter into complex supply chains where they are processed and incorporated by legitimate firms into consumer and industrial goods marketed worldwide. Yet given the technological feasibility of tracking, the businesses involved can now be held accountable right back through the global supply chain to the location, identity and practices of the resource providers. Among the varied topics uncovered in this chapter are conflict-zone mining, mineral resources, blood diamonds, rare earths, coltan, cultural heritage, artefact acquisition, oil smuggling, wildlife poaching, non-state forces, corruption, disarmament, closed-pipe sourcing, technological tracking and global supply chains.

Resourcing Conflicts

Pillage and Plunder

Defined as a perpetrator appropriating property for private purpose, done without the consent of the owner and depriving the latter of its use, pillage has a long history in human conflict. The resources in question often involved metals, precious stones, fuel, timber, animals, food and water, typically scarce resources that more than compensate for the costs of the regional or domestic armed conflict. Procuring exotic animals for work and entertainment can be traced to ancient civilisations, such as by the Egyptians, Greeks and Romans, resulting in reductions in populations, even extinctions in their native habitats. The removal of cultural artefacts has characterised expansionary empires and colonial regimes down through the centuries, including the Conquistadors of Spain, the Napoleonic armies of France and the Nazis of Germany. The crime of pillage first featured in the Lieber Code of 1863, which stipulated that even when taking place after conflict and carried out by an armed force, it was still prohibited on penalty of death. Today pillage and its synonym of plunder are deemed war crimes in international law such as the Hague Convention, and in national laws like the US War Crimes Act.[1] Other countries, including developing economies and failed states with weak institutions, usually cross-reference international treaties in their efforts to stem the trade. Nonetheless, corporations extracting resources in conflict zones tend expediently to ignore the approvals required under national and international legislation in favour of those granted by foreign occupying armies, including insurgent forces.

Catalysts with Consequences

No less than 40 percent of intra-state conflicts alone over the last 60 years and more are linked to natural resources: the access to, exploitation of and trade in which often benefits from and exacerbates the very same conflicts. Consequently, these result in human rights abuses, humanitarian law violations, even war crimes by government forces, separatist movements, warlord militias, terrorist groups, and other armed groups involved in the conflict.[2] Both inter-state and intra-state conflicts continue to be linked to and fuelled by the mineral resources, particularly in developing economies such as those in Africa (Figure 5.1). Significant as mining has been to the economies of those resource-rich developing countries, this has not translated into economic development for the majority of their populations, as exemplified in Nigeria and the Democratic Republic of Congo (DRC). Their contrast with South Africa can only be explained partially by weak government policies, lack of democracy, corruption and historic instability, leaving aside the unremitting demand for their resources in the world economy. Meanwhile poaching for the exotic pet and traditional medicinal markets is a threat to wildlife, while the looting of archaeological and other valuable cultural resources for markets in other continents tends to follow military invasions, as in the Middle East of late. Thus, armed conflicts tend to result in the exploitation of mineral, biodiversity and cultural resources, regardless of whether it is by the eventual victors or the desperate losers.

Reaching Rock Bottom

Corporations Complicit

Although attention has been given to the impact of conflict on artisanal miners and other small-scale operators in war zones, much less has been given to how multinational resource corporations trigger or prolong conflict even unwittingly. These conflicts may further enhance their corporate profitability although reduce their contribution to the economic development of the countries in which they operate. In all contexts of current or potential conflict, mining corporations need to decide whether to invest or to divest from operations, or, if remaining there, to decide on how to prevent, mitigate and resolve the conflict. So, corporations have to assess the risks involving physical assets, employees, work disruption, downstream contracts, litigation, insurance, reputation, consumer boycotts, and more. It is imperative, then,

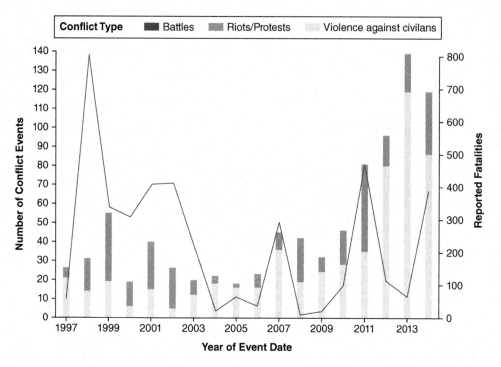

Figure 5.1 Resource-related conflicts in Africa[3]

Copyright © Dr Roudabeh Kishi. Used with permission.

that the corporations adopt conflict management strategies that take into considera-tion such factors as the inequitable distribution of economic benefits, dependence on this one resource, government corruption, environmental impact and sustaining armed groups.[4] Thus far resource corporations in conflict zones have been negligent in working with all stakeholders, including government, community groups, civil society, international organisations, to build trust in their commitment to sustain-able development through transparency in reporting and verification.

Collapsed law and order along with a lack of concern about the environment and human rights during conflict are favourable to trade in resources, particularly if armed groups benefit financially from that trade and are motivated to main-tain the conflict. The extraction of diamonds, gold, timber and the like are not affected adversely by conflicts as much as urban infrastructure or rural farmland are. Because these resources do not depend on a local market and are generic commodi-ties, their conflict origins can be disguised for foreign markets. All this supports the argument that a developing country's dependence on commodities, along with domestic socio-economic inequities, creates prospects for extraordinary financial gain through sales or levies for all parties, perpetuating civil war there. It has been well documented that multinational corporations like BP, Lonhro and Dole, and even aid organisations like the Red Cross, have been known to pay 'war taxes' to government rivals claiming it to be government or 'protection money' to guerrilla movements in conflicts worldwide, from Colombia, Kosovo, Cambodia and Afghanistan to Somalia, Angola and Liberia.[5] Well-intentioned efforts to limit the global trade in conflict resources, whether through government embargoes, corporate audits or consumer boycotts run the risk of adversely affecting legitimate trade in the same goods. Unintended consequences of such neo-colonialist interventions could be those of depriving local owners, workers and traders of livelihoods and causing political instability leading to further conflict.

Indemnifying End-users

Despite embargoes and boycotts, all conflict resources enter complex global supply chains where they are channelled, processed and incorporated by legitimate firms into consumer and industrial goods that are marketed worldwide. Most notably, the almost USD90 million diamond industry worldwide is still bedevilled by the stain of being involved in conflicts, particularly in Africa. Efforts made over a decade ago via the international certification system, better known as the Kimberley Process, to reassure consumers failed due to loopholes that do not recognise local violence and human rights abuses. While the illegal trade in wildlife is facing increasing law enforcement and regulatory intervention from source as well as destination countries internationally, the criminal networks involved in it remain resilient. Yet coffee drinkers, seafood diners and fashion buyers are potentially able to trace their relatively inexpensive consumption back along the supply chain of transportation, processing and manufacture, back to the location, identity and practices of the raw material suppliers. Still, in our information age where the sources of product constituents can be ascertained via block-chain and other technologies, the selective amnesia exhibited by consumers, marketers and governments remains a socio-ethical anomaly.

Human rights breaches have been a widespread concern with the operations of extractive industries around the world, particularly in developing and emergent economies, in violation of extant national and international laws. In the name of protecting assets and operation practices, problematic corporate practices have ranged from people displacement, forced labour, and workplace health and safety to arbitrary detention, rape, murder and torture by armed groups and security staff. These abuses may be permitted by or sometimes carried out by the government or a local business partner or supplier, and usually take place in a developing country context of extreme poverty, corruption, inadequate public administration and political instability. Nonetheless, multinational corporations can be held complicit and accountable in the industrialised countries, where their ownership is typically headquartered. Among the multinational resource corporations that have been made legally liable are: Shell, for killings, torture and detentions of community residents in Nigeria; Total and Unocal, for using forced labour supplied by the local military in Myanmar; Talisman Energy, for the forced displacement of local communities in Sudan; and Nestlé, for child labour on West African cocoa plantations.[6]

Development or Impoverishment

In spite of claiming to provide jobs and to improve the living standards of communities in the developing world, multinational corporations in the extractive industries have long come under criticism for paying considerably low taxes and royalties. In limiting unionism, paying low wages and providing poorer safety to their workers in comparison to similar workers in their home industrialised countries, such exploitative practices foster economic inequity and fuel societal instability. Although stakeholder theory holds that business success is best achieved by balancing the interests of owners, management, employees, customers, government and community, in practice managers prioritise the most powerful group, which may change dramatically, especially in conflict situations.[7] While labour legislation may exist in most developing countries, the means and political will to enforce these are often lacking. Implementation by governments could even be deliberately lax in the context of competing for and retaining multinational corporation investment. Legitimacy theory argues that any corporation is judged worthy of support by society only if it uses its capacity responsibly, and its managers seek to narrow the legitimacy gap between business performance and societal expectation.[8] Where multinational corporations continue to face a legitimacy gap in their employee relations, they can find support in meeting their ethical obligations through ILO guidelines. Meanwhile increasingly democratic governments and responsible unions at home and abroad can be instrumental in bringing about equitable economic development.[9]

Contested Ownership

Mineral Resources

Diamonds and gold

In the 1990s diamond mining in Sierra Leone was controlled by the insurgent Revolutionary United Front, which was noted for its human rights abuses and war crimes. Those forces were supported by the government of neighbouring Liberia, and so Sierra Leonean diamonds were mixed in with those of the latter country and were able to circumvent the UN embargo on the former imposed from 2000 onwards.[10] Research utilising geo-referenced data in DRC indicates that the impact of US legislation against conflict minerals has backfired, supporting instead the proposition that the relationship of mining and conflict in remote areas is highly complex. Violence towards civilians in that country grew by about 200 percent and armed groups moved into unregulated mining areas, even while global prices for various minerals sourced there had been rising. Although geographically far away, India has also been implicated in this shadow trade because its city of Surat processes over 90 percent of the world's diamonds, much of which having bypassed the Kimberley Process, while itself employing almost 500,000 workers in rather unsafe conditions. Paradoxically, the informal exchange by which local miners pay taxes to militias for crude protection seems to make the zone more peaceful and economically productive than the social anarchy that results through well-meaning foreign military intervention.[11]

Coltan and rare earths

Linking the persistent conflict in eastern DRC with the trade in mineral resources, in 2008 the UN Security Council embargoed arms sales to the non-state groups and individuals involved. In spite of clear evidence of culpability provided by NGOs, no individuals, groups or corporations have been subjected to further sanctions. Among the corporations identified by the UN and NGOs as trading in resources from the DRC conflict zones are UK-based Afrimex and Thaisarco, major metals traders and smelters, in defiance of the applicable OECD guidelines, as well as many Congolese exporters.[12] Over and above its diamond industry, which was worth USD8 billion in 2007, Liberia has also been actively involved in the mining of coltan, which is used in a global electronics industry worth USD65 billion. The country thus serves as an intermediary between conflict zones in Africa and the world economy, circumventing legislation that would otherwise require considerable outlay on corporate social responsibility measures.[13] In Latin America, it was only in 2009 that Venezuela's rich reserves of coltan, deep in its Amazonian jungles, were discovered. Since the border area between Venezuela and Colombia is on their well-worn route for smuggling drugs to the US, those crime syndicates controlling it have diversified into the equally profitable trade in coltan.[14] The ban on private mining, which is enforced by their respective militaries, has neither kept away artisanal miners nor prevented the smuggling of coltan ore into Brazil, where it meets local manufacturing demand as well as being exported worldwide. Since socialist, anti-imperialist Venezuela faces diplomatic tensions with the right-leaning, pro-US government of Colombia, overlapping resource claims between the two countries could well spill over into armed conflict.[15]

Oil and energy

In the last half-century, access to oil and gas resources have been notably behind Indonesia's invasion of East Timor, Morocco's of Western Sahara, and Iraq's of Kuwait. Among more current tensions over oil resources are those between various regional claimants to the Spratly Islands in the South China Sea, to parts of the Amazon Basin and to the Arctic Sea floor. Decades of civil protest and armed insurgency in the Niger Delta region over unchecked drilling by the multinational energy corporation Shell, in collusion with corrupt Nigerian military and political regimes, have resulted in extensive pollution but little economic development.[16] Perhaps most troubling in recent years has to be the control by the so-called Islamic State of Iraq and Syria (ISIS) at its height of 60 percent of the rich oil-producing Levant region, using this to fund its terrorist regime. In its heyday ISIS was successful in smuggling and exporting much of this output through neighbouring Turkey, where it was mixed with legally-sourced oil from the Caspian Sea states and Kurdish Northern Iraq also destined for legitimate global markets.[17] Another form of energy widely used in the developing world is coal, and India has had a quietly simmering conflict in its extraction within mineral-rich jungles inhabited by disenfranchised tribal citizens. Government forces have been in armed conflict with Maoist-communist insurgents who have taken up the cause of the tribes and who process the mined coal, bribing the police to be left unmolested. In turn, the Indian government-owned coal-mining corporations are alleged to have been paying the insurgents millions of rupees as 'protection-money' or to exempt their facilities from attack.[18] Given their strategic importance, energy resources are particularly prone to wars, terrorism, civil strife and embargoes, and any resultant disruption of their supply chains results in a consequent shadow trade in smuggling.

Biodiversity Assets

Forestry

Pillage of forest resources can continue well after conflicts are over, as when the Paris Peace Accords that ended the Cambodian civil war left rebel groups, like the Khmer Rouge, which was renowned for atrocities, in control of the resource-rich parts of that country. So after support from China had ceased, the rebel Khmer forces utilised exports of valuable hardwood timbers to fund their resumed conflict with the Vietnamese-installed government. Although a subsequent UN Security Council resolution had supported the Cambodian government's ban on the export of those logs, it inadvertently did not include processed woods. This resulted in the growth of sawmills along the border and a thriving trade of about USD10–20 million per month with the active collusion of corrupt government officials in Cambodia and in neighbouring neutral Thailand.[19] For over 20 years, and in defiance of international protocols, Japan as an industrialised economy exploited timber harvesting in the developing country of Malaysia. In conjunction with businesses from other Asian countries, Japanese firms have fostered local corruption in the granting of land concessions, illegal logging, biodiversity destruction and human rights violations of the indigenous peoples.[20] Besides, the felling of forests in tropical developing countries for valuable wood like mahogany and teak has a long history from colonial occupation and/or imperialistic trade.

Forest looting can prove an invaluable alternative income stream, as when the UN imposed a ban on Liberian diamonds in 2001. Its government turned to harvesting timber to generate income towards funding rebel forces in neighbouring Sierra Leone as well as a civil war within its own country. Ironically, the UN Security Council was not able to take action against this initially due to opposition from its permanent members France and China, which were major importers of Liberian timber. When timber sanctions were finally imposed in 2003, drying up this revenue stream, the Liberian regime collapsed, and notably the 14-year civil war ended. In addition, the pressures to cut down forests in places like Indonesia and Brazil are driven by increasing worldwide consumer and industrial demand for beef, palm oil and timber, as well as several mining resources. The ongoing practice of slash-and-burn is used for efficiency by both corporations and farmers, but this results in dangerous air pollution and risk to the habitat of animals locally, not to mention indigenous communities. Carried by the atmosphere and weather, it has become a global issue, affecting the citizens of most countries, including those in industrialised countries, for whom the final products are manufactured. Loss of tropical rainforests as a major carbon sink has certainly been implicated in climate change and global warming, with their impending social and economic costs.

Agriculture

It is seldom recognised that agriculture can prove equally lucrative in conflict zones, particularly when sanctions are placed on mineral resources. When in 2005 the UN Security Council imposed a ban on the export of Côte D'Ivoire diamonds because its rebel Forces Nouvelles had gained control of the country's diamond mines, the rebels turned to the cocoa trade for revenues to support its armed conflict. Since Côte D'Ivoire is the world's largest cocoa producer and the rebel forces controlled an area that produced 3–4 percent of global output, the rebels earned about USD30 million per year simply from taxing the trade – even more than they had earned through diamonds. Without there being a targeted ban on their commanders in the 10 different conflict zones, the rebel forces had been able to increase their control of the north of the country and to smuggle arms in, allegedly using the very same sacks used to export cocoa.[21] Yet a total ban of the cocoa trade would have affected about 3–4 million Ivorians who were dependent on the crop for their livelihood. Furthermore, the cultivation of cash crops that feed the global narcotics market constitutes another leading shadow trade but one that lies beyond the scope of this book since it has been well documented elsewhere. Nonetheless, the serious environmental consequences of such market-driven reallocation of land-use amid armed conflict seldom features in the discourse on global climate change.

Wildlife

Although wildlife crime is estimated to cost between USD10 billion and 20 billion globally per year, or approximately 5 percent of the size of the international drug trade, the resources for combating it are miniscule by comparison. Rare or endangered species that are targeted include birds, reptiles, insects, fish and large game animals, by both collectors and pet owners, or for their parts, such as fur and skins for fashion products, or their horns, bones and organs for traditional medicine products.[22] Since 1973 the international trade has been regulated by the Convention on International Trade in Endangered Species (CITES), which now has 176 signatories or almost all countries worldwide. Meant to ensure that the international trade does not threaten the survival of animals and plants, the treaty encompasses close to 35,000 species.[23] The wildlife trade, as well as deforestation, has been implicated in the transmission of drug-resistant viruses from animals to humans, such as HIV, Ebola and H1N1, with all the health and economic implications that have been demonstrated more recently with the COVID-19 pandemic.[24]

Poaching networks in developing countries such as in Africa can often encompass locals from nearby communities who slip into national parks, as well as organised gangs using sophisticated tracking technologies. Typically, these poachers pass the animal products to intermediaries who arrange for them to be exported and imported with the collusion of customs authorities, all under the auspices of international crime syndicates which are able to adapt rapidly to changing operational circumstances. Given the involvement of some national military forces with poaching in Central Africa, the inflows of arms there could accelerate the rate at which illicit ivory gets to be harvested. More significantly, the arms can also increase risks to populations through their use in local conflicts.[25] Since wildlife products are integral in East Asian cultural heritage, the population growth and increased affluence of the region have meant that demand is escalating the illegal trade, triggering corruption and illegal hunting. Despite the health risks, the animals or their parts with demand in the region for medicinal and food purposes include pangolins, bats, snakes, seahorses, tigers and bears.[26] Contemporarily, countries like China and Vietnam are major markets for rhino horn, for instance, because this is said to have curative properties in traditional medicine for fever, rheumatism, gout, stroke and even cancer. With their related ethnic minorities growing in North America, the US, Europe and Australasia, the demand for wildlife products has become globalised.

Cultural Heritage

While most countries face some risk from the pilferage of cultural artefacts, those experiencing war or civil conflict and failed states such as Syria, Afghanistan, Iraq and Palestine, whose governments are not able to exercise control over their whole territories, are particularly vulnerable to extensive looting. Newer technologies enabling deep-sea exploration have exposed historic resources lost in oceans to recovery and sale, and these objects are well beyond surveillance and the bounds of national sovereignty. Consistently, this results in contested claims to ownership between various countries over shipwrecks and their valuable treasures, let alone with enterprises which fund their discovery. Despite various UNESCO conventions from 1954 to 2001 to stem the exploitation and erosion of the cultural heritage of nation-states, the global trade has increased over the past three decades and has been estimated to be worth up to USD2 billion per year, second only to the illicit trade in drugs and weapons.[27] Broad interpretation of the UNESCO conventions, as done by Australia and Canada, ensures that all cultural heritage found to be exported illegally needs to be repatriated to the state of origin. Yet many other industrialised economies, including the US, Switzerland and the UK, adopt a much more limited interpretation of the conventions. Their implementation policies on imports are driven primarily by support of their sizeable antiquities industry, which caters to global markets in cultural heritage, comprising both institutional and individual collectors.

International laws that regulate the antiquity industry have failed to prevent the trade in illegally recovered and exported cultural heritage, due to resistance from the industrialised world with its lucrative markets. Salvage operations at sea by commercial interests, which entitle them to have ownership over wrecks, also contribute to the loss of cultural heritage of the countries of origin of the historic ships or of the site of the sinking, despite appeals by the latter. Usually the players and processes involved in the illicit trade in cultural heritage, often from developing-country sources to industrialised-country markets, can be shadowy and the participation of organised crime is periodically speculated on.[28] Only if auction houses and antiquity and museums dealers go beyond national regulations to global ethical best-practice to restore their tarnished corporate reputations ought they be financially rewarded while helping to preserve cultural artefacts.[29] Notably, the definition of cultural heritage by UNESCO is dissimilar to that of the WTO, resulting in the latter being reluctant to resolve disputes between nation-states based on conflicting interpretations of the former.[30] Illogically, then, stringent regulation and enforcement only seem to contribute to the profitability and growth of the market in cultural heritage resources.

Delinking Supply Chains

Auditing the Processing

Tracing the origin of conflict minerals proves a challenge but can be overcome, for instance with the scientific 'fingerprinting' of coltan in tantalum ores. This has been done through the detection of varying combinations of minerals characteristic across regional deposits within Africa, despite being of similar geological age. Since such data on trace minerals allow fine discrimination of deposits on the west of the East African Rift lying in DRC (Congo) from that on the east of the same mineral field lying in Rwanda, this is anticipated to form the basis of certification of the supply chain of coltan. Nonetheless, once the ores from conflict zones have been smelted together with other ores it becomes impossible to identify the source of the refined minerals. Consequently, the Conflict Free Smelter (CFS) programme aids corporations seeking to comply with OECD guidelines and US laws, as well as to address consumer and NGO pressures for corporate social responsibility (CSR), by providing assurance on the sources of minerals like tantalum, tin, tungsten and gold used in electronic end-products. However, assessing the traceability of minerals through tiers of priority suppliers to conflict-free mining sources is not without its challenges. Most smelters failed at their initial audits due to inadequate information systems to cover numerous sources, but corrective action has enabled eventual compliance.[31] Since smelting lies at a narrowing of the supply chain, auditors tend to target smelters of metal producers around the world, including industrialised countries like Australia, Germany, Canada and the US, as well as emergent economies like China, Kazakhstan, Russia and Thailand, although reported compliance across end-users appears sketchy and variable across industry sectors (Figure 5.2).

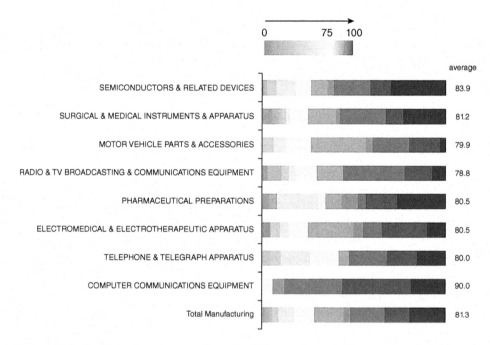

Figure 5.2   Conflict minerals compliance by US manufacturers[32]

Copyright © Development International 2017. Used with permission.

An alternative to supplier auditing, smelter certification and analytical fingerprinting for ensuring conflict-free minerals is the bag-and-tag procedure which requires that immediately upon extraction minerals are certified by an accredited agency, mine or government, and bagged with a label bearing a serial number that is used to track its movement through the supply chain through log books and computer databases updating transactions.[33] Operating under memoranda of understanding with the governments of DRC (Congo), Rwanda and Burundi, the iTSCi Programme is one such bag-and-tag endeavour utilising audits, secured mines, mineral tracking, data analysis and incident monitoring of human rights breaches, corruption, infractions of tagging and security problems. Five years after its launch, it claimed to have 231 members, 1,326 identified mine sites with more than 800,000 miners participating and producing 1,793 metric tonnes of tin, tantalum and tungsten.[34] Although more than 1,000 US firms filed conflict minerals reports, in a research sample of 100 small, medium and large firms, 59 percent did not meet the minimum requirements of legislation, just 21 percent met all the requirements and only 15 percent of the firms actually made contact with the smelters processing their minerals.[35] As an indication of the ineffectiveness of such programmes, while the majority claimed to have policies for identifying risks in their supply chain, such as human rights abuses or support to armed groups, no firm disclosed any violations.

Undermining by Disarming

Due to the fact that shadow trade in resources underwrites the warring parties, a fact seldom acknowledged in its mission mandates, UN peace-keeping forces have had limited effectiveness in resolving a number of conflicts. Instead, control of the mines and related economic activities is typically left in the hands of non-state armed groups or government forces involved in the conflict upon ceasefire. On occasion, the peace-keeping mission has been involved in monitoring the trade in resources from a conflict zone through inspections of export cargoes at airports or border crossings. But most of the staff overseeing this are military or civilian officials with neither a mandate to apply sanctions nor any expertise in customs duties.[36] Although in doing so or even assisting government forces to retake control of resources from armed groups, the peace-keeping forces could paradoxically be said to be complicit in overlooking the abuses in the mines as well in nearby areas affected. As in the case of wildlife exploitation, criminalising the shadow trade is often ineffective due to the under-resourcing of enforcement. Given the financial benefits to local communities in participating in this shadow trade, diplomatic conversation may prove a more productive approach.[37] In any case, this is no guarantee that re-arming will not be fuelled by income from those resources by groups ostensibly under ceasefire, or that even some of the partisan peace-keeping forces drawn from other developing countries, often from within the region, have similar vested economic interests.

Instead of framing conflict as a risk factor to operational security, reputation and costs of resource corporations, the latter have a potential contribution to make in resolving conflict and in the post-conflict reconstruction, which has been relatively under-researched and understood. More than just battle deaths and injuries, disruption through conflict causes long-term social and economic costs resulting from the abandonment of farms and factories, the rise of imports and smuggling, the decline of exports, the breakdown of transportation, a decline in savings, a distrust of the banking system, the failure of government services, and so on. Despite international aid, reconstruction has frequently taken longer than anticipated, partially due to the failure of governments to ensure adequate stability through disarmament and to provide the support required for the private sector to reinvest. Only then will multinational corporations have the potential to go beyond a minimalist CSR agenda to contribute to conflict prevention, resolution and reconstruction through enabling job creation, training, technology transfer, community projects and government dialogue.[38] The potential for post-conflict recovery and economic growth is much affected by damage to productive capacity, infrastructure, human capital, public institutions, democratic participation and more. If not reconstituted and managed well, these can result in a resurgence of conflict to the detriment of the legitimate resources industry and the labour involved, and to the benefit of the illicit trade, military forces and arms industry.

Tracking via Technology

Although coltan has applications in medical devices, optical lenses and weapons, the best known is in mobile phones, laptop computers and games consoles which are now considered consumer staples. While its tantalite ore can be mined in countries like Australia, Brazil, Mozambique, Canada, the DRC and Rwanda, the processed metal coltan comes primarily from China, Kazakhstan and Germany, with an increasing supply also from electronic waste recycled mainly in Estonia, Russia and Mexico. A unique conjunction of economic forces in 2000 resulted in a high demand for coltan, which saw sourcing in the DRC increase. As a result, attention was drawn to the injustices in that country, which are attributable partly to its mining sector. By applying hybrid Life Cycle Analysis along with Multiregional Input-Output analysis, it is now feasible to uncover the path along which coltan moves from the DRC, across porous borders into Rwanda, on to traders and finally processing.[39] Demonstrating resource looting, socio-economic injustice and environmental degradation may be problematic via investigative research, given the distance between the raw material producers and final consumers. However, by combining this with technical analysis and utilising digital technologies, millions of supply chains can be traced definitively across sourcing and processing to manufacture and end-products (Figure 5.3), leading to increased checkpoints for requiring and verifying conflict-free status.

Forensic investigations of wildlife have also gained much from automation and precision in the analysis of geological materials in the last 10 years. Physical, chemical and biological analysis of soils recovered from tools belonging to suspects in badger baiting and from falcon eggs imported from the Mediterranean were instrumental in proving those crimes.[40] Similarly, laboratory-based DNA analysis can be used in forensic casework for implementing species identification and even profiling

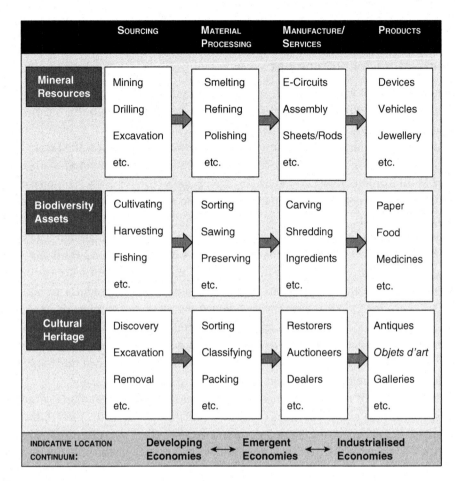

	SOURCING	MATERIAL PROCESSING	MANUFACTURE/ SERVICES	PRODUCTS
Mineral Resources	Mining Drilling Excavation etc.	Smelting Refining Polishing etc.	E-Circuits Assembly Sheets/Rods etc.	Devices Vehicles Jewellery etc.
Biodiversity Assets	Cultivating Harvesting Fishing etc.	Sorting Sawing Preserving etc.	Carving Shredding Ingredients etc.	Paper Food Medicines etc.
Cultural Heritage	Discovery Excavation Removal etc.	Sorting Classifying Packing etc.	Restorers Auctioneers Dealers etc.	Antiques *Objets d'art* Galleries etc.

INDICATIVE LOCATION CONTINUUM: **Developing Economies** ←→ **Emergent Economies** ←→ **Industrialised Economies**

Figure 5.3   Global supply chain of conflict resources

domesticated species.[41] Moreover, wildlife crime enforcement needs to be tailored to the different types of offender. For traditional lone criminals, financial penalties may negate any benefit gained but increased prison sentencing seems to prove ineffective as a deterrent. Yet for economic criminal gang members in the wildlife trade, employment is the basis for their behaviour and any policy approach must place penalties on their employer, so that the offenders risk losing employment. Machismo hunters of wildlife may see prison simply as an occupational hazard and badge of pride which reinforces their male identity, so in their case rehabilitation should be prioritised instead. For hobby hunters, their drive to collect may be so obsessive that penalties might strengthen re-offending to replace the confiscated items.[42] So, while detection and prosecution of wildlife crimes should be paramount, the cultural issues of trophy collecting and health beliefs as well as the environmental degradation need to be incorporated in preventive public education and social communications campaigns.

Conserving Commonwealth

Directives with Enforcement

Comprehensive guidelines from the OECD provide a standard for corporations to establish a responsible supply chain for minerals from conflict and high-risk regions and have been influential in the creation of laws around the world as well as specific industry codes.[43] Subsequently, the EU and China have drafted regulations, the World Gold Council has inaugurated voluntary certification, and the London Bullion Market and Dubai Multi-Commodities Centre have instigated audit requirements. It is noteworthy that OECD guidelines allow multinational corporations to work with artisanal mines and informal traders, so long as there are no armed groups controlling them or serious human rights abuse happening, in the expectation that this will maintain legitimate livelihoods.[44] In the US following the financial crisis of 2008, its Dodd-Frank Act regulating public corporations required them to certify the presence or absence of conflict minerals contained in their products. While not claiming that its products are conflict-free, Apple has reported that after years working to remove conflict minerals, as of 2015 all of its smelters and refiners in Congo (DRC) are audited.[45] Nonetheless the vast majority of suppliers to major electronic device manufacturers like Amazon, Sony, Microsoft, Disney and Google tend not to report on the conflict-free nature of their minerals, often arguing that once refined by smelters this is near-impossible to determine.[46]

Compliance with regulations on conflict-free minerals in industrialised countries, particularly the US and Europe, has occurred at different levels across their industries, sometimes resulting in unintended consequences for their sourcing in developing countries. In Congo (DRC), for instance, Chinese traders became the only ones buying tin for its coltan at discounted prices, as they were willing to accept the higher and more dangerous content of uranium in the ores because they have their own smelter within the country to separate it. They could thus also mask the mineral's origins. In keeping with its practices elsewhere, China has also signed a resources-for-infrastructure contract with the Congolese government to restore infrastructure in the country that has become derelict since independence 60 years ago. The USD6 million deal could be seen as a boon, although how the mineral resources are consequently being priced in repayment remains secretive. Finally, these global regulations on conflict-minerals have resulted in increased smuggling across the border from resource-rich eastern Congo into Rwanda to the benefit of the economic elite in the latter country, although there have been some prosecutions.[47] Overall, the loss of illegal taxes from the artisanal miners often sees militaries and militias move into controlling the mines themselves, and any decline in demand for the conflict minerals tends to drive the jobless miners into joining armed groups. Left largely unsaid is the costly site degradation and waterway pollution of both the mining and the processing in all conflict zones.

Minding the Plunder

Multinational corporations dealing in gold, tin and tungsten in the DRC and a number of other African countries covered by laws on conflict minerals claim to be spending over USD700 million to gather reliable data, unquestionably in an extremely challenging environment. Yet 90 percent of the filings admit to being unable to ascertain whether their minerals are conflict-free and less than 24 percent of firms fully comply. About 43 percent of the corporations do not file at all and 65 percent say they want to see such stringent laws amended, raising doubts about whether these companies wish to succeed in diverting funding away from armed groups and corrupt governments in conflict regions.[48] Some Asian corporations buying resources from Africa are part of an international responsible supply chain initiative that includes a smelter maintaining closed-pipe sourcing and that caters to multinational end-users like Nokia, Intel and Motorola. But other corporations operating in and buying most of their minerals in conflict zones are not compliant with such measures. Once the DRC government had passed a law based on OECD guidelines on conflict minerals in 2012, two Chinese firms were found to be in breach and were suspended. While official Chinese government policy promotes abiding with local laws, the DRC report on the investigation was not published and both firms eventually exported their minerals. Therefore, despite being generally better in the industrialised world than in the emergent and developing economies, governance over mineral resources is highly variable around the world (Figure 5.4).

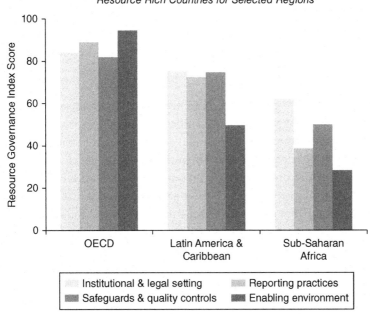

Transparency & Accountability in the Extractive Sector:
*Resource Governance Index (RGI) Component Scores in
Resource Rich Countries for Selected Regions*

Source: Resource Governance Index. Note that the first three components in the RGI index specifically refer to transparency components within the natural resource sector, while the last component (enabling environment) refers to the overall governance environment at the national level.

Figure 5.4 Accountability in resource-rich regions[49]

Treasuring Legacy

Currently some wildlife populations are at all-time lows, such as in South Africa alone where poachers killed 455 rhinos in 2012, compared to only 13 in 2007. Elephant populations are also threatened by the demand for ivory, despite the 1989 trade ban, with tens of thousands being poached in 2011 and 27,000 kg of ivory confiscated in major seizures alone. Global numbers of tigers have dropped from about 100,000 in the early 1900s to an estimated 3,000 presently, driven almost to extinction, even in sanctuaries.[50] Although all countries disapprove of theft of their own cultural property, disputes perpetually arise involving original owners and generally good-faith buyers. Different jurisdictions assign varying rights to these parties, resulting in disharmony as to the interest of nation-states, institutions and persons, with major implications for the collective preservation of global cultural heritage.[51] Hence the depletion of resources and the pollution or ecological damage in countries will continue to run unchecked into untold billions of dollars and the resource pilferage might indeed constitute one of the more valuable shadow trades globally today. Nevertheless, persistent demand for products with conflict-free certification and consumer preparedness to pay a premium for that assurance may result in multinational corporations sourcing similar resources from alternative countries in Europe, the Americas and Australasia. Ultimately, this could reduce global demand for tainted resources and serve as a catalyst for political, social and economic reform in conflict zones, and even in making peace the more economically productive choice.

Commentary in Conclusion

Although multinational corporations together with their financial backers have been instrumental in internal and external conflicts in pursuing access to various natural resources, they are often treated by national and international courts as peripheral to the breaches of human rights laws by the military and political leaders of the countries involved. On the one hand, the present humanitarian laws do not allow for traders, brokers and corrupt officials to be tried as accomplices to atrocities committed in the resource industries on local workers, peasants, tribes and more. On the other hand, once these laws are made more comprehensive and enforcement more effective, not only executives of major global oligopolies in valuable resources but those of manufacturers and marketers of end-products could be held culpable. Another option might be economic truth-and-reconciliation commissions for corporations, such as those held on the Sierra Leone conflict over the mining of diamonds.[52] While participation in such commissions could suit mining and agricultural corporations having corporate social responsibility obligations and accountability to consumers, arms makers and wildlife poachers benefiting from the conflicts would patently not be interested. Ultimately it will take a lowering of the costs of recycled materials relative to the full costs of legitimately acquiring new materials that will mitigate the shadow trade of resource pilferage and its degradation of environments.

--------------------- DIM DOMAIN ---------------------

OILING TERRORISM OPERATIONS

Funding

While its predecessor organisation Al Qaeda in Iraq and Syria, was dependent on sympathetic donor governments and individuals abroad, the Islamic State in Iraq and Syria (ISIS, also known as IS and ISIL) reactivated the black market established earlier by Saddam Hussein. Used in decades past to circumvent US economic sanctions on Iraq, then it comprised a network of crude oil smugglers. Under ISIS this included a further group of middlemen in neighbouring countries through whom they traded their stolen crude oil in return for money and goods. After extraction, the oil was lightly refined on site before the supply chain network took over to bring it to the world economy. Thus, ever since its formation in 2014 ISIS funded its operations to establish an alternate state through a successful dark trade in stolen oil, smuggled through a war zone.[53]

Thus, ISIS became one of the best-funded terrorist groups in the world, which in turn made it able to attract foreign adherents as well as local allegiance. By demonstrating economic self-sufficiency of production and controlling the supply of goods as leverage, ISIS was able to demonstrate legitimacy for their ideology. Besides, fundamentalist religiosity was not sufficient to maintain control; ISIS could not function without providing generously for its citizens and foreign mercenaries. By selling its oil resources, extorting from industry, looting banks, taxing non-Muslim populations, smuggling people, trafficking in slaves, antiquity exports and seized arms, ISIS was said to have accumulated a surplus of about USD2 billion even before the end of 2014. It also commandeered phosphate mining and manufacturing in Iraq and a salt mine in Syria, in addition to maintaining a monopoly on water, electricity and agriculture throughout its territories.[54]

Extraction and Transportation

Definitive oil production figures for huge swathes of territory across Syria and Iraq during ISIS' illegal occupation are understandably unavailable. Its main oil-producing region was Syria's eastern province, where in 2016 production was estimated at around 34,000–40,000 barrels per day. In northern Iraq, ISIS controlled another major field that typically produces about 8,000 barrels per day of heavier oil. As these oil fields were old and the insurgents lacked the expertise and technology to maintain them, production levels soon declined. Russian airstrikes further

(Continued)

contributed to disrupting extraction of crude oil, although not its shipment. Notably, bombardment by the US along with its NATO and Gulf allies were only of oil refinery facilities and not extraction wells, allegedly due to the intricate politics of oil in the Middle East.[55] The price per barrel of ISIS oil varied according to its quality, with some oil fields charging as little as USD25, while others charged as much as USD45 to a captive local market. A key factor in the attractiveness of ISIS crude oil to all players in the supply chain was that the global market price at the time was around USD80-100 per barrel. By earning ISIS about USD1.5-3 million per day, oil was consequently a key revenue stream through control at its peak of 60 percent of Syria's oil assets and seven oil-producing assets in Iraq.[56]

Despite airstrikes targeting collection areas, ISIS managed to maintain its production, even if not its profit margins. Since US and allied strikes did not target trucks in transit for fear of a backlash from locals, the insurgent group allowed convoys quickly past its checkpoints. Smugglers responsible for the transportation and sale of crude oil sent convoys of up to 30 trucks to the extraction sites of the commodity. They settled their trades with ISIS on site, encouraged by customer-friendly discounts and deferred payment schemes. Since collection areas and those trucks waiting were regularly attacked by airstrikes, ISIS capitalised on this by offering licences to skip the queue if traders paid upfront.[57] Thus, crude oil exited ISIS-controlled wells and travelled through insurgent-held parts of Syria, Iraq as well as Turkey, while at the same time catering to local demand. ISIS further used its oil wealth to shore up local support in the areas under its control, by allowing nine influential tribes to tap wells. Since a large trailer carrying 30,000 litres of crude used to make USD4,000 profit per journey of just a few days, this policy of economic largesse promoted unwavering local allegiance to ISIS.[58]

Refining and Export

After collecting their crude, most traders preferred to transport it to sell at nearby refineries, unload it and return to queue at the oil field. Or they could sell the oil on to traders with smaller vehicles, who then sent it to northern Syria or east into Iraq. Alternatively, the traders could sell to a refinery or local oil market on the Syrian-Iraqi border. Most oil refineries were in Syria, although those in ISIS-held territories had a reputation for lower quality output. These refineries produced both petrol and *mazout*, a form of diesel used in generators that was indispensable in the many areas lacking electricity. Since petrol quality could be inconsistent, the less expensive *mazout* was in greater demand. When US airstrikes destroyed crudely made ISIS mobile refineries mounted on trucks, locals made their own simple refineries. Their owners then made contracts with the militants for the purchase of their end-products. In mid-2015 ISIS bought five refineries, retaining their former owners as managers. It had its own tankers to supply crude to the oil refineries and to collect all the *mazout* production, splitting profits with the original owner. With the rise in airstrikes, *mazout* supplies decreased and prices rose, and ISIS benefited.[59]

Concerned primarily with making profits at the retail level, ISIS maintained contracts with unaffiliated gas stations. This left smuggling fuel into neighbouring countries to entrepreneurial Syrians and Iraqis. Most of the smuggling from the Syrian side had gone through areas in the northwest, which were opposed to ISIS. There the locals transferred the oil into jerry cans and carried it over the border on foot, by donkey or on horseback. In Iraq, with most smuggling through the northern Kurdistan region, the route then went south through Anbar province towards Jordan. Towards Turkey, smugglers loaded jerry cans into small rowboats and pulled their cargo across the river using ropes attached to each bank. On the other side, tractors collected the supply and took it to an informal market, where it was picked up by large trucks. Oil was also sold to Iranian traders, overlooking the sectarian religious animosity that underpinned the war. But declining international oil prices made this unprofitable except for the most determined smugglers.[60]

Within Turkey ISIS set up a string of trading hubs along the excellent European West-East route E 90 which extends all the way to Lisbon, Portugal. The supply chain eventually reaches the major tanker shipping port of Ceyhan. This port comprises a marine oil terminal situated in the Turkish Mediterranean that has been operating since 2006. The terminal is the export gateway for legitimate crude oil from offshore assets in the Caspian Sea, transported via the established Baku-Tbilisi-Ceyhan oil pipeline and the new pipeline commissioned in 2013 coming from the Kurdish oil fields in Iraq. With the launch of the ISIS oil business in 2014, tanker charter rates from Ceyhan undercut the ones for the rest of the Middle East. This had consequences for global market demand for ultra-cheap smuggled crude, because whenever ISIS was operating in an area with oil assets, exports from Ceyhan spiked. Regardless, Ceyhan received oil from conflict regions for loading on-board tankers which then transport it to legitimate global markets.[61] The aim for ISIS would have been dubious funds for their urgent need of ammunition and military equipment, presumably imported through the same port.

Crucial Queries

If there were no valuable resources to gain control over, would countries and insurgent forces still go to war? Do oil multinational corporations privately lobby for their governments to go to war for economic benefits rather than to make diplomatic concessions?

When neo-colonial powers use their armed forces to control resources for their corporations, how different is that from insurgent forces defending local ownership? Why is patriotism used to recruit combatants, while the potential economic gains are never mentioned in war rhetoric?

What drives overt enemies in military conflict to still be implicit business partners in shadow trades such as resource pilferage? Why would neighbouring countries avert their eyes from oil smuggling taking place through their own highways and ports?

Why would international refineries and energy companies be willing buyers of smuggled oil from conflict zones despite official embargoes by their home countries? How feasible would it be to identify the source of a commodity like crude or refined oil from an illicit source if it is mixed in with oil from elsewhere?

FURTHER RESOURCES
Research Works

Bieri, F. (2016). *From Blood Diamonds to the Kimberley Process: How NGOs Cleaned Up the Global Diamond Industry*. London: Routledge.

Bruch, C., Muffett, C., & Nichols, S. S. (eds.). (2016). *Governance, Natural Resources and Post-conflict Peacebuilding*. New York: Routledge.

Hufnagel, S., & Chappell, D. (eds.). (2019). *The Palgrave Handbook on Art Crime*. London: Palgrave Macmillan.

Lamarque, F., Anderson, J., Fergusson, R., Lagrange, M., Osei-Owusu, Y., & Bakker, L. (2009). *Human-Wildlife Conflict in Africa: Causes, Consequences and Management Strategies*. Rome: Food and Agriculture Organisation (FAO).

Nest, M. (2011). *Coltan* (Vol. 3). Cambridge: Polity Press.

South, N., & Brisman, A. (eds.). (2013). *International Handbook of Green Criminology*. London and New York: Routledge.

Stone, P. G. (ed.). (2011). *Cultural Heritage, Ethics and the Military* (Vol. 4). Woodbridge, UK: Boydell Press.

Informational Websites

Enough Project [https://enoughproject.org/products/reports/conflict-minerals]

Extractive Industries Transparency Initiative [https://eiti.org/]

Global Witness [www.globalwitness.org/en/campaigns/conflict-minerals/]

National Resource Governance Institute [www.resourcegovernanceindex.org/ data/both/ issue? region=global]

PactWorld [www.pactworld.org/mines-markets/resources]

Statista [www.statista.com/markets/410/topic/954/mining-metals-minerals/]

TRAFFIC [www.traffic.org/about-us/legal-wildlife-trade/]

UK Government [www.gov.uk/guidance/conflict-minerals]

World Wildlife Fund [http://wwf.panda.org/wwf_news/?214033/illegal-wildlife-trade-EU-facts-figures

Annotated Documentaries

RT (2017). *Congo, My Precious: The Curse of the Coltan Mines* [52:00 min.]. Analysing why one of the world's most resource-rich countries runs their mines like slave camps.

Vice News (2018). *Dirty Oil* [14:39 min.]. Explains the chaos, corruption and violence plaguing Nigeria's oil production.

ERT (2015) *Looters of the Gods* [56:50 min.]. Debates the role of the many prestigious museums in the illicit trade of antiquities.

Al Jazeera (2017). *Shadow War in the Sahara* [47:14 min.]. Questions whether the US and French military presence in North Africa is due to the war on terror or competition for natural resources.

BBC (2017). *The True Story of Blood Diamonds* [1 h. 22 min.]. Examines how the symbol of wealth worldwide causes much suffering to the people where it is mined in Africa.

National Geographic (2017). *Crimes against Nature* [44.34 min.]. Every episode explores how different forms of natural resources exploitation have become big business around the world.

Al Jazeera (2016). *The Poachers Pipeline* [47:37 min.]. Investigates how the global network of agents, traffickers and dealers in the lucrative trade is affecting the wildlife populations.

General Reading

Burgis, T. (2015). *The Looting Machine: Warlords, Tycoons, Smugglers and the Systematic Theft of Africa's Wealth*. London: William Collins.

Eichstaedt, P. (2011). *Consuming the Congo: War and Conflict Minerals in the World's Deadliest Place*. Chicago, IL: Chicago Review Press.

Glastra, R. (ed.). (2014). *Cut and Run: Illegal Logging and Timber Trade in the Tropics*. Ottawa: IDRC/Friends of the Earth.

Clarke, C. M., & Szydlo, E. J. (2017). *Stealing History: Art Theft, Looting, and Other Crimes against Our Cultural Heritage*. Lanham, MD: Rowman & Littlefield.

Campbell, G. (2012). *Blood Diamonds: Tracing the Deadly Path of the World's Most Precious Stones*. New York: Basic Books (AZ).

Stewart, J. G. (2010). *Corporate War Crimes: Prosecuting Pillage of Natural Resources*. New York: Open Society Foundations.

Endnotes

1. Stewart, J. G. (2011). *Corporate War Crimes: Prosecuting Pillage of Natural Resources*. New York: Open Society Institute.

2. United Nations Environment Programme (UNEP) (2004). From conflict to peace-building: the role of natural resources and the environment. Nairobi: United Nations Environment Programme [https://postconflict.unep.ch/ publications/ pcdmb_policy_01.pdf – accessed 02 January 2018].

3. Kishi, R. (2014). Resource-related conflict in Africa. *ACLED: Armed Conflict Location and Event Data Project*. [www.crisis.acleddata.com/resource-related-conflict-in-africa/ – accessed 10 August 2017].

4. Switzer, J. (2001). *Armed Conflict and Natural Resources: The Case of the Minerals Sector*. London: International Institute for Environment and Development.

5. Cooper, N. (2001). Conflict goods: the challenges for peacekeeping and conflict prevention. *International Peacekeeping, 8*(3), 21–38.

6. Kaeb, C. (2007). Emerging issues of human rights responsibility in the extractive and manufacturing industries: patterns and liability risks. *Northwestern University Journal of International Human Rights, 6*, 327.

7. Fritz, M. M., & Tessmann, N. (2018). Management of conflict minerals in automotive supply chains: where to start from? In *Social and Environmental Dimensions*

of Organizations and Supply Chains. Cham, Switzerland: Springer International, pp. 153–169.

8. Bhattacharyya, A. (2016). Corporate social and environmental responsibility in an emerging economy: through the lens of legitimacy theory. *Australasian Accounting, Business and Finance Journal, 9*(2), 2015.

9. Eweje, G. (2009). Labour relations and ethical dilemmas of extractive MNEs in Nigeria, South Africa and Zambia: 1950–2000. *Journal of Business Ethics, 86*, 207–223.

10. Thomas, A. O. (2020). Conflict minerals. In S. O. Idowu et al. (eds.), *Encyclopedia of Sustainable Management*. Cham, Switzerland: Springer Nature.

11. Parker, D. P., & Vadheim, B. (2017). Resource cursed or policy cursed? US regulation of conflict minerals and violence in the Congo. *Journal of the Association of Environmental and Resource Economists, 4*(1), 1–49.

12. Global Witness (2010). Sanctions: combating illicit international trade [section 3]. *Lessons Unlearned Report*. London: Global Witness.

13. Kepes, D. (2013). Conflict minerals trade in India. *Pragati*. [http://pragati.nationalinterest.in/ 2013/08/ conflict-mineral-trade-in-india/ – accessed 08 April 2016].

14. Diaz-Struck, E., & Poliszuk, J. (2014). Venezuela emerges as new source of 'conflict minerals'. Washington, DC: The Center for Public Integrity [www.publicintegrity. org/ 2012/03/04/8288/ venezuela-emerges-new-source-conflict-minerals – accessed 04 August 2016].

15. Thomas, A. O. (2020). Conflict minerals. In S. O. Idowu et al. (eds.), *Encyclopedia of Sustainable Management*. Cham, Switzerland: Springer Nature.

16. Kew, D., & Phillips, D. L. (2013). Seeking peace in the Niger Delta: oil, natural gas, and other vital resources. *New England Journal of Public Policy, 24*(1), 12.

17. Kiourktsoglou, G., & Coutroubis, A. (2015). *Isis Export Gateway to Global Crude Oil Markets*. London: University of Greenwich.

18. Lloyd, A. (2015). How coal fuels India's insurgency. *National Geographic*, April. [http://ngm.nationalgeographic.com/2015/04/india-coal/lloyd-text].

19. Global Witness (2010). Sanctions: combating illicit international trade [section 3]. *Lessons Unlearned Report*. London: Global Witness.

20. Global Witness (2013). *An Industry Unchecked: Japan's Extensive Business with Companies Involved in Illegal and Destructive Logging in the Last Rainforests of Malaysia*. London: Global Witness.

21. Global Witness (2010). Sanctions: combating illicit international trade [section 3]. *Lessons Unlearned Report*. London: Global Witness.

22. Wilson-Wilde, L. (2010). Wildlife crime: a global problem. *Forensic Science, Medicine, and Pathology, 6*(3), 221–222.

23. Ayling, J. (2013). What sustains wildlife crime? Rhino horn trading and the resilience of criminal networks. *Journal of International Wildlife Law & Policy, 16*(1), 57–80.

24. Nabi, G., Siddique, R., Ali, A., & Khan, S. (2020). Preventing bat-born viral out-breaks in future using ecological interventions. *Environmental Research*.

25. Nowell, K. (2012). Wildlife crime scorecard. *Switzerland: World Wildlife Fund*.

26. Actman, A. (2019). Traditional Chinese medicine and wildlife. *National Geographic*, 27 February. [www.nationalgeographic.com/animals/reference/traditional-chinese-medicine/ – accessed 20 April 2019].

27. Forrest, C. (2003). Strengthening the international regime for the prevention of the illicit trade in cultural heritage. *Melbourne Journal of International Law*, 4, 592.

28. Dietzler, J. (2013). On 'Organized Crime' in the illicit antiquities trade: moving beyond the definitional debate. *Trends in Organized Crime, 16*(3), 329–342.

29. Clarke, C. M., & Szydlo, E. J. (2017). *Stealing History: Art Theft, Looting, and other Crimes against our Cultural Heritage*. Lanham, MD: Rowman & Littlefield.

30. Voon, T. (2017). Restricting trade in cultural property: national treasures at the inter-section between cultural heritage and international trade law. [papers.ssrn.com]

31. Young, S. B. & Dias, G. (2012). Conflict-free minerals supply-chain to electronics. In *Electronics Goes Green 2012+*, September (1–5). IEEE.

32. Bayer, C. N. (2016). Dodd-Frank Section 1502 – RY2015 Filing Evaluation. *Development International*.

33. Epstein, M. J., & Yuthas, K. (2011). Conflict minerals: managing an emerging supply-chain problem. *Environmental Quality Management, 21*(2), 13–25.

34. Pact (2015). Unconflicted: making conflict-mining a reality in the DRC, Rwanda and Burundi. Washington, DC: Pact [www.pactworld.org/mining – accessed 20 November 2018].

35. Global Witness & Amnesty International (2015). *Digging for Transparency: How US Companies are Only Scratching the Surface of Conflict Minerals Reporting*. London: Global Witness and Amnesty International.

36. Global Witness (2010). Peacekeeping: disrupting the illicit trade at source [section 5]. *Lessons Unlearned Report*. London: Global Witness.

37. Wellsmith, M. (2011). Wildlife crime: the problems of enforcement. *European Journal on Criminal Policy and Research, 17*(2), 125–148.

38. Stenberg, E. (2005). Global corporate citizenship in post-conflict reconstruction. In *Perspectives on Corporate Social Responsibility in International Business*. Turku: Turku School of Economics and Business Administration.

39. McBain, D. (2014). Coltan: a study of environmental justice and global supply chains. *Power, Justice and Citizenship*, 173.

40. Morgan, R. M., Wiltshire, P., Parker, A., & Bull, P. A. (2006). The role of foren-sic geoscience in wildlife crime detection. *Forensic Science International, 162*(1–3), 152–162.

41. Wilson-Wilde, L. (2010). Combating wildlife crime. *Forensic Science and Medical Pathology, 6*, 149–150.

42. Nurse, A. (2011). Policing wildlife: perspectives on criminality in wildlife crime. In *Papers from the British Criminology Conference, 11*, 38–53. The British Society of Criminology.

43. OECD (2013). *Due Diligence Guidance for Responsible Supply Chains of Minerals from Conflict-Affected and High-Risk Areas*, 2nd edn. Luxembourg: OECD Publishing. [http://dx.doi.org/10.1787/9789264185050-en – accessed 03 January 2018].

44. Gillard, T., & Nieuwenkamp, R. (2015). Responsible gold also means supporting livelihoods of artisanal miners. *Huffington Post*, 22 June.

45. Chasan, E. (2016). Apple says supply chain now 100% audited for conflict minerals. [www.bloomberg.com/news/articles/2016-03-30/ – accessed 04 August 2016].

46. Sinclair, B. (2015). Conflict minerals: the real link between games and violence. [www.gamesindustry.biz/articles/2015-06-03-conflict-minerals-the-real-link-between-games-and-violence – accessed 04 August 2016].

47. Magistad, M. K. (2011). Why Chinese mineral buyers are eyeing Congo. *Public Radio International* [www.pri.org/stories/2011-10-26/slideshow-why-chinese-mineral-buyers-are-eying-congo – accessed 04 August 2016].

48. Bayer, C. (2015). *Dodd-Frank Section 1502 Post-Filing Survey*. New Orleans, LA: Tulane University.

49. Kaufmann, D. (2015). The time is now for addressing resource governance challenges in Latin America. Washington, DC: Brookings Institution. [www.brookings. edu/blog/up-front/2015/02/09/ – accessed 02 September 2016].

50. Akella, A. S., & Allan, C. (2011). Dismantling wildlife crime: executive summary. *TRAFFIC, 2012*(15).

51. Fincham, D. (2008). How adopting the Lex Origins Rule can impede the flow of illicit cultural property. *Columbia Journal of Law & Arts, 32*, 111.

52. Schabas, W. A. (2005). War economies, economic actors, and international criminal law. In *Profiting from Peace: Managing the Resource Dimensions of Civil War*. Boulder, CO: Lynne Rienner.

53. Kiourktsoglou, G., & Coutroubis, A. (2015). *Isis Export Gateway to Global Crude Oil Markets*. London: University of Greenwich.

54. Stergiou, D. (2016). ISIS political economy: financing a terror state. *Journal of Money Laundering Control, 19*(2), 189–207.

55. Solomon, E., Kwong, R., & Bernard S. (2016). Inside Isis Inc: the journey of a barrel of oil. *Financial Times*, 29 February. [https://ig.ft.com/sites/2015/isis-oil/ – accessed 15 August 2018].

56. Stergiou, D. (2016). ISIS political economy: financing a terror state. *Journal of Money Laundering Control, 19*(2), 189–207.

57. Solomon, E., Kwong, R., & Bernard S. (2016). Inside Isis Inc: the journey of a barrel of oil. *Financial Times*, 29 February. [https://ig.ft.com/sites/2015/isis-oil/ – accessed 15 August 2018].

58. Kiourktsoglou, G., & Coutroubis, A. (2015). *Isis Export Gateway to Global Crude Oil Markets*. London: University of Greenwich.

59. Solomon, E., Kwong, R., & Bernard S. (2016). Inside Isis Inc: the journey of a barrel of oil. *Financial Times*, 29 February. [https://ig.ft.com/sites/2015/isis-oil/ – accessed 15 August 2018].

60. Solomon, E., Kwong, R., & Bernard S. (2016). Inside Isis Inc: the journey of a barrel of oil. *Financial Times*, 29 February. [https://ig.ft.com/sites/2015/isis-oil/ – accessed 15 August 2018].

61. Kiourktsoglou, G., & Coutroubis, A. (2015). *Isis Export Gateway to Global Crude Oil Markets*. London: University of Greenwich.

CHAPTER 6

WASTE TRANSHIPMENT & HAZARDOUS RECYCLING

Credit: Alex Fu/Pexels

Overview in Introduction

Growth of the international trade in waste has been stimulated progressively by more stringent environmental laws enacted in the industrialised world, resulting in larger volumes being classified thus. The outsourcing of its transhipment for disposal and recycling to countries in the developing world has been possible with the latter's need for economic opportunities coupled with their political negligence to regulate health and safety issues. This shadow trade is one which encompasses everything from household trash, e-waste and organic waste to industrial chemicals, ship-breaking and nuclear by-products, shipped by land, air and sea through multiple ports and countries. Exports of toxic wastes has been surreptitiously included within bilateral free-trade agreements between industrialised and developing countries, despite international treaties, which each country had previously signed, banning these. Thus, this is another exemplar of neo-colonialism. More subtle than the dumping of solid wastes but no less deadly is the related field of pollution or the jettisoning of waste into the air, earth and water, which has local, regional and global consequences regardless of their origin. Hence this chapter highlights the need to tackle the issue of export, transit, storage, recycling and disposal of all wastes produced currently or in the past, through international regulation, manufacture re-engineering and citizen awareness. Major aspects of this shadow trade explored in this chapter include waste generation, environmental regulation, dumping, forms of waste, pollution, contamination, health risks, shipment directionality and improper recycling.

Discarding Responsibility

Historical Propensities

The practice of dumping toxic wastes at sea has an extensive history, dating from the imperial powers dumping industrial waste along shipping routes to their colonies as well as the waters of the latter. In the post-World War II era, the US military routinely jettisoned surplus chemical and biological weapons in the world's oceans. In the first half of the 20th century dismantling ships at the end of their economic life was done mainly in the USA and the UK, but pollution regulations and labour costs pushed the industry initially towards the Mediterranean, such as Turkey, and then to developing countries like Bangladesh, India, Pakistan and China.[1] In the 1970s and 1980s, when multinational oil companies were banned by local legislation from discarding wastes around the coast of the Gulf of Mexico, they began experimenting with incinerating at sea. Eventually it took growing awareness of their practice of surreptitiously exporting the resultant toxic ash to developing countries for there to be global pressure for the enactment of the Basel Convention.[2]

Under the rubric of such 'brown crime' can be subsumed other urban-based environmental crimes such as the residues of oil pollution, as in the Niger Delta, radioactive waste in Russia, chemical warfare, as with Agent Orange in Vietnam, asbestos production in Europe and the like. The Basel Convention of 1992, which resulted from a coalition of Greenpeace and developing countries as well as others from Eastern and Western Europe, has had admittedly limited impact. Analysis of the world trade in e-waste between 206 territories using the United Nations ComTrade database, for instance, reveals a changing geography between 1996 and 2016 that undermines the key notion of uni-directionality that lies behind various international regulations. While the export of e-waste from industrialised countries to developing countries constituted 35 percent of total trade worldwide in the mid-1990s, two decades on this had dropped dramatically to less than 1 percent, while its trade between industrialised countries had risen to 82 percent of the world total.[3]

Current Impetus

The illicit transportation of the detritus from mining, manufacture and consumption continues unabated, usually from industrialised countries where these are generated to developing countries for unsafe storage or recycling, is yet another manifestation of neo-colonialist exploitation. Its adverse consequences for the environment of the latter countries and the health of their people typically characterises this present-day shadow trade. While there has been a decades-old series of international guidelines, declarations, recommendations, and even a treaty, all of these have proven weak in enforcement, as demonstrated by periodic media reports of waste catastrophes *post-hoc*, whether chemicals, plastic, municipal, oil, medical or radioactive. Most published academic research on this shadow trade seems to be in the biological, health and chemical sciences and in environmental engineering, rather than in management, economics and the social sciences. Their agenda has been the abatement of consequences, rather than on pre-emption, oversight or penalisation of dubious entrepreneurs, criminal groups, legitimate businesses and negligent governments that allow this shadow trade to thrive.

While higher-income or industrialised countries may be the largest generators of waste but the slowest in its growth, it is the lower-income countries that remain the smallest generators of waste per capita, even if the growth rates are similar off a much smaller base (Figure 6.1). At the same time, waste shipment and dumping among developing countries has risen, along with some waste from emergent economies increasingly being re-exported in the reverse direction to industrialised economies for specialised treatment. What this seems to suggest is that regulations like the Basel Convention, which are framed largely around hazardous waste export from industrialised to developing countries causing harm, are no longer sufficient. According to the UN Environment Programme (UNEP), the value of the global waste sector from collection to recycling is estimated to be around USD400 billion.[4] Arguably the focus in this shadow trade should now shift to issues of re-use, refurbishment, repair and recycling in efficient waste-recovery economies that incorporate technology, education and employment.

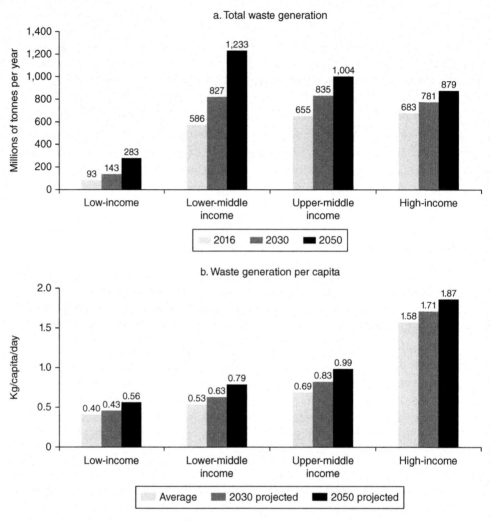

Figure 6.1   Global waste generation projections[5]

Copyright © World Bank. Used with permission.

By-products Unwanted

Industrial Waste

Manufacturing and mining

While all industrial processes generate waste and those that pollute air and water can be removed within the factories themselves, these can still result in the generation of solid wastes like the slag, sludge and dust being disposed of in landfills. As is typical in other developing countries, open-cut coal mines in Vietnam dump their solid waste as side-hill fills, which have negative environmental health impacts. Dust emissions from such hills as well as from the blasting and their transportation affect nearby populations, while contaminated water from surface flows and seepage cause stability risks for workers.[6] Emissions from smelting waste slag include toxic metals that cause harm to both health and the environment, even though their recovery could be a valuable source of zinc and lead. Hence environmental legislation worldwide has gradually sought to discourage this practice and instead to promote the further treatment of industrial waste for re-use, preferably in steel-making if not another industrial process, prompting research on materials recovery that could reduce costs and make production more competitive.[7]

Ships and steel

Ship-breaking is now a valuable sector of the economy for some developing countries because of the low investment outlay for local business and dependence on manual labour that generates needful employment. At the port of Aliaga in Turkey, 1.1 percent by tonnage of the worldwide fleet is scrapped per year, and the recycled steel from ship-breaking yards is a crucial resource for this country, the 12th largest steel-producing in the world.[8] At one of the largest ship-breaking yards worldwide, Alang in India, 241 obsolete ships ranging from bulk carrier, general cargo, container and refrigerator ships to passenger liners were dismantled during 2011–13, each type generating different quantities of the waste types.[9] Likewise, in Bangladesh, which is the leading country for ship-breaking presently, less-old oil tankers and bulk carriers are preferred for their higher steel content, on which its domestic steel industry is dependent.[10] But for ship owners, shipyards and governments, ship-breaking in an environmentally-sound way poses a challenge because ships contain a range of hazardous materials, such as asbestos, rubber, glass-wool, oily sludge, and numerous other chemicals, including residues of their past cargoes. In response, the European Parliament has passed the Ship Recycling Regulation, while the International Maritime Organization drafted the Hong Kong Convention on the issue, compelling the ship-breaking industry and the governments in countries where it is located to conform. However, the results have been mixed.

Construction Waste

Although a concomitant of economic development and infrastructure growth, construction waste is often overlooked as having dire outcomes. The urban boom in China in the 2010s resulted from a government stimulus of the economy worth

USD600 billion following the global recession, not to mention ongoing massive infrastructure programmes. A consequence has been a significant increase of construction waste within a context of limited regulations and low industry awareness of waste management.[11] In Turkey, 13 million metric tonnes (Mt) were generated by one earthquake alone, as well as significant contributions from demolitions of illegal construction and frequent household modifications due to deterioration from poor labour or materials.[12] While Thailand produces over 1 Mt of construction waste, most of which ends up dumped in undesignated sites, it is estimated that up to 4,000 jobs could be created if waste management and recycling were practised.[13] When the government in Hong Kong introduced a levy on construction waste to provide an economic incentive for developers and contractors to recycle, in just one district surveyed for over a year construction waste in landfills was reduced by about 60 percent.[14] Public education campaigns targeting householders on not discarding materials before the end of their life-span, training contractors on quality construction and encouraging the use of recycled materials, as well as ample provision of landfills for the collection of unrecoverable waste, are all invaluable for mitigating construction waste.

Municipal Waste

Inorganic trash

With economic development comes greater urbanisation and better living standards, although the accompanying increased consumption results in greater trash in cities. In many developing and emergent countries there is inadequate collection and uncontrolled dumping, leading to environmental and health issues. Dioxin and similar chemicals have been found in the breast milk of women living near municipal dumping grounds in India, Cambodia, Vietnam and the Philippines, among other Asia countries[15]. With over 280 Mt of plastic produced internationally per year and less than half sent to be recycled, much ends up polluting land and sea, continents and oceans, harming wildlife and, through entering the food chain, being harmful to humans.[16] Reducing the use of virgin plastic and recycling plastics through existing technologies keeps this waste from being consigned to landfills, thus improving environmental sustainability.[17] However, decisions on municipal waste tend to be based on local knowledge on such matters as waste quantities, technical expertise, outputs marketability, public awareness and finances.[18] Mapping the downstream flow has revealed that material losses and functionality can be considerable in recycling processes, but that these are opportunities for reduced material use through re-manufacturing, with benefits for material efficiency and global warming.[19] Subsequent resource scarcity and technological efficiency have stimulated interest in the end-of-life management of products through re-use, re-manufacturing and recycling such as of steel, plastic and glass in component manufacture.

Organic garbage

The processes that governments use to deal with this form of waste include source reduction, collection, recycling, composting, incineration and landfills, each of which has implications for greenhouse gas emission. In the Asian context and elsewhere, where the purported benefits of the waste trade are outweighed by the environmental costs, economic cooperation may be a means of developing countries achieving environmentally-sound waste management. In Indian cities, population growth, urbanisation and industrialisation are causing a rise in the generation of heterogeneous solid waste, which is typically disposed of untreated in open dumping and is found to contain both pollutants and nutrients.[20] Although Romania has acceded to the European Union, its rural areas still lack sanitation facilities, resulting in uncontrolled household waste polluting the mountain rivers, affecting the communities in close proximity and reducing any tourism potential.[21] Methane from food waste has the potential to increase global warming, but since different pre-treatment processes seem to have a marginal impact on this, other considerations – such as economics and practicality – influence decisions. [22] Nevertheless, there is scope for the proper selection and management of wastes, especially the removal of pollutants, before these can be applied as nutrients to the land.

Plastic Waste

While the pollution of oceans, rivers and beaches comprises various materials, about 90 percent of floating marine debris is plastic, of which 62 percent comprises packaging for food and drink.[23] Plastic only came to be widely manufactured about 60 years ago, and being resilient to decomposition, its products and packaging will continue to pollute land and sea for many decades and even centuries. Even those plastics that are ostensibly biodegradable do not decompose fully because of insufficient exposure to light, oxygen and warmth in the ocean depths.[24] If not retrieved in time, due to that being characteristically difficult, plastic eventually breaks down into minute pieces that enter into the food chain and represent a serious health hazard to fish and humans. Land-based sources account for about 80 percent of marine litter, which originated in waste dumps, landfills, stormwater, untreated sewage, manufacturing and tourism.[25] In the early 2010s, an estimated 32 million tonnes of plastic waste originated from waterways draining land and coastal areas, causing between 4.8 and 12.7 million tonnes to enter into oceans.[26] Unfortunately, the use of plastic is increasing as a means of oil industry diversification and consumer affluence, while much plastic waste is not recyclable or else its recycling is either polluting or uneconomic. Hence inadequate collection and disposal systems, particularly in developing and emergent economies, results in plastic waste dumping on land and into water.

Electronic Waste

The specialised area of electronic waste (e-waste) is where business growth has been triggered by the relatively recent enactment of environmental laws in the industrialised world requiring manufacturers and their distributors to take back used products at the end of their useful life. The latest estimates for e-waste generated worldwide in 2014 was 41.8 million metric tonnes (Mt), with the top producers being the US at 7.1 Mt, followed by China at 6.0 Mt. While Asia generated the most e-waste at 16.0 Mt in total, Europe generated the highest e-waste on a per capita basis at 15.6 kg, followed by Oceania (Australia, New Zealand plus the Pacific Island nations), although that may reflect the more regulated processes for collection and measurement in industrialised countries of the latter regions. As might be expected, there has been a clear correlation between the amount of waste generated and the GDP of a country, namely its level of economic development, but not with its population size.[27] Of the international total, 9.3 Mt or about a quarter by weight came from personal devices like smartphones and computers, with household appliances such as refrigerators and air-conditioners contributing the balance. Perhaps most concerning must be that generation of e-waste worldwide was expected to rise by 2.0 Mt per year, thus reaching 50.0 Mt by 2018.[28]

The impact of e-waste recycling on health is dependent on the type and quantity, the locations of various activities and the methods of processing, which typically involves using acid baths, burning cables, breaking apart toxic solders, and dumping consequent waste material without the workers wearing protective clothing.[29] Skin exposure to chemicals such as lead and mercury, air pollution from fumes and dust, and contamination of water and food can all have long-term consequences for the wider community and eco-system, invariably affecting the physically vulnerable most, such as pregnant women and children.[30] Still, a comprehensive review of 57 research papers on the health of populations living near recycling sites found that evidence of a causal relationship with hazardous waste was limited for cancers, asthma and adverse birth outcomes, and presently inadequate for other alleged health outcomes.[31] Resulting air pollution particles have been alleged to have been instrumental in conveying the deadly coronavirus across greater distances than through human-to-human contagion.[32] Notably, the continents generating the lowest per capita waste, Asia and Africa, are the ones to which most e-waste is shipped riskily, along with other forms of hazardous waste, to be recycled in primitive ways and unsafe conditions, adversely affecting the workers' health as well as the environments *en route* and at the destination (Figure 6.2). Much less noted are the implications of exported waste from industrialised economies together with hazardous recycling practices in developing and emergent economies for global environmental degradation and climate change.

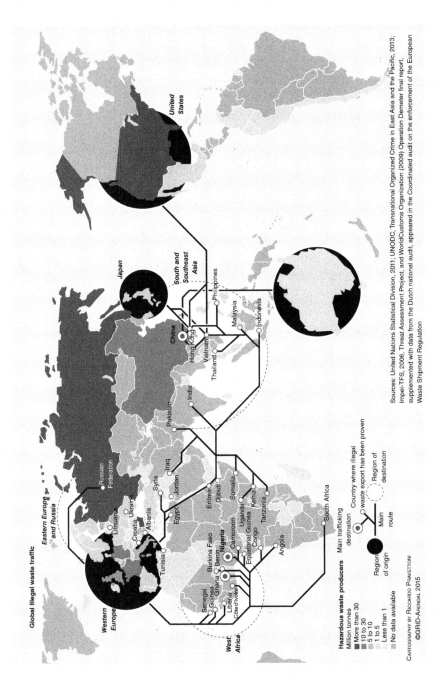

Figure 6.2 Global illegal waste traffic routes[33]

Source: GRID-Arendal/UNEP

Radioactive Waste

Nuclear waste disposal is a particularly sensitive societal issue linked to national security and the environment, and so is seldom talked about as a recycling business. Still, low to immediate level radioactive waste comes from medical institutions, research laboratories, industrial processes and ancillary power-plant equipment, and is reasonably easy to process and store. Low-level waste is defined by the long timespan of its harmful radioactivity, which may extend for up to 100,000 years. Nevertheless, the processing of nuclear waste to a minimal extent requires its transportation to selected industrialised countries which have the appropriate technology and this requires shipping it around the world, at some risk of radioactivity to populations of coastal countries and their maritime resources. Ultimately there is no solution to the disposal of radioactive waste apart from burying it under mountains without any certain knowledge of its impact on humans over another 100 millennia.[34] Nuclear energy is being touted as non-polluting, but it is certainly not sustainable since periodic disasters like Three Mile Island (1979), Chernobyl (1986) and Fukushima (2011) have resulted in serious harm to lives and health, not to mention radioactivity rendering of vast tracts of land unusable for occupation and cultivation indefinitely.

Parties to Disposal

Ineffectual Legislation

Despite a long-standing tradition of dumping waste in the sea, China has come to recognise the impact on both the maritime and coastal environments, especially since ratifying the international conventions in the 1990s. Subsumed under its political agenda of promoting a 'harmonious society', comprehensive national legislation in China has since required permits for the transport and disposal of domestic, industrial, radioactive, ship, aircraft and other hazardous wastes.[35] As of the late 2000s, India had no legislation directly addressing e-waste, leaving its Hazardous Waste Rule to apply. This has proved inadequate because it fails to define e-waste and to require producers and users to recycle or to identify who bears the costs involved.[36] Although NGOs have been working with governments to keep toxic wastes out of Africa, these have had limited long-term success. Having been the end-destination of most waste exports, despite the various pronouncements on the matter by the industrialised world, members of the Organisation for African Unity (OAU) drafted the Bamako Convention.[37] But its concentration on the precautionary principle of reducing the generation of waste on the African continent may well be redundant because most production of waste occurs in other continents. Nonetheless, this convention is quite unique worldwide in not excluding the import of radioactive waste typically generated in industrialised economies. Furthermore, while multilateral economic agreements within regions have been instrumental in promoting environmental governance, the rise of bilateral trade treaties between industrialised and developing countries often masks the permitting of their shadow trade in various hazardous wastes, as with Europe (see Table 6.1).

Table 6.1   Waste exported from the EU in 2019[39]

MAIN DESTINATIONS	MILLION TONNES	TYPES OF WASTE	MILLION TONNES
Turkey	11.4	Ferrous metals	15.6
India	2.9	Paper	5.8
UK	1.9	Plastics	2.4
Switzerland	1.6	Other wastes	2.4
Norway	1.5	Copper, aluminium, nickel	1.5
Indonesia	1.3	Textiles	1.5
China	1.2	Wood	0.5

Source: Data extracted from EuroStat (2020)

Questionable Logistics

The privatisation of public services such as garbage collection and disposal creates opportunities for business involvement with government, and the possible corruption of officials in both sending and receiving locations. The creation of waste crises, such as through worker strikes or civil unrest, is cynically used as an opportunity to trigger the by-passing of the normal contractual process. Where governments relinquish their responsibility for waste collection and disposal, criminal gangs tend to get involved in the distasteful business, which proves lucrative in receiving payment upfront for removal while lacking any monitoring of disposal abroad. For a number of unique reasons, Italy has a well-established reputation for the illegal trafficking in waste. Industrial wastes emanating from the more developed central and northern regions are handled largely by mafias from the less institutionalised south of the country. With the collusion of entrepreneurs, professionals and officials, these wastes are either dumped locally or exported, usually to developing countries. Among the circumventions of the law are recycling undertakings that are done only on paper, the accumulation of huge amounts of waste before declaring bankruptcy or dumping in small roadside dumps, natural caves and abandoned industrial areas.[38] Since the legislation requires firms lacking their own ability to process their wastes to transfer it to specialised providers, this expensive requirement gives rise instead for opportunities to use intermediaries. The latter then illegally under-declare the amounts, reclassify the waste or claim to recycle them while actually dumping them at home or more likely abroad. Through convoluted routes according to type of waste, transhipment takes place via major ports in the world, including in industrialised and emergent economies where interventions may also be made to curtail this shadow trade.

Eco Smugglers

Given the lucrative profits, organised crime syndicates entered into waste smuggling because it came with a lower risk of punitive prosecution than in their customary trades, such as in drugs, prostitution and arms. By corrupting governments and corporations abroad for the cheap disposal of waste, the syndicates were able to offer lower prices at home, thus growing the waste trade into a global market.[40] Furthermore, the criminals have been able to diversify into waste disposal by using the same channels as other illegal goods in their illicit operations. According to Europol, the illegal trade in hazardous waste involves a network of criminals with specialist tasks from collection, transportation and disposal, as well as legal and financial services. Working in close cooperation with client corporations, such organised crime syndicates earn EUR18–26 billion per year in income from the hazardous waste trade alone. As manufacturing corporations that produce hazardous waste prefer to avoid responsibility for any health consequences and environmental degradation, the eco-mafias facilitate its disposal overseas, typically in developing countries.[41]

In addition, these eco smuggling organisations work with corrupt governments and officials at home and abroad, regarding the issuance of falsified certificates, whether on the corporation responsible for generating the waste or on the non-hazard nature of the waste, all the way to their final destination for disposal. Corruption extends to port authorities, custom agencies and the police forces, freight-forwarders and laboratories, all of which facilitates the process of illicit waste disposal. Thus, hazardous waste is typically transhipped to South-Eastern Europe and then on to the Balkan states. However, some EU member states remain transit points for shipment abroad, such as Italy with electronic waste *en route* to Africa and Asia, despite its customs officials having seized over 40,000 tonnes of hazardous waste intended for shipping illegally and disposal permanently, mainly in China and Hong Kong, as well as ports in Africa.[42]

Site Apartheid

Although the location of hazardous production facilities in areas of poor or minority citizens has invariably been pointed out in environmental justice research, it reflects just a snapshot in time rather than the long process by which this came about, even in industrialised countries. In the case of polluting industrial facilities that relocated to the American South in the 1960s, there seemed then no significant relationship between location and race, and only a weak relationship with income. But by the 1990s all such locations had significantly higher minority and lower income populations than the rest of the state, suggesting that they came to live around the avoided facilities for economic reasons.[43] In the context of illegal dumping in Chicago over a century, corporations, with the support of government, targeted ethnic-minority and immigrant low-income neighbourhoods because of their political vulnerability and the availability of unwanted land. While activists campaigned for environmental justice against the waste dumping, and did succeed ultimately in getting relevant laws enforced, other locals were enabling the dumping, including corrupt local politicians, cash-strapped residents and unscrupulous recycling businesses.[44]

Arguably, similar exploitative principles apply, and outcomes occur on a global scale when waste disposal and recycling are directed towards poorer developing economies from richer industrialised economies in a characteristic neo-colonialist manner. Developing countries constitute an obvious destination of waste shipments since manufacturers there often use superseded technologies that already generate effluents, emissions and hazardous wastes of their own. Having neither the finances nor capacity to store, dispose and recycle such waste, their governments overlook the threat to the health of citizens and the environmental degradation in order to attract investment or remain part of transnational supply chains that cater to the demand for consumer and industrial goods. Besides, much industrial waste shipped mostly from the industrialised world is declared as being destined for recycling in the developing world even though it may end up in wastelands, polluting land, air and water with heavy metals and toxic chemicals. Thus, in the waste shipment and hazardous recycling trade as with other shadow trades, illegal entities such as crime syndicates and other operators are parasitic on legitimate ones, such as corporations and governments, and might even be symbiotic.

Intercepting Passage

International Monitoring

The Basel Convention treaty does define the unregulated transnational movement and disposal of hazardous waste as a crime, although the onus is on the signatory countries to monitor, enforce and prosecute. The lack of resources and of political will to do so, particularly in developing and emergent economies, constitute loopholes through which global waste traders find devious means to circumvent laws through bribery, false documents and outright smuggling. Driven by poverty, residents around dumpsites and workers in unsafe recycling enterprises may be unwilling to complain and might even be complicit in hiding the practice. Furthermore, a significant limitation of the Basel Convention is that radioactive waste lies conspicuously outside its remit, and so its disposal remains secretive, possibly at the behest of the industrialised countries that generated it. Given that specialised disposal facilities are scarce around the world, waste from nuclear plants has to be transported long distances across land and sea at considerable risk to populations and environments *en route*.

Before existing regulations are jettisoned, it is worth scrutinising whether the classifications of industrialised and developing countries are still valid. Since there is no prohibition of trade between developing countries under the Basel Convention, Singapore serves as a key node in the global e-waste trade. Often still treated as a developing country despite its industrialised-economy status by gross domestic product (GDP), this semi-periphery country is allegedly able to export high-quality e-waste that has been domestically generated, as well as transhipments from industrialised countries, to buyers in developing countries in Africa and Asia for a variety of purposes from re-use and refurbishment to parts recovery and material recycling.[45] However there are many other countries and ports that are actively involved at various stages of transhipping waste, from generation to disposal (see Table 6.2). The costs and technology for processing waste closer to its production and collection have changed, and yet borderless shipment, storage and recycling of waste has become increasingly opaque to governmental scrutiny.

Table 6.2   Waste transhipment stages

	GENERATION & EXPORT	TRANSIT & CONSOLIDATION	IMPORT &DISPOSAL
Typical Regions	Industrialised Economies	Emergent Economies	Developing Economies
Major Players	Factories/Mines	Shipping Lines	Recycling Firms
	Cities/Governments	Customs/Ports	Cottage Industries
	Households/Offices	Logistics Providers	Landfill Scavengers
Intermediaries	Freight-forwarders	Agents/Brokers	Vendors/Buyers
	Local Gangs	Crime Syndicates	Local Gangs
Likely Ports	Rotterdam, Netherlands	Singapore	Lagos, Nigeria
	New York, USA	Colon, Panama	Karachi, Pakistan
	Yokohama, Japan	Durban, South Africa	Guanzhou, China
	Naples, Italy	Hong Kong	Bangkok, Thailand
	Newcastle, Australia	Dubai, UAE	Sao Paulo, Brazil

Citizen Agitation

In the context of limited data, ambiguous laws and general ignorance on the world geographies of waste, individual citizens have come to be recognised as the key agents in protecting environments and the workers involved. This could be via their consumer choices as well as recycling practices, favouring green economics and ethical trade, regardless of whether these have a significant effect in the short term. Meanwhile rival certification actors, along with their activist and industry sponsors, are framing the debate surrounding e-waste to developing countries as either a toxic trade or a digital development, allowing corporations to deflect any potential pressure that arises to make more effectual changes to design and manufacture through new legislation.[46] Deemed less topical in the public mind than climate change abatement, waste management only marshals political action when seepage from landfills, fumes from dumpsites, dust from incinerators and the like reach crisis point.

Nonetheless, the growing lack of suitable space for landfills near population centres is compounded by the not-in-my-backyard concerns of the more aware and knowledgeable citizens. A rare journal article analysed the decision-making process of an ordnance manufacturer in the US which sought to ignore the community surrounding their facilities in storing and transporting its hazardous waste. Demonstrating that the damage to reputation and costs of correction could have been avoided, the authors offer corporations contentious tips for reaching ethical decisions.[47] The collaboration in Canada of domestic urban garbage, a dump in a remote community and an abandoned gold mine illustrate well the mix of political, economic and cultural contexts in waste management within the wider context of free-market world capitalism. Even when ostensibly dialogue is engendered, this is framed by governments and multinational corporations, through their feasibility studies and public relations, as essentially an engineering problem. Accordingly, citizens are asked to accede to intermediate solutions funded by their own taxes that fail to recognise their colonial history, political economy and indigenous socio-cultural perspectives on the practice of waste dumping.[48]

Trade Re-orientation

Increased regulations, whether on a global, regional and national basis, have sought to encourage conserving resources, reducing environmental damage and preventing harm to health. Nonetheless these have created varying classifications, valuation testing and enforcement, leading to the unintended consequences of increased costs to importers, delayed shipments and loss of trust, all of which act as obstacles to the legitimate waste trade.[49] It is noteworthy that transhipment of toxic wastes has been unobtrusively included within free-trade pacts between industrialised and developing countries, in contravention of international banning treaties that each country has signed amid much publicity. Perhaps the focus of the debate on borderless waste dumping and recycling on the adverse health and environmental effects caused abroad represents some patronising lack of balance. For, from the developing world perspective, there could be some positive aspects, such as their contribution to reconditioned products, replacement parts and materials for manufacturing new products through the trade. On the one hand, industrialised countries can alleviate the negative effects of e-waste by curbing its export, often disguised as technology donations and second-hand products, to developing countries which are ill-equipped to reject them. On the other hand, industrialised countries can help developing countries to attain the capacity to enhance the positive benefits through the training of workers for recycling and health regulation of the processes.[50]

Most research on hazardous waste focuses on the environmental harm of poorer communities through the siting of hazardous waste processing and on the government regulation necessary to mitigate this, albeit in a context of a world economy dominated by neo-liberal ideas of marketisation. Far less attention has been paid to how costs and other compliance requirements of the same laws have driven waste management underground and facilitated the collaboration of legitimate corporations, informal-economy entrepreneurs and organised crime, whether on a national, regional and global scale, in what has been described as green criminology and dirty-collar crime.[51] Longer term, a more sustainable approach to the environment would be waste anti-growth regulation that constrains corporations by promoting new values of de-manufacturing or the reduction of production and consumption, as well as holding them accountable for the full costs of the resources used and the pollution caused.[52] While recycling tends to be couched in positive terms, such as recovering materials for manufacturing new products, the process disguises corporate exploitation of resources and pollution by product waste, a cycle which regulation seems ineffective in managing. Accordingly, this calls for greater societal interventions to moderate the global drivers of the waste trade that exploit domestic catalysts, leading to consequences for those sites selected for disposal and/or recycling (Figure 6.3). In the longer term, policy commitment to sustainability, conservation and cleaner technologies would seem to hold a greater potential than legislation on the disposal and recycling of waste for addressing this shadow trade.

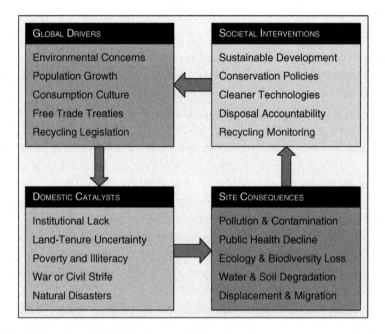

Figure 6.3   Cycle of waste disposal

Changing Course

Progress *sans* Pollution

The international trade in waste is a concomitant of the high consumption lifestyles and accompanying industrial production promoted by the growth logic of the capitalist world-economy. At the same time the trade has been fostered not just by the increase of waste production, but by the more stringent environmental laws in the industrialised world and the developing-emergent world's need for revenue. It is worth bearing in mind that every waste product has its origins in legitimate, even essential products in our economies or the by-products of their manufacture. E-waste comes from our high use of computers, phones, televisions and other such consumer electronics. Plastic is an indispensable material in all sorts of products, from vehicles to receptacles, as well as a packaging for consumer products, including food and drinks, that we often discard after use. Municipal wastes have a high content of discarded food by affluent homes, supermarkets, restaurants and hotels, much of which is still edible. Ships are the means of transportation for about three-quarters of all goods in international trade, and are themselves a generator of waste as they have to be disposed of at the end of their economic life. More subtle than the dumping of solid wastes, yet no less alarming is the related pollution of air and water, which has no borders, as exemplified by acid rain thousands of miles away from the source.[53] Yet the implications of environmental pollution and degradation for the global climate were largely overlooked until the turn of the 21st century and are still unrecognised in some influential quarters of corporations and government in countries at all economic development levels.

Manufacture Re-engineered

Given the directionality of this shadow trade from the industrialised to the developing-emergent world, it is important to tackle the issue of export, transit, storage, recycling and disposal of such wastes produced currently or in the past. But the ultimate question to be addressed is how less toxic products and by-products can be produced in the future. Extended Producer Responsibility (EPR) is also an attempt to implement a 'polluter-pays principle', which shifts the costs of collecting, treating and disposing of hazardous wastes away from governments towards corporations. Although such laws in the industrialised world are based on notions of sustainable development and consumption, no equivalents exist in the developing countries to which such wastes are transported, ostensibly for recycling, where this is often done crudely and dangerously.[54] The idea of establishing 're-manufacturing centres' in emergent economies for recycling of products to be done under the supervision of their original manufacturers is commendable, though possibly naïve regarding the political and economic dynamics. It may well take the impending scarcity of raw materials for industrial production to give waste greater value in the global marketplace and so move sustainable recycling and re-use closer to where the product or waste has been generated.

In the context of heightened ecological concerns about recycling and waste disposal in the industrialised world, businesses make claims to their various publics about endeavouring to be green in all their operations. Yet design innovations like multifunctionality, compactness and durability, which drive the marketability of electronic products from phones to computers and televisions, are at the same time major challenges for production, recycling and materials recovery. As e-waste contains precious metals like silver, gold and palladium, as well as dozens of rare earth minerals for which there is high demand for the manufacture of electronic products and scarce supply in global markets, there is considerable interest in their recovery, although the processes are quite specialised and are dependent on the bulk supply of waste to be economic.[55] Thus, blame is often strategically placed by the same corporations on the extremely strict national environmental regulations which necessitate the export of wastes for recycling and disposal abroad instead. Then there is a role for business academia not only in advocating the responsible marketing, trading and logistics of harmful wastes, but also in being at the forefront of the progressive 'greening' of refining, processing and manufacture of consumer and industrial products, and possibly also lower and more sustainable levels of consumption.

Commentary in Conclusion

Even where certain waste shipments are banned, as in industrialised countries, the regulations can be circumvented via falsified documents and repackaging, making all forms of waste indistinguishable from legitimate exports. Besides, toxic waste dumping is done via complex borderless networks which may or may not include organised crime or illegal businesses.[56] Failed states or developing countries without functioning governments are particularly vulnerable to having toxic wastes dumped on land or within their unmonitored territorial waters. Ironically, this is usually because industrialised countries have put in place more stringent pollution laws and their citizens are more aware of the health consequences of proximity to wastes. Historically, both colonial governments and their corporations have exploited resources for their industries, without regard for pollution, waste and harms to health caused at home or abroad, although the economic neo-colonialism in recent decades has seen this become particularly rapacious.

Environmental clean-up is a futile, endless exercise for communities and countries if even more waste is being produced elsewhere and disposed of irresponsibly. Simplistic as it may sound now, perhaps firms involved in extracting resources from the earth could be persuaded to explore ways for non-contaminating storage of unrecyclable waste, including the gaseous, in exhausted open-cut mines, extensive tunnels and deep drill-shafts as an alternative income stream while being socially responsible in rehabilitating the environments they degraded. The prospects for minorities, especially those living under authoritarian regimes, to combat transnational waste dumping are less optimistic, and a safe living environment needs to be framed within international human rights.[57] Although all parties to any economic exchange are supposed to share the full costs under a capitalist system, sadly neo-liberal economists conveniently deem the costs of waste to eco-systems and to the people affected as incidental externalities, while governments collude in not pricing these in the unquestioned pursuit of economic growth.

DIM DOMAIN

SHIP GRAVEYARD OR MATERIALS RESURRECTION?

As most of the international trade in goods is transported by sea, the shipping industry is essential to all economies. Such ocean-going ships are typically owned in the more developed countries and when redundant or ageing are sold by their owners through brokers operating in London, Dubai, Singapore and Hamburg. Consequently, ship-breaking or the dismantling of vessel structures for scrap and removal of equipment tends to be done in developing countries for lower cost and with less regulation. Regardless of whether this legitimate process is variously termed as recycling, dismantling or scrapping, this shadow trade invariably encompasses illicit operations of labour exploitation and environmental degradation, not to mention money laundering and tax evasion. Whether conducted at piers, in dry dock or on the beach, the industry represents the graveyard of ships, be they oil tankers, bulk carriers, general cargo, container ships, military vessels or passenger liners.

Site and Environment

Accounting for 47 percent of the world's tonnage dismantled every year, the port of Alang is the second largest ship-breaking site in the world. Along the 12 kilometres geographically located on the western coast in the State of Gujarat in India, ship-breaking has taken place here for 160 years. The gradual slope of the beach with a rocky bottom is suitable for beaching ships right up to the scrap yard at minimum cost and low risk. Over two decades, 4,327 cargo vessels, oil tankers, passenger liners and warships, totalling about 26-27 Mt of light dead tonnage, were broken up there. The ship-breaking industry claims to contribute 10-15 percent of India's steel production, by melding traditional ship recycling practices, modern engineering and management knowledge.

Presently, the inter-tidal zone around Alang has no vegetation because the mangroves died out soon after the industry began. The coastal water has become harmful for fish populations, and only species tolerant to petroleum have survived, while foreign species have been introduced through ship ballast water. Fishing is the main livelihood for about 10,000 people, many from scheduled tribes which are discriminated against and who live in poverty despite being protected by the Constitution of India. The absence of sanitation facilities for the workers has led to the presence of pathogenic and non-pathogenic bacteria in surface and underground water around the district, making it unsafe for consumption and unsuitable for recreation.[58]

(Continued)

Living and Working

In the 1980s, most of the 300 or so villagers in Alang were involved in agriculture and animal farming, with a minority engaged in fishing. Since the establishment of the ship-breaking industry, these industires have deteriorated because the water table has dropped from 15 to 130 metres and water quality has been affected by saline intrusion. By the end of 2003, around 15,000 workers were employed in 80 working yards, over 90 percent of these being migrants from underdeveloped states of North India. Their wages are between USD1 and USD6 per day, the variation due to industry arbitrariness, given the sub-contracting system and the fact that there are no unions. Since the work is seasonal, about 8 percent of them stay in rented shanty dwellings without adequate potable water, electricity and drainage systems.

Ship-breaking makes for an unsafe work environment with a high risk of injury and accidents due to unsafe machinery, inadequate equipment, worker illiteracy and lack of safety devices. Often the workers work overtime without pay, leading to decreased productivity, an increase in accidents due to fatigue and a life expectancy of about 40–50 years. Workers have no insurance for health or life, and upon accidents occurring in the shipyard, they are only transported to hospital. Neither the employer nor the government accepts responsibility for medical expenses and workers do not receive any wages while on medical leave. Workers are neither compensated nor provided with medical treatment for the chronic diseases, such as tuberculosis, malaria, dengue fever, hepatitis and respiratory infections, arising from the unsafe working practices and unhealthy living conditions.[59]

Recycling for Reuse

During the process of ship recycling, the prime objective is to recover materials that can be sold for reuse. There are two types. First, there are materials that are sellable without modification, such as changing their physical or chemical characteristics. Examples of these are wooden furniture, kitchen items, life-saving equipment, electrical appliances, office equipment and communications devices. Secondly, there are materials which require re-manufacturing in re-rolling mills, such as into steel bars, channels, girders and other structures for sale. In principle reusing or recycling huge quantities of materials should result in minimal waste dumped into the environment, the conservation of resources and a contribution to the economy.[60]

French Warship

The *Le Clemenceau* was built in 1957, decommissioned in France in 1997 and sailed for Alang in 2005. Its 22,000 tonnes of steel were expected to fetch a good price and thus its ship-breaking was financially attractive. But ships built prior to the 1960s contained toxic materials for fire-proofing and certain metals used in paints. Before it reached India, environmentalist groups campaigned against it, alleging that it contained more than 500 tonnes of asbestos and some polychlorinated biphenyls (PCBs). France had banned all forms of asbestos in 1977, while the import of asbestos waste was banned by the EU in 2005. Although it is possible to decontaminate asbestos and other toxic materials in their own countries, most ship-owners prefer to send it to developing countries where the costs are low and regulations lax. Still, traditional sites in Turkey, Greece and Bangladesh would not accept Le Clemenceau for ship-breaking.

A court in France approved sailing the vessel to India for ship-breaking because the authorities argued that it was a warship, had been decontaminated and was not considered as waste, and so was not subject to the Basel Convention. Environmentalists blamed the French authorities for not conducting a full inventory of toxic waste on board and for not assessing the impact on workers and on the marine environment at Alang. The Indian Supreme Court invited the French company Technopure, which had carried out the decontamination of the ship, to appear and provide details. The company testified to having removed 70 metric tonnes of asbestos from the ship, but admitted that there was still a minimum of 500 metric tonnes on board, which could have been removed safely in France. Finally, the Court issued an order to prohibit the entry of Le Clemenceau into Indian waters, the Supreme Court of France ruled against the decision to send the ship to India, and the French president recalled it.[61]

Norwegian Liner

The SS France was built in 1960, had a mass of 45,000 tonnes and was then the longest passenger ship ever built, comprising 16 floors and 1,400 rooms. In 1979 it was sold to Norwegian Cruise Line, renamed SS Norway and transformed into a glamorous cruise ship. Seriously damaged in 2003 by a boiler explosion in Miami, it was towed to Germany for repairs, but in 2004 it was found that decontaminating the in-built asbestos would cost EUR17 million. So, in 2005, the ship departed Germany with its official destination declared as Singapore for reuse, even though the ship-owner planned to discard the ship. Given its ownership, the SS Norway came under the EU Waste Shipment Regulation, besides the fact that the export of such ships from OECD countries to non-OECD countries was illegal. Nonetheless, the ship arrived in Malaysia instead of Singapore and its planned ship-breaking in Bangladesh was also protested by environmental lawyers there.

When the SS Norway departed for Dubai in early 2006, the owners informed the relevant authorities that it was going there for repairs, but instead it sailed towards Alang for ship-breaking. Meanwhile its parent company, Norwegian Cruise Line (Bermuda), sold it to a subsidiary, Star Cruise (Malaysia), which resold it to Bridgeed Shipping (Liberia), officially for a token USD10 despite a valuation of about USD15 million. A month later Bridgeed sold on the ship to the Indian ship-breaking company Hariyana Steel Demolition, which soon after transferred ownership to another ship-breaking company, Priya Blue Industries, which renamed it Blue Lady. In May 2006 the ship was prevented from entering Indian waters by an activist application to the Supreme Court of India, although, on humanitarian grounds of an impending

(Continued)

monsoon storm, the ship was permitted to anchor at another port nearby. Eventually it was beached at Alang without permission in August 2006 and allowed to be dismantled by a final court order in September 2007.[62]

Crucial Queries

Is the local authority or national government responsible for ensuring minimum wages, a safe workplace, healthcare insurance and other employee rights? What is the liability of the foreign ship-owner and its ship-breaker to these contracted workers?

Are the cost-savings and environmental benefits on recycling the ship for steel production or as second-hand equipment worth the exploitation of workers and the degradation of the local ecology? Should old ships be readily scrapped for metal without exploring the feasibility of refurbishing and repairing them for re-use in shipping, recreation or housing?

Can a ship that is being disposed of be variously classified as a 'vessel' or as 'waste' depending on what would best serve the interests of the owner at the time? Should a decommissioned warship be exempted on grounds of military secrecy from international regulations on the movement of hazardous waste?

Was the implementation of national regulations on the part of the relevant local authorities commendable or inadequate in either of the two ship cases? What is the likelihood that there was money laundering or tax evasion involved in the rapid re-sales at questionable prices of these ships heading for recycling?

FURTHER RESOURCES

Research Books

Dauvergne, P. (ed.). (2012). *Handbook of Global Environmental Politics*. London: Edward Elgar Publishing.

Hieronymi, K., Kahhat, R., & Williams, E. (eds.). (2012). *E-waste Management: From Waste to Resource*. London: Routledge.

Kojima, M., & Michida, E. (eds.). (2013). *International Trade in Recyclable and Hazardous Waste in Asia*. London: Edward Elgar Publishing.

Lepawsky, J. (2018). *Reassembling Rubbish: Worlding Electronic Waste*. Cambridge, MA: MIT Press.

Norris, L. (2010). *Recycling Indian Clothing: Global Contexts of Reuse and Value*. Bloomington, IN: Indiana University Press.

Pellow, D. N. (2007). *Resisting Global Toxics: Transnational Movements for Environmental Justice*. Cambridge, MA: MIT Press.

Informational Websites

European Commission [http://ec.europa.eu/trade/import-and-export-rules/export-from-eu/waste-shipment/ index_en.htm]

Institute of Scrap Recycling [www.isri.org/recycling-commodities/international-scrap-trade-database]

National Geographic [www.nationalgeographic.com/environment/global-warming/toxic-waste/]

Recycling International [https://recyclinginternational.com/category/research/]

Waste Atlas [www.atlas.d-waste.com/]

World Bank [www.worldbank.org/en/topic/urbandevelopment/brief/solid-waste-management

Our World in Data [https://ourworldindata.org/faq-on-plastics]

Annotated Documentaries

Basel Action (2013). *Exporting Harm: The High-Tech Trashing of Asia* [23:04 min.]. On the dumping of global e-waste in developing countries, including China.

DW Television (2018). *The Rich, the Poor and the Trash* [28:26 min.]. Investigates the lives of people both working with and living off trash in Kenya as well as the USA.

Europe Documentary (2015). *Nuclear Waste Disposal* [52:29 min.]. Explores the problem of past nuclear waste disposal on Europe's coasts and in sites across our oceans.

National Film Board of Canada (2017). *Shipbreakers* [1h 12 min.]. Investigates how workers dismantling the world's largest ships have no protection from injury or death.

PBS NewsHour (2019) The Plastic Problem [54:08 min.]. Explains how plastic use has become widespread, how it is affecting the environment and how its impact can be mitigated.

Sky News (2018). *Dirty Business: What Really Happens to Your Recycling* [46:00 min.]. Follows the trail of UK plastic waste through the country and around the world.

General Reading

Alexander, C., & Reno, J. (eds.). (2012). *Economies of Recycling: The Global Transformation of Materials, Values and Social Relations*. London: Zed Books.

Electronics TakeBack Coalition (2009). *E-Waste Briefing Book*. Electronics TakeBack Coalition.

Minter, A. (2013). *Junkyard Planet: Travels in the Billion-Dollar Trash Trade*. New York: Bloomsbury Publishing USA.

Pasternak, J. (2010). *Yellow Dirt: An American Story of a Poisoned Land and a People Betrayed*. New York: Simon and Schuster.

Mauch, C. (ed.) (2016). *Out of Sight, Out of Mind: The Politics and Culture of Waste*. Munich: Rachel Carter Center.

Endnotes

1. Sujauddin, M., Koide, R., Komatsu, T., Hossain, M. M., Tokoro, C., & Murakami, S. (2015). Characterization of ship breaking industry in Bangladesh. *Journal of Material Cycles and Waste Management, 17*(1), 72–83.

2. Müller, S. M. (2016). The 'Flying Dutchmen': Ships' tales of toxic waste in a globalized world. In C. Mauch (ed.), *Out of Sight, Out of Mind: The Politics and Culture of Waste*. Munich: Rachel Carter Center. pp. 13–19.

3. Lepawsky, J. (2015). The changing geography of global trade in electronic discards: time to rethink the e-waste problem. *The Geographical Journal, 181*(2), 147–159.

4. Rucevska, I., Nellemann, C., Isarin, N., Yang, W., Liu, N., Yu, K., & Bisschop, L. (2017). *Waste Crime–Waste Risks: Gaps in Meeting the Global Waste Challenge*. Nairobi and Arendal: United Nations Environment Programme and GRID-Arendal.

5. Kaza, S., Yao, L., Bhada-Tata, P., & Van Woerden, F. (2018). *What a Waste 2.0: A Global Snapshot of Solid Waste Management to 2050*. Washington, DC: World Bank Publications.

6. Ahmad, S., Martens, P. N., Fernandez, P. P., & Fuchsschwanz, M. (2009). Mine waste dumping and corresponding environmental impacts at Chinh Bac waste dump in Vietnam. Paper presented at 8th ICARD (International Conference on Acid Rock Drainage), June, Skelleftea, Sweden.

7. Lobato, N. C. C., Villegas, E. A., & Mansur, M. B. (2015). Management of solid wastes from steelmaking and galvanizing processes: a brief review. *Resources, Conservation and Recycling, 102*, 49–57.

8. Neşer, G., Ünsalan, D., Tekoğul, N., & Stuer-Lauridsen, F. (2008). The shipbreaking industry in Turkey: environmental, safety and health issues. *Journal of Cleaner Production, 16*(3), 350–358.

9. Hiremath, A. M., Tilwankar, A. K., & Asolekar, S. R. (2015). Significant steps in ship recycling *vis-à-vis* wastes generated in a cluster of yards in Alang: a case study. *Journal of Cleaner Production, 87*, 520–532.

10. Sujauddin, M., Koide, R., Komatsu, T., Hossain, M. M., Tokoro, C., & Murakami, S. (2015). Characterization of ship breaking industry in Bangladesh. *Journal of Material Cycles and Waste Management, 17*(1), 72–83.

11. Yuan, H. (2013). A SWOT analysis of successful construction waste management. *Journal of Cleaner Production, 39*, 1–8.

12. Esin, T., & Cosgun, N. (2007). A study conducted to reduce construction waste generation in Turkey. *Building and Environment, 42*(4), 1667–1674.

13. Kofoworola, O. F., & Gheewala, S. H. (2009). Estimation of construction waste generation and management in Thailand. *Waste Management, 29*(2), 731–738.

14. Hao, J. L., Hills, M. J., & Tam, V. W. (2008). The effectiveness of Hong Kong's construction waste disposal charging scheme. *Waste Management & Research, 26*(6), 553–558.

15. Ray, Amit (2008). Waste management in developing Asia. *The Journal of Environment and Development, 17*(1), 3–25.

16. Rochman, C. M., Browne, M. A., Halpern, B. S., Hentschel, B. T., Hoh, E., Karapanagioti, H. K., & Thompson, R. C. (2013). Policy: classify plastic waste as hazardous. *Nature, 494*(7436), 169.

17. Singh, N., Hui, D., Singh, R., Ahuja, I. P. S., Feo, L., & Fraternali, F. (2017). Recycling of plastic solid waste: a state of art review and future applications. *Composites Part B: Engineering, 115*, 409–422.

18. Bhada-Tata, P., & Hoornweg, D. (2016). Solid waste and climate change. World-watch Institute (ed.), *State of the World 2016*. Washington, DC: Island Press/ Center for Resource Economics, pp. 239–255 [https://link.springer.com/chap ter/10.5822/978-1-61091-756-8_20 – accessed 26 June 2020].

19. Diener, D. L., & Tillman, A. M. (2015). Component end-of-life management: exploring opportunities and related benefits of remanufacturing and functional recycling. *Resources, Conservation and Recycling, 102*, 80–93.

20. Goswami, U., & Sarma, H. P. (2008). Study of the impact of municipal solid waste dumping on soil quality in Guwahati city. *Pollution Research, 27*(2), 327–330.

21. Mihai, F.-C., Apostol, L., Ursu, A., & Ichim, P. (2012). Vulnerability of mountain rivers to waste dumping from Neamt county, Romania. *Geographica Napocensis, 2*(2).

22. Naroznova, I., Møller, J., Scheutz, C., & Lagerkvist, A. (2015). Importance of food waste pre-treatment efficiency for global warming potential in life cycle assessment of anaerobic digestion systems. *Resources, Conservation and Recycling, 102*, 58–66.

23. Galgani, F., Hanke, G., & Maes, T. (2015). Global distribution, composition and abundance of marine litter. In M. Bergmann, L. Gutow and M. Klages (eds.), *Marine Anthropogenic Litter*. Cham, Switzerland: Springer International, pp. 29–56.

24. Hopewell, J., Dvorak, R., & Kosior, E. (2009). Plastics recycling: challenges and opportunities. *Philosophical Transactions of the Royal Society B: Biological Sciences, 364*(1526), 2115–2126.

25. Arcadis (2014). Marine Litter study to support the establishment of an initial quantitative headline reduction target – SFRA0025. Brussels: European Commission DG Environment Project number BE0113.000668.

26. UNEP and NOAA (2012). *The Honolulu Strategy: A Global Framework for Prevention and Management of Marine Debris*. Washington, DC: United Nations Environment Programme/National Oceanic and Atmospheric Administration.

27. Kumar, A., Holuszko, M., & Espinosa, D. C. R. (2017). E-waste: an overview on generation, collection, legislation and recycling practices. *Resources, Conservation and Recycling, 122*, 32–42.

28. Balde, C. P., Wang, F., Kuehr, R., & Huisman, J. (2015). *The Global E-waste Monitor 2014: Quantities, Flows and Resources*. Bonn: United Nations University, IAS – SCYCLE.

29. StEP Initiative (2011). *Annual Report 2011: Five Years of the StEP Initiative*. United Nations University/Solving the E-Waste Problem Initiative. [Available at: www. step-initiative.org/files/step/_documents/ – accessed 02 January 2018].

30. Zheng, J., Chen, K. H., Yan, X., Chen S. J., Hu, G. C., Peng, X. W., et al. (2013). Heavy metals in food, house dust, and water from an e-waste recycling area in South China and the potential risk to human health. *Ecotoxicology and Environmental Safety, 96*, 205–212.

31. Fazzo, L., Minichilli, F., Santoro, M., Ceccarini, A., Della Seta, M., Bianchi, F., & Martuzzi, M. (2017). Hazardous waste and health impact: a systematic review of

the scientific literature. *Environmental Health, 16*(1), 107. [License: Creative Commons Attribution CC BY 3.0 IGO].

32. Carrington, D. (2020). Coronavirus detected on articles of air pollution. *The Guardian*, 24 April. [Available at: www.theguardian.com/environment/2020/apr/24/coronavirus – accessed 25 April 2020].

33. Rucevska, I., Nellemann, C., Isarin, N., Yang, W., Liu, N., Yu, K., & Bisschop, L. (2017). *Waste Crime – Waste Risks: Gaps in Meeting the Global Waste Challenge*. Nairobi: United Nations Environment Programme and GRID-Arendal.

34. Vidal, J. (2019). What should we do with radioactive nuclear waste? *The Guardian*, 01 August.

35. Zhu, K. (2009). Regulation of waste dumping at sea: the Chinese practice. *Ocean & Coastal Management, 52*(7), 383–389.

36. Krishna, M., & Kulshrestha, P. (2008). The Toxic Belt: perspectives on e-waste dumping in developing nations. *UC Davis Journal of International Law & Policy, 15*, 71.

37. Clapp, Jennifer (1994). Africa, NGOs, and the international toxic waste trade. *Journal of Environment & Development, 3*(2), 17–46.

38. Massari, M., & Monzini, P. (2004). Dirty businesses in Italy: a case-study of illegal trafficking in hazardous waste. *Global Crime, 6*(3–4), 285–304.

39. Data extracted from EuroStat (2020). Turkey: main destination for EU's waste. [https://ec.europa.eu/eurostat/en/web/products-eurostat-news/-/DDN-20200416-1 – accessed 30 June 2020].

40. Shebaro, I. (2004). Hazardous waste smuggling: a study in environmental crime. Transnational Crime and Corruption Center (TraCCC). Washington: American University [www.american.edu/traccc/resources/publications/students/shebar01.pdf].

41. Obradović, M., Kalambura, S., Smolec, D., & Jovičić, N. (2014). Dumping and illegal transport of hazardous waste, danger of modern society. *Collegium Antropologicum, 38*(2), 793–803.

42. Obradović, M., Kalambura, S., Smolec, D., & Jovičić, N. (2014). Dumping and illegal transport of hazardous waste, danger of modern society. *Collegium Antropologicum, 38*(2), 793–803.

43. Mitchell, J. T., Thomas, D. S., & Cutter, S. L. (1999). Dumping in Dixie revisited: the evolution of environmental injustices in South Carolina. *Social Science Quarterly, 80*(2), 229–243.

44. Pellow, D. N. (2004). The politics of illegal dumping: an environmental justice framework. *Qualitative Sociology, 27*(4), 511–525.

45. Lepawsky, J., & Connolly, C. (2016). A crack in the facade? Situating Singapore in global flows of electronic waste. *Singapore Journal of Tropical Geography, 37*(2), 158–175.

46. Pickren, G. (2014). Political ecologies of electronic waste: uncertainty and legitimacy in the governance of e-waste geographies. *Environment and Planning A, 46*(1), 26–45.

47. Magasin, M., & Gehlen, F. L. (1999). Unwise decisions and unanticipated consequences – case study. *Sloan Management Review, 41*(1), 47.

48. Hird, M. J. (2017). Waste, environmental politics and dis/engaged publics. *Theory, Culture & Society, 34*(2–3), 187–209.

49. Milovantseva, N., & Fitzpatrick, C. (2015). Barriers to electronics reuse of transboundary e-waste shipment regulations: an evaluation based on industry experiences. *Resources, Conservation and Recycling, 102*, 170–177.

50. Amankwah-Amoah, J. (2016). Global business and emerging economies: towards a new perspective on the effects of e-waste. *Technological Forecasting and Social Change, 105*, 20–26.

51. Ruggiero, V., & South, N. (2010). Green criminology and dirty collar crime. *Critical Criminology, 18*(4), 251–262.

52. South, N. (2016). Green criminology and brown crime: despoliation, disposal and de-manufacturing in global resource industries. In Wyatt. T. (ed.), *Hazardous Waste and Pollution*. Cham, Switzerland: Springer International, pp. 11–25.

53. Critharis, M. (1990). Third World nations are down in the dumps: the exportation of hazardous waste. *Brooklyn Journal of International Law, 16*, 311–339.

54. Nnorom, I. C., & Osibanjo, O. (2008). Overview of electronic waste management practices and legislations, and their poor application in the developing countries. *Resources Conservation & Recycling, 52*, 843–858.

55. Tansel, B. (2017). From electronic consumer products to e-wastes: global outlook, waste quantities, recycling challenges. *Environment International, 98*, 35–45.

56. Naim, Moises (2005). *Illicit: How Smugglers, Traffickers and Copycats are Hijacking the Global Economy*. London: Random House.

57. Adeola, F. O. (2000). Cross-national environmental injustice and human rights issues: a review of evidence in the developing world. *American Behavioral Scientist, 43*(4), 686–706.

58. Sonak, S., Sonak, M., & Giriyan, A. (2008). Shipping hazardous waste: implications for economically developing countries. *International Environmental Agreements: Politics, Law and Economics, 8*(2), 143–159.

59. Deshpande, P. C., Kalbar, P. P., Tilwankar, A. K., & Asolekar, S. R. (2013). A novel approach to estimating resource consumption rates and emission factors for ship recycling yards in Alang, India. *Journal of Cleaner Production, 59*, 251–259.

60. Hiremath, A. M., Tilwankar, A. K., & Asolekar, S. R. (2015). Significant steps in ship recycling *vis-à-vis* wastes generated in a cluster of yards in Alang: a case study. *Journal of Cleaner Production, 87*, 520–532.

61. Sonak, S., Sonak, M., & Giriyan, A. (2008). Shipping hazardous waste: implications for economically developing countries. *International Environmental Agreements: Politics, Law and Economics, 8*(2), 143–159.

62. Moen, A. E. (2008). Breaking Basel: the elements of the Basel Convention and its application to toxic ships. *Marine Policy, 32*(6), 1053–1062.

CHAPTER 7
ARMS CONVEYANCE & MILITARY CONTRACTING

Credit: H. Assaf/Freeimages

Overview in Introduction

The arms business ranges from nuclear arms on the one hand to small arms on the other, and increasingly encompasses the privatisation of soldiering or use of mercenaries. Valued at almost USD2 trillion and accounting for about 10 percent of total world trade in legitimate merchandise, the revenues from the global arms export are considerable compared to other shadow trades. Despite the efforts of some inter-government organisations and NGOs to develop initiatives on arms control, this shadow trade in all its forms is thriving. This chapter seeks to identify major arms exporter and importer economies, the forms of government support, the mechanics of arms transfers as well as to foreground the socio-economic costs of war. Both governments and the arms industry stereotypically cite foreign policy objectives, national sovereignty and domestic economic contribution in justification for mutual collaboration. Consequently, this chapter will debate the application of corporate social responsibility and sustainability principles to arms businesses, and the extent of their compliance. In particular it queries why the arms industry has been largely exempt from such accountability and argues how measures like transparency, audits and capacity conversion may be applied to restrain its transnational harm without necessarily inhibiting the survival of the firms. Thus, the chapter investigates the wide-ranging and interwoven issues of arms spending, government subsidies, military contracting, corruption, social costs, infrastructure damage, legal liability, sustainability, economic decline, investment discrimination and industrial conversion.

Projecting Power

Weapon Fabricators

Throughout history, it has been those countries that are better able to equip their armed forces and artificially supplement their numbers that have invariably succeeded in wars. Hence leaders and governments have always pushed for innovative design and mass production in weaponry – even of arrows, swords, cannons, guns, armour and ships – that would increase enemy casualties rather than their own. With the coming of the industrial age in the late 19th century came the further mechanisation of war that enabled the killing of large numbers of people, both military and civilians, indiscriminately.[1] While the industrialised countries became autonomous in such arms production through promoting and subsidising domestic manufacturers, post-colonial developing countries around the world lacked that capacity and were discouraged from acquiring it. Instead the latter have been compelled to purchase military equipment, ranging from missiles to aircraft, from the former, thus fostering growth of the shadow trade in arms. Intractable civil, national and regional conflicts in the late 20th and early 21st centuries have drawn attention to the extensive role of small arms in guerrilla-style warfare, including by mercenaries. Thus, submachine guns, land mines (or IEDs) and grenade launchers (or RPGs) have become progressively a more pressing international issue, superseding prior preoccupation with large weapons like fighter aircraft, naval destroyers and long-range missiles. Collectively, global arms conveyance today encompasses nuclear bombs on the one hand and automatic rifles on the other, with cyber-security and military contractors as yet unplaced in the hierarchy of options for militaries.

Political Overlords

The major exporters, particularly of heavy arms, are based in the industrialised economies, and often are firms that are highly subsidised, even owned fully or in part, by their governments in keeping with their hegemonic foreign policies. The buyers are largely from developing countries, often diverting revenue earned through their natural resources from social spending, thus exacerbating economic instability. Emergent economies, however, tend to be both buyers from the industrialised world as well as sellers to developing economies, including as agents and re-exporters of the former, demonstrating the core–periphery economic relations of the capitalist world system. The secrecy surrounding strategic arms conveyance particularly leads to a lack of accountability of their numbers and movements, and includes multiple intermediaries, such as manufacturers, brokers, financiers, armies and government departments. The commercial contracting of services ranging from private militaries to logistical support are another shadow trade for corporations to profit from, under the guise of national security and strategic interests. Generally, the stance of governments on subsidising the development and sale of arms, as well as the attendant confidentially of contracts, seems prompted as much by their foreign policy objectives in international relations as supporting the competitiveness of their domestic arms industry and corporations in global markets.

Besides, the source of the global demand for arms is no longer just nation-states but includes rival claimants to power – dissident groups, terrorists, organised crime, local warlords, tribal factions and the like – in an age of asymmetric warfare. In the 1990s, small arms sold corruptly by Argentina and Peru via European, American and Middle East middlemen ended up being used in conflicts as far apart as Croatia and Colombia.[2] The rise of Islamic fundamentalism from North Africa to East Asia, plus the availability of arms following the dismembering of the Soviet Union and Eastern Bloc in the late 20th century, has been a cause of particular concern to the European Union.[3] One controversial issue is the conveyance of arms to non-state organisations without the approval of the nation-states in which they operate, which quite a few countries, including the US, refuse to sanction.[4] In fact, allegations as well as proof exist that former 'Western' allied powers regularly purchase arms used by their former Eastern Bloc enemies during the Cold War to supply insurgent forces that they support clandestinely in proxy wars, using third-country arms brokers and factories so as to avoid traceability in their exercise of geo-political hegemony.

Pursuing Supply Routes

Weighty versus Nimble

Mass obliteration

The trade in nuclear arms ranges from the complete device, fissile material, production components and missile delivery, to the scientific expertise to build such systems. All of these are ostensibly governed under the international Nuclear Non-Proliferation Treaty (NPT) set up by the nuclear powers and ratified by most nation-states worldwide, but more recent developers of nuclear arms, such as India, Israel and North Korea, are not signatories. While the completed nuclear arms are sought by even non-state terrorist groups which lack the facilities to develop one on their own, such weapons are understandably the hardest to transport and the most zealously guarded by nation-states. In addition, the advanced technology needed to reproduce such arms is technologically sophisticated and the know-how would require the expatriation of scientists, which has had limited success as a strategy.[5] Enriched weapons-grade material has instead been the focus of nuclear arms smuggling, but still has been difficult to obtain and ship in the quantities required for weapons production. Although the term 'weapons of mass destruction' (WMDs) is often identified with nuclear arms, other types of weapon unquestionably share this categorisation, even though they attract less attention. Biological, chemical and radiological weapons are also deliverable by missiles and bombs from conventional land, sea or air vehicles, and they are all much in demand as military hardware for their comparable destructive effect.

Targeted incursion

While their impact on populations may not seem as devastating or as feared as heavy weapons, small arms or light weapons have the potential for social disorganisation. Indeed, they could be conceptualised instead as 'weapons of mass disruption' and thus are the weapons of choice in terrorism.[6] The shadow trade in small arms is said to be responsible for the deaths of 300,000 persons per year in armed conflicts alone, and another 200,000 persons per year as a result of other forms of violence, including domestic forms. Actually, in 97 percent of regional or intra-state conflicts since 1990 solely light weapons were utilised.[7] Markedly easy-to-handle compared to large arms, no comprehensive training is needed for anyone to use them. While powers with imperialistic ambitions such as the US and Russia remain major suppliers of arms both large and small, many other countries are able to manufacture and export small arms without any stipulations, such as China, Czech Republic, Sweden, Israel and Brazil.[8] Yet despite the intermediations of governments, regional organisations, IGOs and NGOs, resulting in a treaty on small arms control, this shadow trade is said to be growing surreptitiously.

Valuing the Transactions

Revenues of the mostly legal global arms conveyance are significant, totalling USD1.7 billion or about 10 percent of total world trade in merchandise, in contrast to the relatively low revenues of the shadow trade of human trafficking. In recent decades, the US has been by far the biggest buyer, comprising about 50 percent of global military expenditure, primarily from its own arms industry. At the same time, US manufacturers constitute the largest global exporter of arms, totalling USD45 billion, followed in the latter closely by Russia at USD40 billion.[9] The list of top 10 arms-producing corporations includes such well-known corporations as Boeing, Lockheed, BAE Systems and EADS,[10] yet this aspect of their business seems to interest largely those in political science and military studies. China's arms industry is shrouded in secrecy, but just four of its top 10 firms investigated are estimated to have combined sales of USD54.1 billion, and these firms would be ranked among the world's top 20 arms producers.[11] Although much of this substantial shadow trade is among industrialised economies, the larger importers of arms include Saudi Arabia, China, India, Egypt, Iraq, Qatar and the United Arab Emirates, countries involved in conflicts regionally or in civil wars (Table 7.1). For these, plus other developing and emergent economies, such spending on arms imports forestalls spending on economic development, demographic reform, environmental sustainability and social justice, which are often at the root of conflicts within and between such nation-states.

Outsourced Soldiering

Modernising mercenaries

Even if its roots in mercenary forces date back in history around the world, what is different in its present manifestation as the private military industry is the corporate structure of the entities operating from the industrialised world. These bid for government contracts to provide a range of services from logistics through training to actual fighting, driven by profitability and linked to investor-shareholders and financial markets. Particularly abhorrent is the outsourcing by governments of the imprisonment of 'enemy combatants' and the torture of political prisoners to these firms, as well as to foreign armed forces, their intelligence agencies and their secret police, in order to circumvent laws in their home country. The privatisation of the military can be traced to the ideological shift in the 1980s during the Thatcher and Reagan administrations' right-wing commitment to free-market economics in the UK and US respectively. It was to receive further impetus with the end of the Cold War and the consequent downsizing of military forces which saw a growth in supply of trained soldiers in search of relevant new employment to make up for their low pensions. Subsequent intra-country conflicts, such as in Africa and Eastern Europe, drug wars in Latin America and post 9/11 interventions in Central Asia, the Middle East and North Africa, created ample demand for out-sourced mercenary forces in lieu of national armies.

Table 7.1   Leading countries in arms export and import 2015–2019[12]

RANK	EXPORTER	USD (MILLIONS)	%	RANK	IMPORTER	USD (MILLIONS)	%
1	United States	53,033	36.0	1	Saudi Arabia	17,694	12.0
2	Russia	30,069	21.0	2	India	13,412	9.2
3	France	11,544	7.9	3	Egypt	8,396	5.8
4	Germany	8,518	5.8	4	Australia	7,133	4.9
5	China	8,080	5.5	5	China	6,300	4.3
6	United Kingdom	5,415	3.7	6	Algeria	6,150	4.2
7	Spain	4,539	3.1	7	South Korea	5,004	3.4
8	Israel	4,331	3.0	8	UAE	4,982	3.4
9	Italy	3,134	2.1	9	Iraq	4,960	3.4
10	South Korea	3,085	2.1	10	Qatar	4,943	3.4
	Top 10 Total	131,748	90.2		**Top 10 Total**	78,974	54.0
	Global Total	**145,755**	**100.0**		**Global Total**	**145.775**	**100.0**

Source: Extracted and compiled by the author from the SIPRI Arms Transfers Database with permission.

Soldiers of misfortune

Citizens in the industrialised world are especially unwilling to see more soldiers from their own country involved in such active combat abroad. So, by claiming troop withdrawals abroad, political leaders are able to use private military contractors as surrogate 'boots on the ground'. Hence, there has been an increase in the contracting of mercenary forces, now marketed under urbane brand names such as Executive Solutions and Blackwater Worldwide, that recruit and deploy worldwide with impunity former soldiers who have not found employment after serving on active duty, and who are possibly traumatised by their past experiences. Apart from officers, who tend to be special-forces veterans from industrialised countries, these soldiers are largely drawn from developing countries. Often demobilised combatants from civil wars there, including former child soldiers, they represent a form of post-colonial exploitation of labour, which is sometimes condoned by their home-governments as the expatriation of potential domestic 'trouble-makers'. Reliable global statistics simply do not exist, not because the US as the largest commissioner of private military services does not collect data, but because it keeps much of the data highly classified. Accordingly, the clandestine growth of privatised military services as a shadow trade in recent years has gone somewhat under-addressed in academic research and policy studies. While not private armies themselves, the deployment of UN peace-keeping forces from developing countries in need of hard currency, paid for by industrialised countries in lieu of sending their own soldiers, could arguably be another form of contracted soldiering and neo-colonial practice.

Camouflaging spending

What data are available through various agencies are that, at its peak, there were almost 110,000 private contract personnel in Afghanistan in 2010 and 150,000 in Iraq in 2008, matching the number of military personnel deployed there.[13] In 2000, the sector was estimated to be worth USD1 billion and this was expected to double in a decade.[14] But a more recent estimate in 2016 values the private military sector at USD200 billion,[15] or an exponential increase in less than two decades. However, the wide range in estimates may reflect the perennial problem of definitive figures in the shadow trades, rather than rapidly escalating growth. Yet another related area of this shadow trade is the presence in developing countries of military bases belonging to the industrialised world, such as the US and France, and increasingly also established by emergent economies like China and Turkey. Meant to project strategic political power and protect economic interests, these bases are prudently constructed, maintained and staffed by their own military contractors. Whether or not involved in actual conflict, these bases tend to distort the local economy and foster a market for non-essential consumer goods as well as questionable services like prostitution and illicit drugs.

Underwriting the Destructive

Government Subsidy

Support for arms export can take subtle forms, such as military attachés, defence marketing agencies, use of armed forces, underwritten official visits, domestic procurement choices and export credits assistance. Overt government subsidies in the form of loans, research and development (R&D) grants, merger/restructuring compensations, low-cost facilities and promotional activities enable their domestic manufacturers to sell competitively abroad in arms and non-arms products with dual-use technologies.[16] An examination of major Pentagon contracts found that the proportion awarded under competition declined from a peak of 60.7 percent in 2009 to 55.4 percent in 2015, when the total spending was above USD273 million.[17] The resultant risk-free business context provides little incentive for arms manufacturers to produce economically and efficiently. Even more scandalous is the production of over-requisitioned and thus redundant weapons in return for political campaign contributions and through claiming job creation.[18] Defence contractors collectively spent USD126 million in 2018 alone on lobbying, including campaign contributions, mostly to influential members of the US House of Representatives and Senate committees that approve the generous Pentagon budget. In return, defence firms, comprising nine of the ten biggest beneficiaries of government contracts, enjoyed about a 125-to-1 return on their lobbying and campaign contributions.[19] The relocation of their production to states with high levels of unemployment creates dependency on the arms industry and results in Congress members' support for greater military spending.[20] So despite the end of the Cold War, US spending on arms goes on unabated and much is made by politicians and lobbyists of the domestic jobs that these arms exports generate in justifying subsidies by the government.

In the UK, subsidies to its arms industry in 2009–2010 amounted to about GBP136.5 million, excluding research and development funding of another GBP698.9 million, by the best estimates, since there is much opacity in official data reporting.[21] The export subsidies by the government were made via multiple means, such as defence marketing agencies, armed force displays, official visits, domestic procurement choices and export credits assistance. Even less noted are the sanitised military parades, navy visits, air-shows, war games and battle footage that propagandise defence spending as patriotism, security and national prowess while suppressing any reflection on the obscenity of injury, damage and death that the weapons cause. All of these are in contravention of the European Union Anti-Subsidy Rules that then applied and which subsidies non-EU arms makers argue distort competition,[22] although it is unclear whether these arguments should not apply also to other EU member states. The most recent study in 2016 by SIPRI provides the composite estimate of direct UK subsidies of its arms industry, less the levy the government charges for commercial benefits gained from its research and development subsidies, but not counting the invariable cost overruns of 15–45 percent in most procurement projects (Table 7.2). All of this is underscored by the high incidence of government ministers, officials and military personnel who have later found employment in the arms industry as well as of senior members of defence trade agencies, advisory councils and related government bodies which have been seconded from that industry to government.[23] While it is speculated to be the case also with other countries with an arms industry, no similar data are available publicly, as acknowledged by SIPRI on a personal enquiry.

Table 7.2   Direct UK government subsidies to the arms industry[24]

FORM OF SUBSIDY	ESTIMATED COST GBP (MILLIONS)	USD (MILLIONS)
UKTI Defence & Security Organisation	3.4	4.6
Defence Assistance Fund	7.6	1.2
Defence Attachés	3.4–17.4	4.6–23.3
Other government support, e.g. official visits	10.0	13.4
Net ECG subsidy	49–73	66.7–97.9
Less Commercial Exploitation Levy	–9.5	12.7
Total	**64–102**	**86–137**

Source: Extracted and compiled by the author from the SIPRI Arms Transfers Database with permission.

Counting all Costs

Loss accounting

Comprehensive econometric modelling of various civil, inter-nation, regional and world wars over the 19th and 20th centuries proves that their social impact and economic costs are consistently immense, statistically significant and regularly persistent beyond the period of conflict.[25] Although challenging to estimate, the full costs must surely include the resultant destruction of physical capital and other economic losses, but they seldom do. Existing trade flows tend not to explain whether or when two countries might go to war and what the consequences for their economies might be, despite research efforts to try to demonstrate this. Still, noting the high trade-related costs might prove a disincentive to advocates of war as a solution to political conflict of interests. Yet the experience from numerous regional wars in recent decades must augur against the hope that inter-government institutions may be instrumental in persuading countries against all forms of war using economic arguments.

Adventurism expenditure

The costs of war are seldom ever fully added up because apart from the budgeted purchase of arms by governments, in part to replace arms expended, there are the ongoing operational costs. Costs prior to war include maintenance of the military, such as the salaries, allowances, medical rehabilitation and pensions of military personnel, paramilitary forces, civilians employed in the military, as well as procurement, operation and maintenance of weapons, research and development, construction expenses and military aid to foreign countries, among other costs. Accounting for the full cost of war, including the consequences of damage and harm caused to infrastructure, economy and people, is a complex endeavour. Hence the actual costs and duration of wars tend to be grossly underestimated in advance,[26] often deliberately so in order to gain public support and political approval of the initiative. Most assessments of the cost of war focus on the resources applied to waging the actual conflict and only peripherally on the human lives lost, despite the indirect losses being considerable and rarely appreciated.

Societal impact

In estimating the societal costs of war, it is not a matter of totalling the number of dead and wounded, but considering the loss of their intangible value to society and their potential contribution to the country's wealth. In addition to that must be their foregone consumption of goods and services in the economy during the conflict, their confidence dented by arms supplied under this shadow trade. Moreover, the loss of earnings to others in society as a result of war occurring must be accounted for by comparing all earnings prior to and during the war. The nature of the weapons utilised can contribute to costs as their residues, such as radioactivity and chemicals, reduce the health and life expectancy of those exposed to them, including increases in infant mortality. The cost of providing long-term healthcare for all those who are casualties of the war, civilian and military, must also be factored in. Finally, environmental and ecological degradation caused by war, such as the burning of oil wells and poisoned fields, have to be included in the estimated cost, for instance the reduction in income through the loss of farmlands and fish-catch.[27] Ironically, the impact of weapons use in warfare is never accounted for independently in statistics on pollution that ultimately contributes to global climate change.

Infrastructure destruction

Damage assessments, whenever done, invariably confirm the dire situation facing the people remaining in conflict areas. For Yemen, preliminary estimates as of late 2015 showed the damage in four cities over six sectors – education, energy, health, housing, transport, and water and sanitation – to be in the range of USD4–5 billion. For Iraq, damage assessment for the four cities liberated from ISIS over four key sectors, such as water and sanitation, transport, public buildings and municipal services, and housing is estimated at around USD363–443 million. As for Syria, about a third of its 780 health facilities in the major cities, ranging from hospitals to pharmacies, were damaged by the products of this shadow trade, leaving the country short of medical supplies and lacking in healthcare professionals. During 2015, as a consequence of further attacks, more than 50 percent of hospitals were either destroyed or left partially functioning. In the education sector in Syria, almost 15 percent of the 1,417 educational institutions in six major cities alone, ranging from kindergartens to universities, suffered damage. The total damage for just six major cities in Syria over seven selected sectors was estimated in 2016 to be up to USD7.3 billion, simply on the basis of original construction costs, an unrealistically low assessment for post-conflict reconstruction (Table 7.3).

Table 7.3   Total damage by sector for six cities in the Syrian civil war[28]

SECTOR	EDUCATION (USD) (MILLIONS)	ENERGY (USD) (MILLIONS)	HEALTH (USD) (MILLIONS)	HOUSING (USD) (MILLIONS)	ROADS (USD) (MILLIONS)	WATER/ SANITATION (USD) (MILLIONS)	TOTAL (USD) (MILLIONS)
Low Estimate	176	1,182	321	4,056	128	99	5,962
High Estimate	215	1,445	392	4,958	156	121	7,287

Note: Damage estimates of physical infrastructure using historical unit cost. Reconstruction needs would be higher due to inflation, security premium, scarcity of material/labour, etc.

Copyright © Syrian Center for Policy Research, 2014 and UNDP Syria. Used with permission.

Economic impact

The economies of countries experiencing civil war have been shown to shrink 2.2 percentage points from their size in peacetime. Thus, a civil war of seven years would see incomes drop by about 15 percent, resulting in a 30 percent increase in poverty, and a cumulative loss of income of as much as 60 percent of the annual GDP.[29] Another study of countries enduring civil war found an even greater decline in GNP per capita – at the rate of 3.3 percent. Additionally, 15 out of 16 countries at war saw a fall in per capita income, and 13 out of 17 such countries had a reduction in food production. All such countries saw external debt increase to a substantial percentage of GDP, trade patterns changed in 12 out of 18 countries, while export growth declined.[30] In addition to losses from the interruption of trade and factors of production, civil wars damage physical capital, although estimations of this depend on the methodologies used and the assumptions made, resulting in divergent figures. The most widely used are either calculations based on economic models for estimating damage on capital stock or on aggregation of data on the actual damage to infrastructure.

Regional consequences

Countries bordering war zones, which are already fragile economically from the conflict, face further pressure from refugee inflows. In addition to the damage to physical capital, the civil war in Syria triggered the displacement of more than 12 million people (or half its population) in 2010, both internally and externally. The two-thirds displaced within the country by the conflict, which has been fuelled by this shadow trade, encounter threats to life, deteriorating livelihoods and low access to basic needs. Over 2.1 million refugees have fled to regional neighbours, 80 percent of these to Lebanon and Jordan, plus another 2.5 million to Turkey,[31] straining all the resources of these countries. Syrian refugees were estimated to cost Jordan over USD2.5 billion per year, causing government debt to rise to about 90 percent of GDP in 2015.[32] Another 800,000 Syrians have sought asylum in Europe, mostly in Germany, Sweden, Hungary and Austria, resulting in long-reaching social, political and economic outcomes. Established oil exporters in the region, such as Saudi Arabia, Qatar, Kuwait and the United Arab Emirates (UAE), have financial reserves to run budget deficits in the short term, although at current spending levels these reached 9.4 percent of GDP in 2015.[33] With smaller oil exporters, like Syria, Yemen, Libya and Iraq, being no closer to peace, lower oil prices affect their war economies much more. A major source of export earnings and employment to non-oil economies in the Middle East and North Africa (MENA) region is tourism, which has declined precipitously, reducing employment opportunities and stifling economic growth.[34] With the greater repatriation of migrant workers from the more affluent Gulf countries, their remittances to their poorer home countries, such as Egypt, Lebanon and Jordan, have deteriorated, impacting on dependent economic growth there.

Strategic Re-direction

Treaty Entreaties

Warring illegally

It is rarely acknowledged that ever since the Peace Pact of 1928, which was incorporated into the United Nations Charter in 1946, war has been strictly illegal worldwide. This is in contrast to the old world order up to the World War I, where nation-states had the legal right to pursue war to set right perceived wrongs with impunity. While national laws may be thought of as hard regulation enforceable by governments, international laws tend to be softer, comprising voluntary standards and best practice at least, till eventually written into national laws.[35] Under this new world order, only the UN Security Council can authorise war or economic sanctions against a country that had committed aggression against another or on its own people, such as genocide. Still, the Charter has been by-passed by the major powers in the industrialised world seeking to intervene extra-legally in countries such as Iraq and Kosovo more recently, thus eroding its effectiveness.[36] Nonetheless, this somewhat radical new world order in which war is strictly outlawed has been responsible for some seven decades of freedom from world wars, even if it has been replaced by numerous regional and civil wars. Despite being undermined by innumerable inter- and intra-state wars, the UN Charter is still worth preserving. The various international institutions that are charged with its implementation are key to its peace-keeping and peace-enforcement remit.

Law dilution

Expertise and capacity are essential to governance of any laws, but further attributes of independence and representativeness are critical to it being done in the public interest and not subject to capture by any vested interests in the international sphere. It has been argued that governance under international laws between nation-states does not take place or is at least ineffective unless a hegemon like the US participates, for example with arms and security.[37] But this is inadequate to explain why international laws on small arms have proved less effective than those on military-security services, both of which the US participates in. Due to intense lobbying by special interests such as national gun lobbies, which are funded by arms manufacturers, the Arms Trade Treaty (ATT) was watered down despite the valiant efforts of NGOs like Oxfam and IGOs like the European Union.[38] Likewise, it will take self-interest prompted by political crises and national scandals to prompt countries, organisations and other relevant partners to form collaborative international networks to engage in the pragmatic process of regulating the related shadow trade in private military-security services. Without such unity of purpose, national or regional initiatives like the Montreux Document on mercenaries will never be translated into viable international and national laws.

Incentives for Disarmament

Declassifying subsidy

Doubtless the strategic nature of this shadow trade mitigates against transparency and yet financial, employment and sales data are critical for government assessment and civil society oversight of arms subsidy. One of the issues faced is that much arms manufacturing is still state-owned or part-owned, and so the firms are not obligated to divulge strategically sensitive information. While such information is routinely required of all publicly listed firms in most industrialised economies and disseminated by industry associations, even this is often incomplete for such firms in the arms industry, which are quick to claim that full disclosure would jeopardise national security. There is also a difference in terms of corporate governance of arms firms, with the Anglo-American model of diffused ownership being more open than the relationship-based model that is prevalent in continental Europe and Asia, where ownership is closely held by banks and other related firms. Still, cultures of business transparency vary greatly among countries, with Nordic ones, the UK and France having the highest levels, the US being fairly transparent, while Russia and Japan are among the least so.[39] Furthermore, there is the challenge of scrutinising industry sectors such as electronics, shipbuilding, aircraft manufacture, computing, communications and food supply to ascertain what percentage of their economic output is ultimately used for military purposes.

Curtailing destination

The official statistics on importing nation-states belie the actual destination of the arms, which might be third countries or rebel forces and need not be of large quantity and value. After all, in a world of what can be termed 'new wars', there are a multiplicity of players, including remnant armies, paramilitary groups, self-defence forces, foreign mercenaries and international forces, mingling with organised crime, all of them abusing human rights with impunity.[40] While these forces might largely be in the market for small arms, this is not exclusively what is bought, particularly given the wide range of surplus weapons since the end of the Cold War and after other conflicts cease. Small arms like rifles, pistols, landmines, grenade launchers and the like remain weapons of choice in most conflicts worldwide between and within nation-states.[41] Yet being of low-cost, small arms do not feature in most global arms transfer statistics, and being lightweight, they are easily smuggled long distances transnationally through illegal brokers. As small arms are highly durable, these often remain in circulation long after there is conflict resolution, facilitating criminality, if there is no systematic disarmament, buy-back and destruction of weapons. Relatively inexpensive landmines severely curtail access by subsistence farmers to productive land for food generation and therefore have implications of poverty, malnutrition, and even famine. Despite the international ban on the sale of landmines, these continue to kill and maim the civilian population of a region, especially children, long after the armed conflict is resolved.

Collusion capture

The Arms Trade Treaty is different from the conventions against landmines and cluster bombs in that it does not eliminate any category of weapons. While presenting an opportunity for achieving compatibility of processes and a level playing field for competition, it will be a challenge to implement the ATT internationally without equivalent national regulations. Given that this shadow trade encompasses transnational supply chains and that emergent economies are increasingly involved in arms production and sales, the ATT could prove a mixed blessing. Since the treaty serves only to regulate trade in small arms, quite broadly defined, the global arms industry should advisedly be brought into consultation about its implementation.[42] That may seem compatible with promoting corporate social responsibility initiatives by arms manufacturers and provide guidance to investors and financial institutions. Positive intentions routinely expressed by the arms industry about supporting the maintenance of peace and claims that many of its products are used in humanitarian crises do not detract from their actual negative long-term impacts in conflicts. So, the consultation could prove counter-productive to the treaty if it is manipulated to result in the private capture of what are essentially goods that should only be produced in the public interest and thus brought under civil society and government scrutiny.

Divestment or Diversification

Investment discernment

Discriminating against investment in firms by applying the criteria of involvement in the arms industry proves problematic because the industry is typically opaque for purported security considerations. Since liability has to be shared by the state for using the products in furthering national interests, it is conflicted as both buyer and regulator. Through the mining of subscriber-only databases such as Amadeus and Orbis, major UK consumer banks have been revealed to hold shares in or grant loans to both domestic and international arms firms. For instance, as of 2008, Barclays Bank held GBP7.3 billion (or USD12 billion at the time) in global arms industry equity. Ranking among the top 10 investors in US arms firms, it was banker to three major arms manufacturers and part of 43 syndicated loans to the arms industry. Barclays was joined in these practices by notable banks such as HSBC, Royal Bank of Scotland, Lloyds TSB and Halifax Bank, insurers like AXA and Prudential, as well as firms as diverse as British Airways and British Telecom.[43] Pension funds have been found to be investing in firms that persist in the manufacture of cluster munitions that have long been prohibited by international conventions. One proposal to discourage the practice has been that of creating a more realistic index of corporate social irresponsibility (CSI) rather than attempting to assess such firms by the more traditional notion of CSR.[44] In the face of such businesses disseminating dubious CSR reports claiming impeccable credentials, proactive investors in equities, individual clients of banks and savers in pension funds may hold an invaluable key to persuading ethical change through their investment preferences.

Responsibility audits

Apologists for the arms industry may try to show that in terms of CSR orientations its managers comply with legal strictures to a higher extent and with the economic, ethical and discretionary ones to a similar extent as managers in other industries.[45] That merely reflects the highly regulated nature of their own industry in recognition of its capacity for harm, conflict and corruption. In fact, the arms industry has generally been exempt from being held accountable on the grounds that it serves higher national goals. This is a questionable proposition, because the industry invariably fails to meet conventional CSR criteria on the environment, social equity, political power and profitability. Arguably the benefits of products from the arms industry are not primarily security for the citizens of the countries purchasing these, but rather for the profitability of the shareholders of foreign firms selling them.[46] The arms industry has been quite aggressive in promoting the security benefits of their products to the wider public, with 88 percent of the top 100 firms using corporate videos online. Even in supposedly neutral Sweden, cinematic videos created by Saab use images, sounds and text to persuade of the needful military intervention of its planes for good ends in international conflict resolution, humanitarian aid abroad, and even for the protection of families at home from an unnamed but widely perceived neighbouring power.[47] Given its track record for being complicit in the loss of human lives and damage to property, not counting ongoing environmental harm and economic decline, demonstrating corporate social responsibility would appear a quite unreachable goal, verging on the farcical, for this shadow trade.

Diffusion fudged

Often the argument is made by political leaders who support the arms industry and its vital exports that it is beneficial for wealth creation through various knowledge, markets and networks effects. Yet measuring this diffusionary impact of the arms industry in both exporting industrialised countries and importing developing and emergent countries is challenging due to differences in the societal context and analytical tools, as illustrated by quite divergent positive and negative findings by researchers. While technology diffusion may appear unrelated to the stage of a country's economic development, the impact of subsidised military technology is far more variable than civilian technology, or rather technology in general given the latter's commitment to efficiency and technical change.[48] A comprehensive review of 170 papers over four decades from 1973 to 2013 on both industrialised and developing economies found an ambiguous relationship between defence spending and economic growth, with studies in the post-Cold War era showing instead marked negative outcomes.[49] Furthermore, defence spending creates fewer jobs than an equivalent investment in other industries, and fewer civilian-applicable innovations, despite the generous funding of research. Supposed benefits of financial offsets, namely reciprocal investment by arms manufacturers in the countries that purchase their arms, have proven to be near non-existent or nowhere close to what they are purported to be in political pronouncements and corporate public relations. Ultimately, the disproportionate impact of the fallout from infrastructure damage, economic decline, injury and death, population displacement and other consequences of war on both countries involved and their allies, and the costly interventions needed to rectify these, go largely ignored (Figure 7.1).

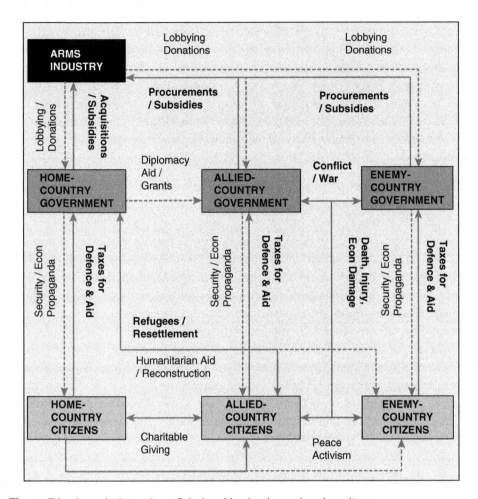

Figure 7.1 Arms industry beneficiaries, blowbacks and underwriters

Peace Dividends

Reimagining War

Liberal argument

Theories promoting economic interdependence in the capitalist world system prefer to argue that trading countries are less likely to go to war because this could impede, if not eliminate, economically-valuable mutual trade. Time-series research conducted on 14 conflict-country dyads showed that while there was some decline in trade between the pre-war and post-war periods, this was less so in the case of 13 non-major power dyads.[50] This lack of a sustained decline in trade may be explained by analysis made by the political leaders of the countries involved regarding the dire impact of cessation of trade on their economies. Awareness of their own inability to sustain the war indefinitely and the adverse impact on the economy of their respective allies, risking alienating the latter, would be further reasons for ending hostilities. Controversially, some research finds that war does not disrupt trade, except in the short term, but that trade sometimes continues despite the conflict, and even that mutual trade actually increases on the cessation of hostilities.[51] Unfortunately, countries sometimes go to war to open up markets in imperialistic style and so privileged trade can indeed grow through their rebuilding of the economy of defeated enemies.

Realist critique

These viewpoints tend more credibly to contend that trading countries are prone to go to war in order to keep the other from using the economic gains to build up its military strength. Only recently has research been conducted on 88 countries using a comprehensive causal model, which incorporates multi-factor dimensions of human development, governance and democracy. This has demonstrated that arms have been sold by industrialised and emergent economies to developing economies that are scarcely able to afford the financial outlay. But more crucially, the transfers have a negative relationship to nation-state stability and democracy, which is in contradiction to and undermines the US policy of promoting those goals for the client or allied nation-states and its own national security.[52] The aggressive marketing of arms by hegemonic powers is commonly believed to be responsible for undermining stability in the post-colonial regions of Asia, Africa, the Middle East and Latin America. By contrast, it is those countries whose armed forces have been limited or eliminated, such as Germany, Japan and Costa Rica, that demonstrate economic development, social services and life expectancy that are superior to many others. Just as war disrupts economic growth, its cessation tends to result in a peace dividend for all parties involved, as demonstrated after World War II and elsewhere since, through renewed trade and investment between these and other countries that were previously cautious.

Capacity Conversion

Spears into ploughs

The end of the Cold War and the subsequent decline in arms spending did foster debate by economists, civil society, trade unions, peace activists and the like about the conversion of military production to civilian purposes. Since then, conversion proposals have encountered the barriers of firms being overly specialised in military production and lacking engineering and managerial skills, of governments following poor industrial policies, and of politicians showing an ambivalent commitment to disarmament. In addition to its contribution to political parties and election campaigns mentioned earlier, the arms industry spent a further USD30 million towards lobbying politicians, an effort usually fronted by former government officials, military officers and politicians.[53] Therefore, it could be imperative for the conversion of industrial capacity to be spearheaded instead by networks of worker-led firms, supportive government infrastructure and relevant academia-led R&D.[54] Commendable as such ideas and initiatives may prove, the ongoing conflicts in the Middle East, the ill-defined Global War on Terror, renewed tensions with North Korea and periodic Russian belligerence have undermined any prioritisation of industrial conversion since arms manufacturers subsequently experience a return to more lucrative defence contracts.

Casualty of truth

The propaganda, public relations or political spin on arms conveyance is that it promotes the security and stability of the recipient countries, while in actuality the arms build-up has often fuelled border conflicts, civil wars and inter-ethnic strife. While other variables, such as semi-democracy, regime transitions, previous conflicts and ethno-political groupings, are contributory to the incidence of wars, multivariate regression analysis in sub-Saharan Africa found military spending, weapons acquisition and arms transfers to be the necessary and significant factors.[55] Instead of the strength of the armed forces of one country deterring aggression by another country, sadly it tends invariably to trigger similar levels of arms purchase by the latter. Thus, incorporating the arms transfers into models of military conflict, alongside political, economic and cultural variables, results in the better prediction of military conflict.[56] Mutual arms build-up has the propensity in turn to precipitate military conflict instead of taking a more pragmatic and far less costly settlement, negotiated proactively ahead rather than after inconclusive hostilities, through diplomatic means leading to economic sustainability, much to the chagrin of the arms industry.

Commentary in Conclusion

While management research may have borrowed strategic insights from military studies, it seems not to wish to lend its critical analysis to the role of arms transfer in the uneconomic business of war. In a neo-liberal capitalist era where light regulation of business and free trade are promoted as the ideal, ironically, the arms industry lobbies aggressively and benefits generously from government subsidies, protectionism and support with marketing abroad. Much of the arms trade is undergirded by the impe-rialistic ambitions of some countries for political and economic hegemony over other countries within their region and beyond, rather than the purported defence of their own national sovereignty. Were the industry not to be subsidised but instead taxed for producing socially undesirable products, its growth may be constrained, while the harm from war is mitigated through pre-emptive diplomacy and the reduction of military expenditure can result in the availability of social services. While countries, non-state entities and their leaders are periodically hauled before international courts for crimes against humanity, these tend to be from developing countries, while the foreign governments and multinational corporations supplying the arms are never prosecuted. Furthermore, if the arms industry and their executives were to be held co-liable jointly with their clients for the societal and economic harm caused, includ-ing war crimes, and for financial restitution of war damage and deaths, there could be greater incentive for firms comprising this shadow trade to diversify investment into more sustainable and responsible businesses.

DIM DOMAIN

PACIFIST SELLER TO COMBATIVE BUYER

For such a relatively pacifist and small country economically, Sweden hosts a sizeable arms industry and is among the highest exporters of arms on a per capita basis – topping the list in 2011. Strictly speaking, arms exports have been prohibited under Swedish law since World War I, although this has been eroded since Sweden joined the EU and has participated in UN military missions abroad.[57] There is also a loop-hole of arms exports being permitted for 'security reasons' or if there is no conflict with Swedish foreign policy. Therefore, the government policies dictate that arms are not to be exported to a country currently or potentially involved in a conflict and where there are significant breaches of human rights. Nonetheless throughout the early 2010s, Sweden has been documented as having exported arms to and been involved in 'defence cooperation' with over 20 regimes in countries known for such violations, with yet more in the decade since.

Defence Industry

While Europe and North America still account for about 50 percent and 10 percent of Sweden's exports respectively, as sales in those regions stagnate, their arms indus-tries are turning to the rest of the world, with 30 percent of exports now going to Asia (including the Middle East) and 10 percent to Latin America and Africa.[58] The companies involved in the production and marketing of arms and other defence equipment and services, even if not exclusively in such products, tend to be members of the Swedish Security and Defence Association. With over 70 member companies, including some of major multinational parentage, employing over 30,000 workers in

Sweden alone and a turnover of EUR3.5 billion, this is a not insignificant lobby group and player in its international trade.[59] Materials imported for the manufacture or maintenance of products for Swedish military use are duty-free, which represents a subsidy towards export sales. Perhaps the best known of these arms manufacturers is Saab, which produces a wide range of military products such as Gripen aircraft and Carl Gustav rifles, and accounts for 50 percent of all Swedish arms sales. Aircraft represent the largest share of Swedish exports, followed by armoured vehicles and radar equipment.[60]

Swedish Politics

While parliamentary democracy in Sweden dates back to the 16th century, it has only known universal suffrage in the last 100 years or so, with elections held every four years. Elected by proportional representation rather than by constituencies, parliament selects a prime minister who in turn forms a cabinet, often in coalition with other parties. Although also a constitutional monarchy, all policy decisions in Sweden are taken by the prime minister as the head of government and cabinet, not by the king serving as the head of state. There are eight parties represented in the 349-member parliament, with the Social Democrats, Centre, Moderates, Sweden Democrats and Greens being the more dominant. In its history, Swedish politics has generally been dominated by the left-of-centre parties, although on occasion right-of-centre coalitions have gained government. Since the early 20th century, Sweden has maintained a policy of non-alignment in peace time, such as in not joining the North Atlantic Treaty Organisation (NATO), and neutrality in war, as in World War II and the Cold War thereafter.

Saudi History

The Kingdom of Saudi Arabia has been in existence from the early 1900s as a result of the consolidation of power by the Saud family over the tribes in the interior, condoned by Britain so long as they respected the latter's control over the small Gulf sheikdoms and South Yemen (then Aden). The discovery of oil in the 1930s and subsequent concessions to American oil companies resulted in royalties being paid directly to the Saud family, consolidating their control over the country. This wealth allowed it to contribute to the budgets of major countries in the wider Middle East region, such as Egypt, Syria and Jordan, enabling Saudi Arabia to influence foreign domestic policies and religious practice. At home, the Saudi regime is beholden for its grip on power to leaders of the Wahabi sect, and so conforms to their enforcement of strict observance via the religious police. This extends to preventing men and women socialising together, requiring women to wear a full covering in public, forbidding the sale of alcohol and pork, prohibiting fornication, adultery and homosexuality, and the practice of other religions, even by expatriates, among other strictures. The draconian punishments meted out by these religious authorities include lifetime prison sentences, the kidnapping of dissenters, public whippings, the mutilation of limbs and the execution by beheading

(Continued)

or stoning, the last of which can be applied for robbery, drug use, sexual misconduct and perceived blasphemy.[61]

Gulf Conflicts

The invasion of the small but oil-rich neighbouring emirate of Kuwait in the Persian Gulf by the dictator Saddam Hussein of Iraq in the early 1990s and his consequent alleged threat to Saudi Arabia was the basis of the First Gulf War. The consequent stationing of US troops on Saudi soil or the Islamic holy land to protect the oil resources of its ally and its own supplies led to the radicalisation of its citizens, notably Osama bin Laden and his followers in Al Qaeda. Hence bin Laden's attacks on the US in the early 2000s led to the US invasion of Afghanistan where he had found refuge. Under the pretext of links between Al Qaeda and the Saddam Hussein regime, and claims that the latter had weapons of mass destruction, Iraq was invaded in the Second Gulf War of the mid-2000s. The Arab Spring of 2013 saw many authoritarian regimes toppled only to be replaced by civil war or the emergence of new authoritarian regimes. The rebellion in Syria against the Assad regime and the vacuum following the US withdrawal from Iraq in the mid-2010s saw the unexpected rise of the Islamic State in Iraq and Syria (ISIS, also known as ISIL, Da'esh or simply Islamic State), a fundamentalist caliphate which, being Sunni Muslim, was supported by Saudi Arabia. Being Alawite and supportive of the religious minorities, including the Shiite, the Assad regime was supported by Iran and Russia, which has a base in Syria. Dominated by the majority Shiites, the Iraqi government found itself at war with ISIS, ironically supported by both the US and Iran. Meanwhile in the strategic southern tip of the Arabian Peninsula, a civil war in Yemen broke out between Houthi rebels of Shiite persuasion supported by Iran against the Sunni government supported by Saudi Arabia.[62]. Hence sectarian conflicts in the Middle East are rife, making it a major market for global arms export.

Diplomatic Crisis

Soon after the Social Democrat party regained power in 2014, Sweden recognised the State of Palestine and this led to much admiration worldwide, culminating in an invitation to address the Arab League conference in early 2015. However, its new foreign minister Margot Wallström had previously announced that she would be pursuing a feminist foreign policy, one that would make gender equality a precondition for development and security collaboration with other countries. In keeping with that, she made a speech in the Swedish parliament in early 2015 pointing out well-known facts about Saudi Arabia, including that the monarchy held absolute power, that public floggings were acceptable and that women were repressed. This caused a furore, resulting in condemnation, at Saudi Arabia's urging, by the Gulf Cooperation Council and the Organisation of Islamic States, as well as by the Arab League, which 'disinvited' Wallström from addressing them. Perhaps most significantly, it was alleged that in criticising Saudi Arabia she had condemned Sharia law and derided Islam itself.[63]

Corporate Peace-making

As a consequence, the Swedish government – facing pressure from its Green coalition partner – announced immediately thereafter that it would not be renewing its arms treaty with Saudi Arabia. This caused considerable consternation within the Swedish defence industry about the loss of significant revenue from potential business deals, leading 30 leaders of arms manufacturers to take out a newspaper advertisement to protest against the decision. Soon after, a delegation of Swedish officials was dispatched to Saudi Arabia, bearing letters from the King to his counterpart, apologising for any misunderstanding caused and emphatically denying any intention of criticising Islam. The message that the Persian Gulf states and other emergent economies with non-democratic governments were too valuable as trade partners to be offended seems to have been noted by Sweden, and has served as a lesson to other liberal European states. Nevertheless, the non-renewal of the previous arms treaty had little immediate impact on Sweden's arms industry since it had already brought long-term benefits, with approximately EUR1 billion in its last year (2014) alone. Still, the prospect of future arms sales in the Middle East Gulf region and with other emergent markets could well be impacted by the ongoing Swedish feminist foreign policy on human rights.

Crucial Queries

How effective have wars been historically in settling disputes between countries permanently? To what extent does 'violence begat violence' both internationally and societally indefinitely after any conflict?

What are the economic benefits underlying the political rhetoric about the reason for going to war? If peace-making were to break out on an international scale, what could happen to the existence and growth of the arms industry?

Is the arms industry inclined from self-interest to lobby for military aggression over political diplomacy? Does the availability of a well-armed military tend to reduce government preference to exhaust all opportunities for diplomatic negotiations before declaring war?

If the arms industry cannot be profitable without government subsidy, how is this justifiable within a neo-liberal free-market economy? On what basis should citizens pay taxes to subsidise exports of the arms industry at the expense of getting adequate education, health and housing themselves?

Why is it that governments protest that there are insufficient funds for social spending and yet this is not a factor in decisions to subsidise the defence industry, buy arms, fund militaries and to go to war? For what reasons do governments not acknowledge the evident economic dividends of peace?

If wars are increasingly carried out by non-state forces such as insurgents and terrorists, what are the implications for governments and inter-government bodies abiding by international treaties and conventions? How feasible would it be for arms manufacturers to be held financially and criminally liable for infrastructure damage and civilian harm by the countries and forces they supplied?

FURTHER RESOURCES

Research Works

Avant, D. D., & Avant, D. D. (2005). *The Market for Force: The Consequences of Privatizing Security*. Cambridge: Cambridge University Press.

Kinsey, C. (2006). *Corporate Soldiers and International Security: The Rise of Private Military Companies*. London: Routledge.

Sandler, T., & Hartley, K. (eds.). (2007). *Handbook of Defense Economics: Defense in a Globalized World*. Oxford: Elsevier.

Stohl, R., & Grillot, S. (2009). *The International Arms Trade* (Vol. 7). Cambridge: Polity Press.

Tan, A. T. (ed.). (2014). *The Global Arms Trade: A Handbook*. London and New York: Routledge.

Yihdego, Z. (2007). *The Arms Trade and International Law*. London: Bloomsbury.

Informational Websites

Amnesty International [www.amnesty.org/en/latest/campaigns/2017/09/killer-facts-the-scale-of-the-global-arms-trade/]

Centre for Responsible Politics [www.opensecrets.org/industries/indus.php?cycle=2018&ind=D]

European Union: Defence Industry [www.europarl.europa.eu/factsheets/en/sheet/65/defence-industry]

Royal Institute of International Affairs [www.chathamhouse.org/ research/ topics/ all? page=2]

Safer World [www.saferworld.org.uk/effective-arms-control/effective-arms-control]

Stockholm International Peace Research Institute [www.sipri.org/research/ armament-and-disarmament/arms-transfers-and-military-spending/international-arms-transfers]

Transparency International [http://ti-defence.org/]

Annotated Documentaries

Campaign Against Arms Trade (2013) *The Military and Corporate Takeover* [10:13 min.]. ForcesWatch. Presentation detailing links between government, the arms industry and society.

Journeyman Pictures (2016). *Executive Outcomes: The War Business* [51:25 min.]. Video on the mercenary armies available for hire to governments and multinational companies.

Alper, L., & Earp, J. (2007). *War Made Easy* [1 h. 13min.]. Exposing the pattern of US government deception leading the country into one war after another over five decades, from Vietnam to Iraq.

Vice News (2012). *The Business of War: SOFEX* [2012] [20:10 min.]. Exploring the annual trade show where weapons from handguns to laser-guided missile systems are on sale to all.

Feinstein, A. (2017). *The Shadow World of the Global Arms Trade* [1 h. 28 min.]. The Wall Exchange. A film about the systemic corruption and secrecy in the global trade in weapons.
Al Jazeera (2018). *Who Controls the Arms Trade?* [24:56 min.]. Reveals how the permanent member countries of the UN Security Council are collectively sellers of the most arms around the world.

General Reading

Armstrong, S. (2009). *War PLC: The Rise of the New Corporate Mercenary*. London: Faber & Faber.
Farah, D., & Braun, S. (2007). *Merchant of Death: Money, Guns, Planes, and the Man who Makes War Possible*. Chichester, UK: John Wiley & Sons.
Feinstein, A. (2011). *The Shadow World: Inside the Global Arms Trade*. Basingstoke, UK: Macmillan.
Holden, P. (2016). *Indefensible: Seven Myths that Sustain the Global Arms Trade*. London: Zed Books.
Pelton, R. Y. (2007). *Licensed to Kill: Hired Guns in the War on Terror*. New York: Broadway Books.
Stavrianakis, D. A. (2013). *Taking Aim at the Arms Trade: NGOs, Global Civil Society and the World Military Order*. London & New York: Zed Books Ltd.

Endnotes

1. Plamondon, A. (2012). *Defence Industries*. Oxford: Oxford University Press.
2. LaFranchi, Howard (2001). Small wars, small arms, big graft. *Christian Science Monitor, 93*(157).
3. Haqhaqi, J. (2004). Small arms and regional security in the Western Mediterranean: reflections on European views. *Mediterranean Quarterly, 15*(3), 55–74.
4. Saveedra, B. O. (2007). Transnational crime and small arms trafficking and proliferation. In K. L. Thachuk (ed.), *Transnational Threats: Smuggling and Trafficking in Arms, Drugs and Human Life*. Westport, CT: Praeger/Greenwood Publishing, Chapter 5.
5. Smigielski, D. (2007). Addressing the nuclear smuggling threat. In K. L. Thachuk (ed.), *Transnational Threats: Smuggling and Trafficking in Arms, Drugs and Human Life*. Westport, CT: Praeger/Greenwood Publishing, Chapter 4.
6. Santoro, D. (2005). Rethinking the concept of 'weapons of mass destruction': an assessment of the weapons of concern. *Journal of Contemporary Analysis*, November–December, 21–40.
7. Shah, A. (2006). Small arms – they cause 90% of civilian casualties. *Global Issues, 21*, 1–7.

8. Holtom, P., & Pavesi, I. (2017). *Trade Update 2017: Out of the Shadows*. Geneva: Small Arms Survey, Graduate Institute of International and Development Studies.

9. SIPRI (2006). *Year Book on Armaments, Disarmament and International Security for 2005*. Stockholm: Stockholm International Peace Research Institute (SIPRI).

10. SIPRI (2008). *Year Book 2008 on Armaments, Disarmament and International Security*. Oxford: Oxford University Press.

11. Tian, A., & Su, F. (2020). *Estimating the Arms Sales of Chinese Companies*. SIPRI Insights on Peace and Security 2020/2 (January).

12. SIPRI (2020). *Arms Transfers Database*. [www.sipri.org/databases/armstransfers – accessed 03 March 2020].

13. SIE Center (2017). Statistics on the Private Security Industry – US Composite Data. [http://psm.du.edu/articles_reports_statistics/data_and_statistics.html – accessed 28 December 2017].

14. Singer, P. W. (2003). *Corporate Warriors: The Rise of the Privatized Military Industry*. Ithaca, NY: Cornell University Press, p. 78.

15. Statistica.com (2016). Outsourcing security: private military and security companies. [www.statista.com/chart/4440/private-military-and-security-company-sector/ – accessed 27 December 2017].

16. Hartley, K. (2015). Defence economics and the industrial base. *World, 185*, 8–700.

17. US Department of Defense (2015). *Competition Report 2015*. Washington: Department of Defense.

18. Hartung, W. D. (1999). *Corporate Welfare for Weapons Makers: The Hidden Costs of Spending on Defense and Foreign Aid*. Washington, DC: Cato Institute.

19. Vittori, J. (2019) *A Mutual Extortion Racket: The Military Industrial Complex and US Foreign Policy*. London: Transparency International.

20. Thorpe, R. U. (2014). The American Warfare state: The Domestic Politics of Military Spending. University of Chicago Press. [http://fpif.org/warfare_vs_welfare_subsidies_to_weapons_exporters – accessed 12 January 2017].

21. Jackson, S. (2011). *SIPRI Assessment for UK Arms Export Subsidies*. London: Campaign Against Arms Trade.

22. European Commission Directorate-General for Trade (2017). Anti-subsidy. [http://ec.europa.eu/trade/policy/accessingmarkets/tradedefence/actions-against-imports into the eu/anti-subsidy – accessed 01 December 2017].

23. Campaign Against Arms Trade (CAAT) (2005). *Who Calls the Shots? How Government-Corporate Collusion Drives Arms Exports*. London: Campaign Against Arms Trade. [www.caat.org.uk/resources/publications/government/who-calls-the-shots-0205.pdf – accessed 01 December 2017].

24. Perlo-Freeman, S. (2016). *Special Treatment: UK Government Subsidy for the Arms Industry and Trade*. Stockholm: SIPRI; London: CAAT. [www.sipri.org/publications/2016/other-publications/special-treatment-uk-government-support-arms-industry-and-trade – accessed 02 December 2017].

25. Glick, R., & Taylor, A. M. (2010). Collateral damage: trade disruption and the economic impact of war. *The Review of Economics and Statistics, 92*(1), 102–127.

26. Crawford, N. C. (2016). Are we safer? Measuring the costs of America's unending wars. *Cognoscenti*, 23 June.

27. Sieglie, C. (2007). Economics costs and consequences of war. In *Encyclopedia of Violence* (2nd edn). Oxford: Elsevier. [www.ncas.rutgers.edu/economic-costs-and-consequences-war – accessed 28 December 2017].

28. Syrian Center for Policy Research (2014) *Syria, Alienation and Violence: Impact of Syria Crisis Report*. United Nations Development Programme/United Nations Relief and Works Agency (UNRWA), March.

29. Collier, P. (2006) Post-conflict economic recovery. Paper for the International Peace Academy. Oxford: Department of Economics, Oxford University.

30. Stewart, F., Huang, C., & Wang, M. (2001). Internal wars in developing countries: an empirical overview of economic and social consequences. In F. Stewart & V. Fitzgerald (eds.), *War and Underdevelopment* (Vol. 1). Oxford: Oxford University Press, pp. 67–103.

31. The figures are sourced from the United Nations High Commisioner for Refugees (UNHCR), the International Organisation for Migration (IOM), governments and NGOs.

32. The figures are sourced from the Jordanian government.

33. Devarajan, S., & Mottaghi, L. (2015) Plunging oil prices. *MENA Quarterly Economic Brief*. January. Washington, DC: World Bank.

34. Data from the United Nations World Tourism Organisation (UNWTO).

35. Matti, W., & Woods, N. (2009). In whose benefit? Explaining regulatory change in global politics. In W. Matti & N. Woods (eds.), *The Politics of Global Regulation*. Princeton, NJ and Oxford: Princeton University Press.

36. Hathaway, O. A., & Shapiro, S. J. (2017). *The Internationalists and their Plan to Outlaw War*. London: Penguin.

37. Krahmann, E. (2003). Conceptualizing security governance. *Cooperation and Conflict, 38*(1), 5–26.

38. Avant, D. (2013). Pragmatism and effective fragmented governance: comparing trajectories in small arms and military and security services. *Oñati Socio-Legal Series, 3*(4).]

39. Surry, E. (2006). *Transparency in the Arms Industry*. Stockholm: Stockholm International Peace Research Institute (SIPRI).

40. Kaldor, M. (2006). *New & Old Wars: Organised Violence in a Global Era* (2nd edn). Cambridge: Polity Press.

41. Cukier, W. E., & Chapdelaine, A. N. (2002). Small arms, explosives and incendiaries. In B. S. Levy & V. W. Sidel (eds.), *Terrorism and Public Health*. New York: Oxford University Press, pp. 155–174.

42. Kytomaki, E. (2014). The defence industry, investors and the Arms Trade Treaty. Research Paper. London: Chatham House.

43. War on Want (2015) Banking on bloodshed: UK high street banks' complicity in the arms trade. [www.waronwant.org/ sites/ – accessed 18 April 2017].

44. Taylor, N. A. J. (2012). A rather delicious paradox: social responsibility and the manufacture of armaments. In R. Tench, W. Sun, & B. Jones (eds.), *Corporate Social Irresponsibility: A Challenging Concept*. Bingley: Emerald Group Publishing, pp. 43–62.

45. Halpern, B. H., & Snider, K. F. (2012). Products that kill and corporate social responsibility: the case of US defense firms. *Armed Forces & Society, 38*(4), 604–624.

46. Byrne, E. F. (2007). Assessing arms makers' corporate social responsibility. *Journal of Business Ethics, 74*(3), 201–217.

47. Jackson, S. T. (2017). Selling national security: Saab, YouTube, and the militarized neutrality of Swedish citizen identity. *Critical Military Studies, 5*(3), 1–19.

48. Li, H. C., & Mirmirani, S. (1998). Global transfer of arms technology and its impact on economic growth. *Contemporary Economic Policy, 16*(4), 486–498.

49. Dunne, J. P., & Tian, N. (2013). Military expenditure and economic growth: a survey. *The Economics of Peace and Security Journal, 8*(1).

50. Anderton, C. H., & Carter, J. R. (2001). The impact of war on trade: an interrupted times-series study. *Journal of Peace Research, 38*(4), 445–457.

51. Barbieri, K., & Levy, J. S. (1999). Sleeping with the enemy: the impact of war on trade. *Journal of Peace Research, 36*(4), 463–479.

52. Reeder, B. W. (2009). Arms transfers and stability in the developing world: a causal model. *McNair Scholars Research Journal, 5*(1), 8.

53. Open Secrets (2018). *Defense Long-term Contributions*. Washington, DC: Center for Responsive Politics. [www.opensecrets.org/industries/totals.php?cycle=2018& ind=D – accessed 01 November 2018].

54. Feldman, J. M. (2006). Industrial conversion. In G. Geeraerts, N. Pauwels, & E. Remacle (eds.), *Dimensions of Peace and Security: A Reader*. Brussels: PIE-Peter Lang.

55. Craft, C., & Smaldone, J. P. (2002). The arms trade and the incidence of political violence in sub-Saharan Africa, 1967–97. *Journal of Peace Research, 39*(6), 693–710.

56. Craft, C. (2002). The arms trade and the incidence of political violence in Sub-Saharan Africa. *Journal of Peace Research, 39*(6), 693–710.

57. SIPRI (2014). *The SIPRI Top 100 Arms-producing and Military Services Companies, 2014*. Stockholm: Stockholm International Peace Research Institute.

58. Bromley, M., & Wezeman, S. (2013). *Current Trends in the International Arms Trade and Implications for Sweden*. Stockholm: Stockholm International Peace Research Institute.

59. Nordstjernan (2014). *Facts on Arms Exports from Sweden*. [www.nordstjernan.com/ news/education%7Cresearch/6945/ – accessed 30 December 2015].

60. Swedish Security & Defence Industry Association website [http://soff.se/about-soff/ – accessed 01 January 2016].

61. Sluglett, P., & Farouk-Sluglett, M. (1996). *The Times Guide to the Middle East.* London: Time Books.

62. Shah, Anup (2006). The Middle East conflict – a brief background. *Global Issues* [www.globalissues.org/article/119/ – accessed 02 January 2016].

63. Norberg, Jenny (2015) Who's afraid of a feminist foreign policy? *The New Yorker*, 15 April. [www.newyorker.com/news/news-desk/swedens-feminist-foreign-minister – accessed 29 December 2015].

CHAPTER 8
FINANCIAL SLEIGHT & MONEY LAUNDERING

Credit: Drozdin Vladimir/Shutterstock

Overview in Introduction

The deregulation of financial markets late in the 20th century, which artificially boosted world economic growth, helped multinational corporations and the mega-rich to move their funds around the world, particularly to tax havens abroad. Drug barons, political dictators, warlords, terrorist organisations and corrupt officials, among others, have also been enabled to shift dubious income with much greater ease. Money laundering could have reached almost USD2 trillion by the late 2010s, making this shadow trade a significant part of the world economy. This chapter traces how the legitimate banking sector has enabled corrupt local officials, corporate embezzlers and organised crime to move funds to the detriment of socio-economic growth, especially of developing countries, by depriving them of productive investment. To this flight of capital may be attributed monetary volatility, shifts to high-risk investments, market uncertainty, reputational tarnishing, and significant other damage to all the economies involved. Since the other shadow trades covered in this book are dependent on tax havens, money laundering and other forms of financial sleight for safeguarding the proceeds, then their business model can surely be undermined through more stringent financial controls and harmonised tax regimes. The critical issues addressed in this chapter encompass illicit financial flows, offshore financial centres, tax evasion, transfer pricing, free-trade zones, sports and gambling, real-estate investing, private banking, the informal economy and internet transfers.

Capital Adrift

Parking Profits

A study that included non-financial transactions and unrecorded capital outflows found that since the late 1990s, significant capital flight has occurred from developing countries towards industrialised countries, undermining the former's capacity for economic growth. Over the years developing countries have lost USD13.4 trillion through leakages in the balance of payments, trade mis-invoicing and the use of tax havens, though the method of estimation cannot distinguish between illicit and licit financial flows.[1] Although there have been inflows from industrialised economies in turn, the investors behind these extract a high return and enjoy tax concessions in developing countries, as is typical with economic neo-colonialism (Figure 8.1). Subsequent profit outflows drain resources from the latter countries, which remain poor economically, causing the living standards of their citizens to stagnate or decline. Inter-government organisations like the UN and OECD may have been able to persuade most countries that the problem of money laundering needs to have a multilaterally coordinated policy response, but the effectiveness of these protocols is questionable.[2] Since the turn of this century, policies against finance flight, including money laundering, have diffused across most countries worldwide, although in the developing world at least this has not been because of enlightened thinking or economic benefits. Hegemonic powers like the US and the EU in the world economy have been particularly insistent on compliance, with the attendant financial penalties and rewards, so the policies adopted have largely been due to coercion by mimicry of, and competition with, the industrialised world.

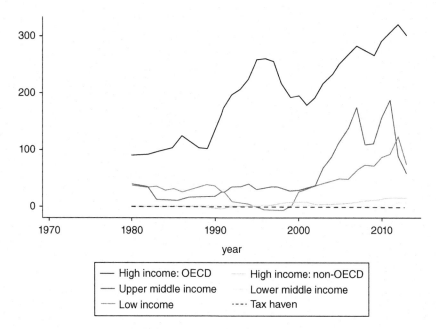

Figure 8.1   Tax revenue loss by national income level in USD billion[3]

Source: This figure is reproduced with full acknowledgement of UNU-WIDER, Helsinki. The original study was commissioned under the UNU-WIDER research project Macro-economic management (M-EM)

Cleansing Currency

Money laundering and its close relation of tax havens are no new shadow trades, as merchants have historically sought to conceal the profits of their legitimate businesses as well as disguise those from illicit ones from rapacious city politicians, port officials and country royalty. In the early 20th century, the mafia in the US was said to have recycled their bootleg liquor, drug and other dubious income via the establishment of legitimate laundry shops, hence the alleged etymology of the term. As a conduit for money laundering, tax havens grew phenomenally in the 1960s, largely in the Caribbean and South Pacific, due to a conducive conjunction of secrecy and regulatory and political conditions. Attempts by their former colonial overseers to limit these operations were tempered by the recognition that these microstates had no alternative economic activities and hence any regulations would prove non-viable.[4] The much-hyped developments in communications technologies and the deregulation of the global financial markets in recent decades have given the klepto-crats and the corrupt of dysfunctional states in developing and especially transitional economies, the mega-rich of the industrialised and emergent economies as well as criminal syndicates, warlords and terrorist organisations, greater facility to hide their misbegotten wealth abroad. Notably by the early 2000s the UN had estimated that transnational money laundering had reached USD1.6 trillion annually or about 2–5 percent of world GDP,[5] with no sign of that growth abating.

Accounting for Flight

Defining the Dodge

Money laundering

As commonly understood, money laundering is any process by which the illicit source of income and/or its illegal use is made to appear as if it was from a legitimate source. In many jurisdictions, any party that obtains, stores or uses assets thus obtained for themselves or other parties can be held responsible for prosecution for money laundering, including forfeiture of the funds. Layering, or the use of complex transactions, often in jurisdictions that allow financial secrecy, such as tax havens, is typically used to launder money, and this has been helped by newer methods of payment aided by digital technologies[6]. In decades prior, investigations into these practices were primarily concerned with the illicit drugs trade, rather than other financial misdemeanours by corporations and the mega-rich, who could be considered monetary bullies for their efforts to get more than their fair share. After the 9/11 terrorist attacks in 2001, the US Patriot Act granted government agencies widespread powers, including to prevent, investigate and prosecute terrorist activities, including potential money laundering to fund these. While expanded global surveillance is still generally supported, there are concerns that definitions of terrorist financing differ worldwide and an understanding of traditional systems for financial transfer and of the role of charitable or social organisations under different economic conditions is lacking.[7]

Tax havens

A closely related issue to money laundering is tax avoidance via offshore financial centres (OFC), which, given their secrecy laws, are often also centres for money laundering via legitimate banks, facilitated by international law firms and accountancy consultancies. Better known as tax havens, such locations are where most of the transactions that are initiated in other jurisdictions by foreign institutions and individuals are accounted for. They are attractive to such non-residents because of tax advantages and other incentives such as secrecy granted to them.[8] Unquestionably, OFCs are benefiting from the deregulation of the financial industry. They provide an essential service to multinational corporations and mega-rich individuals, who can include highly regarded actors, athletes, musicians, entrepreneurs, religious gurus as well as royalty, in conducting tax rates arbitrage. Consequently, it is challenging for governments elsewhere to determine whether or not the funds flowing through such centres involve tax evasion or money laundering.[9] It was alleged but unproven in court that a Sicilian mafia clan had come to own much of the economy of the tiny state of Aruba in the Caribbean and to virtually control its polity for the purposes of money laundering.[10] Attempts by countries in the industrialised world, via inter-government organisations, to regulate OFCs and to blacklist the less cooperative among them, many in developing economies, have been controversial as a form of neo-colonialism. For if offshore financial centres in some developing countries are capable of laundering money, then the much larger sums flowing through onshore centres, such as London and New York, are even more culpable (Table 8.1).

Table 8.1 Financial Secrecy Index – global rankings[13]

RANK	JURISDICTION	FSI VALUE[6]	FSI SHARE (%)[7]	SECRECY SCORE[4]	GLOBAL SCALE WEIGHT (%)[5]
1	Switzerland	1589.57	5.01	76.45	4.50
2	USA	1298.47	4.09	59.83	22.30
3	Cayman Islands	1267.68	4.00	72.28	3.79
4	Hong Kong	1243.68	3.92	71.05	4.17
5	Singapore	1081.98	3.41	67.13	4.58
6	Luxembourg	975.92	3.08	58.20	12.13
7	Germany	768.95	2.42	59.10	5.17
8	Taiwan	743.38	2.34	75.75	0.50
9	Dubai	661.15	2.08	83.85	0.14
10	Guernsey	658.92	2.08	72.45	0.52
11	Lebanon	644.41	2.03	72.03	0.51
12	Panama	625.84	1.97	76.63	0.27
13	Japan	623.92	1.97	60.50	2.24
14	Netherlands	598.81	1.89	66.03	0.90
15	Thailand	550.60	1.74	79.88	0.13
16	British Virgin Islands	502.76	1.59	68.65	0.38
17	Bahrain	490.71	1.55	77.80	0.11
18	Jersey	438.22	1.38	65.45	0.38
19	Bahamas	429.00	1.35	84.50	0.04
20	Malta	426.31	1.34	60.53	0.71

Governments in developing countries as a whole are particularly dependent on foreign direct investment for their tax revenues through royalties, tariffs, pay-roll taxes and corporate income taxes, and yet about a third of all transnational investment is routed by multinational corporations through offshore financial centres. Creative accounting and tax planning appear to have become the *raison d'être* of the accounting function within multinational corporations as well as their management consultants. Their tax avoidance results in a loss of some USD100 billion annually to the developing countries, to the extent that on aver-age every 10 percentage points of offshore funds results in a one percentage point lower tax return on that foreign direct investment.[11] About 31 percent of US cor-porate profits in 2013 or USD650 billion were made abroad even by firms that have no overseas business operations. A break-down of their sources indicates that a growing share of this, or 55 percent, was made in the six tax havens of the Netherlands, Bermuda, Luxembourg, Ireland, Singapore and Switzerland.[12] Notably the UK is closely linked to its crown dependencies, such as Jersey and the Isle of Man, via its global financial centre, the City of London, and locally-domiciled banks. Via correspondent banks, overseas territories like the Cayman Islands, the Bahamas and Bermuda, and even former colonies like Malta, Cyprus and Hong Kong, are prominent offshore tax havens for legitimate UK financial interests, all having extensive secrecy laws.

Totalling the Bill

There have been various estimates made by inter-government organisations and individual researchers of the transnational profit shifting and the consequent tax revenue losses to countries worldwide on the basis of different measurement methodologies. The International Monetary Fund estimated that the loss largely through tax havens for OECD countries in the late 2010s was USD400 billion, while for developing countries this was USD200 billion. The OECD itself esti-mated that about 4–10 percent of corporate income tax was lost in 2014 by its own higher and middle-income member countries, although for low-income countries this was at the much higher rate of 7.7–14 percent.[14] Similarly, the UN Conference on Trade and Development (UNCTAD) appraised that about 8 percent of corporate income tax is lost internationally through tax avoidance schemes, with almost half of this from lower-income countries. Since tax revenues consti-tute a lower amount of the GDP of developing countries, the proportion of such tax lost through profit-shifting by multinational corporations is greater, at about 6–13 percent of their GDP as compared to around 2–3 percent in industrialised and emerging economies.[15]

Specifically, illicit financial flows from developing countries accounted for 14–24 percent of their trade on average, growing between 8.5 percent and 10.1 percent annually over the decade 2005–2014. Outflows were estimated to range between USD2 and 3.5 trillion in 2014 alone, while inflows were substantially less, estimated between USD1.4 and 2.5 trillion.[16] Classically, illicit financial flows are measured from mis-invoicing in merchandise trade and discrepancies in the balance of payments, with the former being more measurable and accounting for about 87 percent of such outflows. About USD3.1 trillion in tax evasion or about 5.1 percent of world GDP results from the shadow economies in every nation-state.[17] To put these figures into context, the illicit financial outflows far exceed the legitimate inflows of overseas development aid from industrialised countries, which is thought to be roughly USD135 billion per year.[18] Thus, evading tax and laundering funds is a major economic impetus for the shadow trades, through resorting to illicit financial outflows and involving tax havens.

Robbing the Poorer

The top 10 countries facing tax evasion in absolute terms include industrialised economies like the US, Germany and Japan as well emerging economies like Brazil, Russia and China. But the countries that lose the greatest proportion of their healthcare budget to tax evasion are mostly developing countries, especially the smaller ones such as Bolivia, Papua New Guinea and Lesotho.[19] Unmitigated financial sleight has implications for life expectancy, healthcare, poverty, crime, illiteracy and a host of other social problems that become intractable over time in developing countries. As identified by the UN Sustainable Development Goals, education can be instrumental in ending poverty and promoting economic justice, but it remains under-funded by governments as a whole. Yet the link of worldwide education resource shortfall of USD39 billion to tax avoidance by large corporations and wealthy individuals through tax havens is conveniently overlooked. Ironically, it is argued that money laundered via targeted investments in the legitimate economy of developing countries can have positive consequences for creating employment and supporting entrepreneurship. This may benefit financially a minority segment of citizens but comes at an enormous social cost to the majority in those countries.

The crime of money laundering only appears victimless until one considers the loss of revenue by governments, which then constrains funding for social services and vital infrastructure. These are the very financial resources of the developing and emergent countries that are misappropriated by kleptocrats and the corrupt, and are then sent abroad to industrialised countries or wealthy tax havens on their periphery. Better exchange controls, more stringent financial sector oversight, effective tax enforcement, greater penalties for corruption and so on, have all long been prescribed as antidotes. Apart from greater transparency and harmonisation of wealth taxes on a regional level, an international tax as low as 1 percent imposed on financial transactions could contribute revenues of between USD60 and USD360 billion, which would adequately fund the UN-based commitments to sustainable development.[20] Nonetheless proposals like the Tobin Tax to curb financial transactions unrelated to actual goods and services have proven anathema to multinational corporations, banks, stock markets and the mega-rich in a neo-liberal capitalist world economy predicated on minimal financial regulation, sadly with some scholarly support.[21] Yet, addressing the incidence of other shadow trades will reduce demand for money laundering, tax havens and other forms of financial sleight worldwide, and certainly vice versa, once their profits cannot be realised as legitimate.

Punters and Dealers

Mainstream Businesses

Multinational corporations

While offshore financial centres or tax havens have been held to account for money laundering in support of terrorism and criminal syndicates, they are left unmolested to facilitate questionable tax avoidance and evasion by multinational corporations (MNCs). Thus, these larger corporations gain an unfair advantage over smaller local enterprises, a challenge faced by governments in developing and emerging economies alike. Among 1500 MNCs operating in India, those that had links to tax havens, systematically reported lower profits and paid less tax.[22] Likewise, a study of over 500,000 manufacturing plants in Europe found that those that were foreign-owned achieved greater tax savings than domestic-owned ones in the same country. Such profit-shifting or debt-shifting by MNCs is achieved via transfer-pricing, royalty payments and licence fees, as well as through public policy like preferential tax schemes.[23] Schemes for the transfer-pricing of intangibles such as services, along with the digitalisation of operations across borders, create even greater opportunities to minimise taxes. Quite evidently national measures against transfer-pricing and profit-shifting have proven ineffective in tackling tax evasion by MNCs, especially since their legal entities in different countries tend to be treated as independent of each other.

Free-trade zones

Strongly prescribed by the World Bank as an efficient means of stimulating economic growth through attracting foreign investment, employment opportunities and export income, free-trade zones (FTZs), export processing zones (EPZs) and special economic zones (SEZs) have been established in over 130 countries. Based primarily in developing and emerging economies, although there are similar free ports and science parks in industrialised economies, collectively these generate an estimated USD500 billion in international trade.[24] However, the incentives offered to multinational corporations and their suppliers by national governments include tax holidays on profits, the duty-free import of raw materials, reductions in trade controls and exemptions from labour regulations as well as domestic laws in general, all of them conducive also to money laundering and tax evasion. Among the illicit operations carried out within FTZs and EPZs are human trafficking, kidnapping, indentured labour, narcotics smuggling, stolen goods, piracy and bulk cash shipping. Reduced oversight over the high volume of containers allows for transhipment and the repackaging of other goods that would normally attract heavy duties, be these contraband or illegal goods. Trade-based money laundering of the proceeds of illicit goods is prevalent in the zones through over-invoicing, phantom shipments and the falsification of documents through front companies, currency exchange and complex transactions.[25] A crucial benefit of such trade-based money laundering is that it can be based within the legitimate economy and no goods need necessarily be moved across borders, at some commensurate risk.

Banking and insurance

Derivatives, currency swaps and hedge funds have come to be almost indispensable for the management of financial risk in global markets through the speculative trading of futures in highly complex packages of dubious intrinsic value divorced from the real economy.[26] Such financial instruments were largely implicated in the global financial recession of the late 2000s, which originated in their packaging of subprime mortgages in the US and led to major financial institutions worldwide having to be bailed out by governments.[27] Typically located in OFCs and relatively unregulated, the same opaque instruments are of interest also to money launderers and tax evaders, including those financing crime syndicates and terrorist groups. Meanwhile another part of the financial sector has avoided scrutiny, namely the insurance industry worldwide, which generates income of up to USD2.6 trillion by providing risk management and investment products to consumers, corporations and governments. Since general insurance, life insurance and re-insurance involves global business, offers a large range of products and uses intermediaries like brokers extensively, the industry is vulnerable to money laundering, including through false policies, overfunded investments and bogus claims.[28]

Sports and gambling

Through the ownership of clubs, the trading of players, betting activities, advertising sponsorships and broadcasting rights, the sports industry provides opportunities for money laundering and tax evasion by illicit business. Among the sports identified as particularly vulnerable are football, basketball, cricket, boxing, wrestling, horse racing and motor racing, some of which have long-standing links with criminal syndicates. Football or soccer is a major global business in its own right, with over 300,000 clubs, 38 million registered players, and 5 million officials, attracting over a billion viewers for its World Cup.[29] Since these sports have high value assets, are largely cash-based and involve transnational financial transactions, these allow for the laundering of money. Furthermore, sports have increasingly become associated with other illicit operations, such as doping, illegal gambling, trafficking in young players and corruption.[30] The global casino industry with its use of chips, cheques, currency exchange, gambling accounts, high-roller junkets and other cash-intensive financial practices is peculiarly vulnerable to money laundering. Although its actual turnover is not known, the global casino industry is said to generate revenues in excess of USD70 billion, mostly from foreign or non-resident clients. While ostensibly earning the over-150 countries in which casinos are located with tax income and licensing fees, this benefit comes at the cost to those countries of eroded scrutiny of these casinos' financial records.[31] Physical casinos are often located in regions of contested governance, political instability, endemic poverty and organised crime, and generally where laws are non-existent or unenforceable. Further, the extension of gambling into the 'high-seas' on cruise liners, slot-machines at clubs, neighbourhood sports-betting shops and online casinos makes the issue of regulatory jurisdiction even more problematic.

Pernicious Predicates

Informal sectors

Although illegitimate enterprises related to natural resources result in the highest economic losses, through financial outflows from the region and goods transiting in trade, causing high-level corruption, not all of the shadow trades can be characterised as criminal.[32] Informal economic activities in many developing countries and emergent regions enjoy low stigma, provide livelihoods and gain legitimacy which can sometimes compete with state authority. In West Africa, for instance, low financial inclusion of the population institutionally results in a large informal economy, at about 60–70 percent of total economic activity, with both legitimate businesses and illicit operations observed to be intertwined. Transnational crime syndicates may earn their funds through various shadow trades, such as drugs, arms and diamond smuggling, but these can be laundered through various informal financial structures in order to be used at least partially in the legitimate economy.[33] Related to this is the practice of carousel fraud, whereby small businesses are set up serially as fronts for illicit operations but are then soon wound-up or declared bankrupt prior to proper auditing, with the proprietors often absconding with valued-added taxes collected or corporate taxes unpaid.

Criminal syndicates

In Europe, the various mafia families play a major role in Italy's grey economy through toxic waste disposal, human trafficking, government fraud, gambling, arms sales and loan sharking, laundering their profits through front companies in legitimate businesses. The Russian mafia equivalents have become active not just in their own country but across Europe and beyond, dealing in crimes as varied as the sex trade, drugs, fraud, forgery, extortion, stolen cars, front businesses and even banking.[34] While no definitive figures exist for capital flight from the Russian Federation, a 'guesstimated' USD133 billion is said to have been shifted abroad in the 1990s immediately after the collapse of the Soviet Union. In Asia, Chinese triad gangs have expanded worldwide from their base in Hong Kong to elsewhere in the continent, Europe, North America and Australasia, and operate in gambling, prostitution, trafficking, counterfeiting, extortion, loan sharking as well as money laundering. The Yakuza criminal organisation which has considerable influence in legitimate Japanese business and banking with an estimate turnover of USD90 billion, has expanded to South East Asia and Australia, is suspected to have invested USD50 billion in US financial markets. In Africa, Nigerian criminal networks are estimated to earn USD3.5 billion per year regionally and worldwide through frauds in oil and gas, banking and finance, housing and benefits, shipping and drugs, not to mention USD100 million per year via online scams such as their infamous 419 appeal emails alone.[35]

Drug smuggling

Overall, drugs smuggling accounts for about half of all transnational organised crime income though this is less than one percent of legitimate world GDP. The cartels in Latin America and Asia sell to regional markets but primarily to international markets in North America and Europe. Most of the profits from the drugs trade is made in industrialised countries with only a small fraction spent on production in developing countries. The main destination of the net outflow in profits from the drugs trade in North America and South America, estimated at around USD6 billion, is the Caribbean, although the socio-economic costs of drug abuse in the former regions is estimated to be twice as high as the criminal income generated there.[36] Pakistan is geographically located amidst Afghanistan, Iran and India, where opium is cultivated and trafficked across porous borders, with the profits often being channelled into financing terrorism.[37] While drug smugglers need to launder large amounts of cash, perhaps more frequently than other criminals, unsurprisingly they tend not to use specialists in money laundering, but self-launder through informal currency traders or at best use businesses in kinship networks. Yet measures against money laundering do not always broaden the search for criminals since, in the drug trade at least, the launderers are essentially the same persons involved in committing the predicate crime.[38]

Covert charities

Since charities enjoy public trust as non-profit organisations, transfer considerable funds transnationally, involve informal cash-collection, are subject to minimal regulation and are granted tax-exempt status, they have been exploited by terrorist groups to finance their activities. Yet many countries find oversight of this form of illicit financial flows problematic, particularly as these charities perform vital services as non-profit organisations in many societies, especially in the developing world. Apart from the known terrorist sympathies of directors and incongruous sources, amounts and purposes of funds, governments have to be cautious that their rigorous intelligence gathering and sharing does not prevent innocent donors contributing to worthwhile causes.[39] Terrorist groups and transnational crime syndicates alike are major players in operating money laundering and financial outflow schemes through charitable channels, both legitimate and illegitimate. Both groups are not averse to using shadow trades like heritage looting, conflict minerals and human trafficking for raising income that is then laundered, with or without charities and tax havens.

Enabling Conduits

Private banking

Offshore banking secrecy facilitates the concealment of the proceeds of illegal, corrupt and other unethical economic activities from governments, as well as legitimate wealth from tax authorities, business partners and family members. Conservatively, about USD7.3 trillion or 8 percent of world household wealth is estimated to be held in tax havens, leading to a loss of tax revenue of USD190 billion. It is among the developing and emerging economy regions of the world that the share of wealth kept offshore is highest, such as in Latin America at 22 percent, in Africa at 30 percent, while in Russia this percentage is 50 percent and in the Persian Gulf states it is 57 percent.[40] Although tax planning via lawyers and accountants to set up convoluted financial structures may arguably be legal, if immoral, tax evasion is definitely illegal in most jurisdictions. But the process of challenging such schemes which circumvent laws, and of recovering unpaid tax, is highly demanding to governments worldwide in terms of time, money and expertise. Especially in developing and emerging countries with weak legal oversight, such as tax havens, these invariably complex and deliberately opaque financial arrangements are susceptible to capital flight and the tax evasion agenda of their clients, although the extent of this has been difficult to quantify.[41] Yet given their role in establishing and managing legal entities that hold and transfer assets, trust and company services providers remain perfectly legal financial intermediaries in the world economy.

Internet transfers

For the purposes of money laundering, the internet allows the easy setting-up of operations, low cost means of communication, deceptively using images from reputable sources, gathering the financial proceeds anonymously, and, critically, it allows the conduct of all these functions in jurisdictions where legal enforcement is weak. The internet arguably does not need to create new opportunities for money laundering; it only has to facilitate traditional informal means of money transfers, such as *hawala* in the Middle East and *chop* in East Asia.[42] Newer payment methods including prepaid cards, internet payments and mobile transfers have also attracted interest by money launderers and terrorism financiers for their anonymity, negotiability and global access through teller machines. Relatively lacking in paper-trails, these financial channels continue to compete with regulated wire-transfer services for migrant remittances and with official banks, where there are foreign exchange restrictions for importers, making them easily adapted for the payment of fictitious goods and other means of money laundering.

Crypto-currencies

Disruptive digital technologies such as digital or crypto-currencies that allow users to transfer value anonymously are attractive to illegitimate businesses for being able to mask transactions with suppliers and clients, and to shift the proceeds. Transactions that have been researched have been found to range from a few thousand to millions of dollars, involving payment for drugs, stolen goods, racist propaganda, extortion, internet fraud, counterfeit and other dubious economic activities.[43] With increasing electronic commerce globally, including on the Dark Web, such currencies make logical economic sense but any belated regulation of them needs to recognise that not all such transactions are illegal.[44] In fact, the underlying block-chain technology has the potential to trace transactions as well as perform ledger-keeping functions for better transparency purposes. However, no universal standards exist to be applied uniformly, with many jurisdictions setting different thresholds or caps for transactions. Identifying the risk of these methods to money laundering, capital flight and tax evasion remains problematic since many of their intermediaries, such as card providers and retailers, are deemed outside current legislation.

Real-estate investments

For the purposes of money laundering, major property purchases, typically in cash, allow criminals to conveniently achieve the process of inserting the illicit funds, disguising the ownership and realising their investment as legitimate money. Often the investment is for properties, even whole private islands, in quite desirable

Caribbean, Mediterranean, Persian Gulf and Pacific Island locations, which serve conveniently as tax havens too. This is not to mention fashionable world-class cities like London and New York, often pricing out locals from home-ownership. Elsewhere it has been proven that Russian oligarchs and kleptocrats laundered their funds with the assistance of the German-based Deutsche Bank, which in turn had generously funded purchases in Trump Organisation property developments.[45] In Canada, drug traffickers were revealed to have invested CAD5 billion in Vancouver real estate, including the provision of unofficial loans to buyers, thus earning high interest while laundering their funds.[46] This did raise questions for Australia, where buyers from China constituted the largest group of investors, placing AUD24 billion in the real-estate market in one year alone.[47] Up to USD1 billion that was siphoned corruptly from Malaysia's 1MDB (1Malaysia Development Berhad) national development fund is said to have been invested in UK and US real estate. Given its lax oversight on businesses, Dubai has been designated by the US State Department as a jurisdiction of concern for this practice. In fact, sanctioned individuals operating in narcotics, financing terrorism, nuclear proliferation and corruption were found to own luxury properties in Dubai worth USD28.2 million, with a further USD78.8 billion held by their business networks.[48] Hence all the major financial centres at the crossroads of financial flows from their regions and internationally provide multiple means for transferring and laundering funds raised from various illicit operations through layering into the legitimate world economy (Figure 8.2).

Curbing the Scam

Penalty Policies

To succeed with measures against money laundering, countries need to recognise that it can only be done through convergence of economic coercion, material incentives and moral argument. The Financial Action Task Force (FATF) set up by the G7 Paris Summit in 1989 initially attempted to combat money laundering by persuading member-countries to adopt uniform standards. But in 2000 it controversially switched to coerce other countries that did not adopt the standards through 'grey-listing' or discriminating against them in international trade. Such economic imperialism was possible through the US exercising its dominance of the world economy. Subsequently FATF has problematised money laundering as a global issue further, by associating it with the financing of terrorism and the drugs trade.[49] Furthermore, emergent and developing countries are encouraged to perceive these measures as imperative for ensuring that illicit financial outflows of up to USD2 trillion do not continue to perpetuate their underdevelopment. Key to tracing, freezing and repatriating such assets has been legislation that allows these to be done – paradoxically – on the basis of

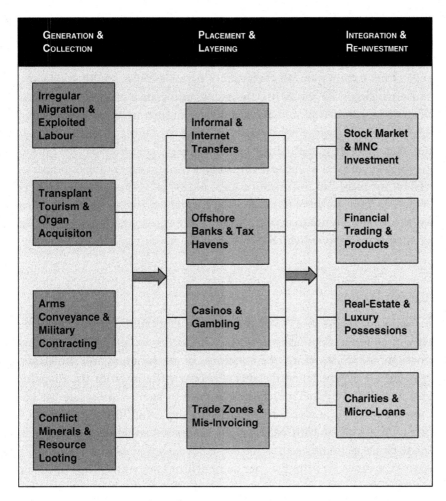

GENERATION & COLLECTION	PLACEMENT & LAYERING	INTEGRATION & RE-INVESTMENT
Irregular Migration & Exploited Labour	Informal & Internet Transfers	Stock Market & MNC Investment
Transplant Tourism & Organ Acquisiton	Offshore Banks & Tax Havens	Financial Trading & Products
Arms Conveyance & Military Contracting	Casinos & Gambling	Real-Estate & Luxury Possessions
Conflict Minerals & Resource Looting	Trade Zones & Mis-Invoicing	Charities & Micro-Loans

Figure 8.2 Processes for laundering money

non-conviction, thus allowing for manipulation by those corporations and individuals who are well resourced financially to reach settlements. Nevertheless, only a limited number of OECD countries have such policies, resulting in the freezing of USD1.4 billion of assets but the return of only USD147 million, or a tenth, to the developing countries from which these were stolen.[50] Since criminal conduct is complex to prove, requiring proof of legitimate wealth acquisition should suffice for identification instead.

Although most banks in tax havens had made progress by the late 1990s towards complying with national and inter-government strictures, there still remain weaknesses with identifying the ownership of accounts and granting access to foreign regulators, with a possible exception made where criminal investigations are involved.[51] Anti-money laundering efforts have gained momentum internationally as various inter-government organisations, such as the OECD, the G20, the World Bank and others, have advocated regulations and promoted best-practice measures. These include transparency of entity ownership, the reporting of transactions, an exchange of tax information, the taxation of financial flows and the curtailment of trade mis-invoicing.[52] By the 2010s, the public intolerance of financial institutions' involvement in laundering and predicate crimes, such as corruption and insider trading, resulted in a policy shift towards greater government enforcement and prosecutions. But in both industrialised and developing countries largely undisclosed settlements were arrived at instead with major banks, corporations, industries and financial centres, offshore and onshore, for tax evasion.[53] Consequently, the expected repatriation of funds onshore has not occurred, and tax havens continue to exist by tax rate competition, if not to expand through innovative financial products devised by accountants and lawyers which circumvent the newer regulatory regimes.[54]

Corruption Watch

While corruption might seem to help grease the moribund wheels of a developing economy, it certainly does adversely affect the efficiency of the financial system, the provision of infrastructure, the collection of tax revenues and the creation of employment, all of which mostly affect its own citizens. Since the illegitimately acquired assets of any public officials often need to be moved outside the country and then masked in the global financial system to avoid discovery, systemic corruption is closely allied with capital flight, money laundering and tax havens.[55] Legitimate banks at home and tax havens abroad, as well as informal funds transfer networks, casinos and the like, are complicit in laundering these illicit funds.[56] Corrupt politicians, officials, police, judges and other authorities can sometimes be in collusion with organised crime syndicates, which may control monopolistic businesses like waste disposal, as well as illegal ones such as contraband, particularly in politically unstable countries. Thus, anti-corruption efforts must have the support of anti-money laundering legislation that emphasises international cooperation on financial intelligence and asset confiscation, with developing countries sharing ownership of such systems along with the industrialised countries where much of the ill-gotten funds are lodged.[57]

Trade Transparency

Whereas anti-money laundering agencies have traditionally focused on monitoring suspicious transactions made through financial institutions, they are increasingly scrutinising the abnormal pricing of imports and exports of merchandise. Based on data mining of trade transactions involving 25 terrorist watch-list countries, the US estimated that the value of money thus moved in the early 2000s as about USD4.27

billion.[58] When Switzerland extended its anti-money laundering policy to all of its financial institutions, the volatility and amount of capital outflow from there towards the US increased significantly. This suggests that merchandise trade had been utilised to shift income through transfer pricing, and also illustrates how corporations are quite adept at finding new ways to launder money in response to legislative changes.[59] Furthermore, lawyers and accountants may deliberately or unwittingly be implicated by their clients in money laundering, and thus be subject to prosecution and the loss of their licence. Ultimately, all regulatory measures must be judged not by how much money laundering and capital flight is reduced, but by whether the criminal activities that generate and use the funds are curtailed.[60] By emphasising prevention, legitimate businesses can be brought under surveillance for possibly abetting money laundering and thus, those in real estate, antiques, jewellery and other luxury goods, must be required to report large cash purchases to the authorities.

Following the Money

Sanctions and Subsidies

Draconian measures of sanctions for non-compliance, such as seizure, prosecution and isolation, can be ruinous for the financial sectors of small developing economies, causing economic recession and political turmoil, which they would be prudent not to collaborate in against themselves.[61] Efforts directed by the OECD to name and shame tax havens in such countries have faced a backlash, with the financial sectors in many of its own member states found not to be complying with those same standards. One radical proposal has been for the OECD to compensate tax havens for financial losses due to their compliance, out of the tax recovered by its member states, although that raises issues of sovereignty and dependency.[62] Despite having already enhanced audit trails and money profiling to identify persons for further investigation, there remains doubt over the effectiveness of such strategies for disrupting illicit finance flows and for prosecution if proven.[63] Proving that money laundering has taken place is crucial for prosecuting the criminals who distance themselves from that, though the task for forensic accounting or auditing is complex and not always understood by legal professionals, who require clear evidence to convict.[64] The critical problem may be that anti-money laundering laws make it easier to track the financial transactions to prosecute the money laundering entities, but these could be quite distinct from those that commit and finance the more serious predicate crimes.

Extra-territorial Reach

Since territoriality remains the main basis for jurisdiction, shadow trades, including money laundering, pose a serious challenge to any national legislation and consequent enforcement because these take place across borders. Sorely needed are international treaties incorporating a binding commitment to hold every parent or holding company accountable for the extra-territorial crimes of its foreign subsidiaries.[65] If the probability of being prosecuted for money laundering as well as the predicate crimes, and the transaction costs become negatively related to the profits of crime, then anti-money laundering policies should in principle deter involvement in the shadow trades and/or related borderless networks. Of all the policy areas assessed through a quantitative model such as rule of law, institutional framework and the private sector role in law enforcement, only international cooperation was found by researchers to be related to lower crime. This implies that further effort in that direction should prove effective.[66] If money laundering is to be rightly treated as a serious transnational crime in and off itself, then its harm to the economy, society and polity needs to be recognised by all countries involved, whether classified as developing, emergent or industrialised economies.[67] Since economic globalisation and finance sleight appear mutually reinforcing, then their regulation and enforcement must be duly de-territorialised and encompass the predicate shadow trades.

Commentary in Conclusion

On the basis of the UN Human Development Index, finance-dependent countries join resource-dependent ones in being among the poorest economic performers. The resource curse has been well documented, demonstrating how many developing countries have failed to translate their natural resource endowments, like oil or gold, for economic development. Arguably the over-sized financial sector comes to capture the politics of the country and there is growing evidence that its contribution to the economy might be far less than claimed, even possibly negative. The dominance of the financial sector tends to displace other productive and entrepreneurial economic sectors, support authoritarian governments in the name of political stability and attract employees away from the public and other private sectors through high salaries.[68] Although small economies serving as tax havens might be vulnerable similarly to what might be termed the finance curse, this has gone largely unaddressed.

Not adequately recognised is the fact that regardless of where the tax havens are located, whether offshore in the Caribbean and South Pacific or onshore in Europe and North America, the substantial funds channelled through them from both the legitimate and illicit economies are worldwide in origin. In spite of the existing capacity to track all financial flows in our digital era, the reluctance of governments and corporations to be fully transparent means that reliable figures are not factored into a realistic geography of global finance.[69] Were the UN or OECD to educate civil society worldwide on how tax havens have caused costly financial crises and on how the seizure of illicit funds can provide funding for developmental goals, this could motivate citizens to hold their own governments, corporations and mega-rich to account.[70] Doubtless an international convention or treaty is no guarantee of establishing an effective multilateral regime on money laundering, but by raising public awareness it would provide impetus for change, in much the same way as is happening with the issue of climate change.

───────────────── DIM DOMAIN ─────────────────

MAP TO HIDDEN TREASURE

Governments around the world keep being pressured by financial markets and international funding agencies to reduce their countries' fiscal deficits, even while their wealthy shift assets into tax havens. About GBP6.3 trillion of assets are held by only 92,000 people or less than 0.001 percent of the world's population. The elite of resource-rich countries tend to stash their wealth into offshore bank accounts instead of investing in the domestic economy. Yet right-wing politicians worldwide peddle the historically discredited idea of trickle-down economics or that greater tax breaks for the rich result in greater investment and spending that eventually benefits poorer citizens with jobs. Closing the financial loopholes exploited by multinational corporations and mega-rich citizens to avoid their fair share of tax will reduce the national fiscal deficit. Only then can governments stimulate the economy by increased public spending, rather than by cost-cutting and tax rises for the 99 percent of people who cannot avoid paying taxes.

Personal Loopholes

According to the Tax Justice Network, the global mega-rich hold GBP13 trillion (or USD21 trillion) offshore, which is equivalent to the combined GDP of the US and Japan. By exploiting cross-border tax rules, they move their funds into secretive jurisdictions such as Switzerland and the Cayman Islands. The top 10 private banks, such as UBS, Credit Suisse and Goldman Sachs, alone managed more than GBP4 trillion (or USD11 trillion) in 2010. Such banks, along with legal, accounting and investment firms, specialise in masking the assets of their high net-worth clients, by capitalising on the varied tax regimes available in the world economy. The Bank of International Settlements and the International Monetary Fund estimate that the capital that has flowed out from developing countries since the 1970s would be more than enough to pay off their international debts.

The substantial mineral resources of many countries are controlled by a small group of mega-rich business and political elites, while national debts have to be repaid by governments through taxing the populace and depriving them of public services. Including their investment returns, almost GBP500 billion (about USD800 billion) has left Russia since the early 1990s, Saudi Arabia has lost GBP197 billion (about USD320 billion) since the mid-1970s, while similarly Nigeria

(Continued)

has lost GBP196 billion (about USD315 billion). Assuming the GBP13 trillion (USD21 trillion) in assets held by the mega-rich and corporations were to earn 3 percent per annum, and governments could tax that at 30 percent, their countries would earn GBP121 billion (about USD200 billion) in revenues. This sum would be greater than what higher-income countries give as aid to the lower-income countries each year. Typically, the tax bills of the mega-rich are paltry and yet they expect to benefit from public services, such as good infrastructure for the running of their business and good public transport for their customers, without paying for it.[71]

If the corporate income taxes were to be abolished, then the wealthy would simply form multiple shell corporations in tax havens, while remaining beneficial owners via extensive networks for opacity. They could allege that their earnings are dividends of the corporation and should not be subject to personal income tax because in some countries, dividends are already paid to tax-exempt companies. It was to preclude such actions that corporate income tax was introduced in many high-income countries just before World War I. Still the mega-rich use many ways to access their wealth by having their shell companies buy luxuries for them, lease them properties or provide loans that need never be repaid. The Panama Papers scandal in the mid-2010s showed how these players hide their funds through shell companies in the Caribbean, the Indian Ocean and South Pacific. In all these remote island nation-states these companies use nominee directors, such that the true identities of the owners are rendered difficult to trace. Through the leaks of over 1.5 terabytes of information from an altruistic and anonymous insider which were authenticated through other independent and ongoing investigations, a law firm was found to have assisted the families, closest friends and business associates of political leaders worldwide, such as of Russia, Syria, Zimbabwe, China, Iceland and Argentina, not to mention other kings, princes, generals and prime ministers still in authority, now in exile or long dead.[72]

Corporate Incentives

Developing countries typically seek to attract foreign direct investment (FDI) by a number of policy measures, including lower corporate tax rates, special tax breaks or via the lax enforcement of tax laws. While such tax incentives do not necessarily make the host-country more competitive, other countries have little choice but to follow suit, in a race to the bottom. Half of all African countries have laws for tax-free investment zones today, compared with less than 5 percent in the early 1980s and yet the evidence is that such zones are of little benefit to and some actually cost low-income countries. In OECD countries, corporate tax revenues constitute about 10 percent of total tax revenues, while in low-income countries these make up just 15 percent. If multinational corporations repatriate profits from the countries-of-operation, they then undermine the development opportunities related to productive reinvestment there. Assuming a conservative reinvestment rate of 50 percent on after-tax profit of USD300–400 billion means a loss of reinvested earnings of about USD150-200 billion or between a quarter and third of the potential value otherwise, the total loss of development finance through the activities of MNCs is about a tenth or USD100 billion. This leakage of financial resources also affects overall GDP and the reinvested earnings component of FDI. Extrapolating this to all lower-income countries, other than the tax havens, translates into a revenue loss estimated at USD70-120 billion.

The Panama Papers further revealed how that tax haven was widely used by legitimate multinational corporations and global banks, their shareholders, even senior management, just as much as by drug barons, arms dealers, corrupt politicians, violent dictators and criminal syndicates.[73] Through the services of an international law firm Mossack Fonseca, multinational corporations such as Siemens were found to have used shell companies in tax havens to hold and move slush funds, abetted by reputable financial institutions like Commerzbank and Deutsche Bank, with which to bribe political leaders and senior government officials. Similarly implicated were international sports federations such as football's FIFA and its regional affiliates, often involving the siphoning of lucrative media contracts to bribe committee members and national representatives to vote in specific ways, for instance in the awarding of event locations. Also identified were links of tax havens to arms suppliers, art dealers and oil smugglers that have broken various embargoes against countries by the United Nations. So, if tax authorities ever wish to recover even a fraction of potential income and corporate taxes hidden through shell companies, they would have to constantly innovate, regulate and enforce to outwit the proponents.

National Policies

Major European countries have attempted to attract some of the tax evasion market away from Ireland. The UK government itself admitted that the cuts to its headline tax rates alone would lose the UK Treasury an estimated GBP7.8 billion annually by 2016-17, while other estimates have been as high as GBP10 billion (USD15 billion). An investigation by Reuters in 2014 found seven multinationals that had relocated to the UK had created less than 50 jobs and that one of the tax-incentivised relocations had even caused the loss of 600 jobs.[74] It could positively identify only one USD200,000 tax payment from the seven corporations. The evidence of other aspects of the tax changes appears to support the view that the UK's tax-cutting corporate model has been a failure. Within Asia, the former British colony of Hong Kong is periodically cited as a model for low tax leading to economic growth, as popularised by the free-market economist Milton Friedman. The city is wealthy because of its strategic position as the leading international entry-point to a booming China and also a location where dubious financial practices occur for a lack of effective regulation and enforcement. Other countries in Asia and elsewhere simply cannot succeed in replicating the Hong Kong corporate tax model.

(Continued)

Structures and Occupants

Ireland's pre-crisis foreign investment-led growth was not solely on account of its tax benefits, but due to its unique position as an English-speaking gateway into the Eurozone. It became a tax haven to the detriment of other European countries even though it continues to deny it. Tax did factor in its attraction to US corporations, which was enhanced by cultural links to the country. Although the country offered corporate tax incentives as far back as 1956, it was not until the European Single Market emerged in 1992 that this grew. Ireland's pre-crisis growth rate was helped by European subsidies which allowed the country to fund infrastructure and other public goods. Another factor was the immigration of professionals, allowing Ireland to gain from the taxpayer-funded education of individuals from other countries. Its economic growth was further fuelled by consumption based on a property bubble which later burst.

League tables of wealthy economies that include tax-haven countries tend to use Gross Domestic Product (GDP) as a basis for their rankings, rather than Gross National Income (GNI). But this measurement includes the profits of multinationals taken there, which cannot effectively be taxed and which is the reason for their headquarters or some subsidiaries being located there and thus deemed tax resident. Especially in smaller tax havens, GDP growth and income figures disguise the fact that most of these tend to be due to a small number of highly skilled and well-paid expatriates. If only a fraction of this trickles down to the original populations, it is questionable whether the wealth of expatriates should count as contributing to economic development in developing countries. Anyway, countries with profitable offshore financial industries decline to reveal details of the assets of the mega-rich to the tax authorities of their home countries or those of the multinational corporations to their headquarter countries.[75]

Thousands of dubious financial structures can be found in tax havens, including ones where locals are proxies for true foreign owners or where firms circuitously own themselves. Leaders of the G20 countries did commit to closing down tax havens in the aftermath of the financial crisis of 2008, where the secrecy in the banking system was credited with exacerbating the meltdown. In 2016 Britain was the first G20 country to introduce a public register for owners of shell companies, revealing even some of its politicians being among them. Among the tax havens in the industrialised world where tracing ownership is also difficult are European micro-states like San Marino, Liechtenstein and Monaco. Generally, information declared by wealthy individuals and multinational corporations has not been counter-checked because of the underfunding of the government and inter-government agencies set up to oversee them, in part due to political lobbying. Yet, unless more stringent regulations are instituted and rigorously enforced, leading to substantial penalties including imprisonment, tax evaders and money launderers as well as their enabler consultancies and financial institutions have no incentive to comply.

Crucial Queries

Is money laundering and the use of tax havens essentially a victimless shadow trade? If not, who suffers as a result of this prevalent practice by mega-rich individuals and corporations? To whom should any funds recovered from kleptocrats be reimbursed, assuming corrupt governments were complicit in the practice?

Should money laundering by criminal organisations and terrorist groups receive higher priority in investigation and penalisation than legitimate corporations and successful businesspersons? How can tax havens be made less profitable for use by those evading taxes or hiding their sources of illicit wealth?

Why are tax havens in small developing countries typically targeted by inter-government organisations and do they deserve to be? How are major financial centres in industrialised countries able to remain active in assisting in money laundering and tax evasion despite the rule of law functioning?

Why would multinational corporations declare losses in the higher tax countries for decades and still choose to continue operations there? Should governments bail-out their corporations during economic crises when these companies have secreted their revenues abroad through various tax planning in better times?

Do tax breaks and other subsidies to multinational corporations by countries benefit their whole economies and citizens? If not, which industry sector or social class stands to gain the most? How can this shadow trade of financial sleight and tax evasion be tackled more effectively than it is at present?

FURTHER RESOURCES

Research Works

Kleinbard, E. D. (2015). *We are Better than This: How Government should Spend our Money.* New York: Oxford University Press, USA.

Masciandaro, D. (ed.). (2017). *Global Financial Crime: Terrorism, Money Laundering and Offshore Centres.* London: Taylor & Francis.

Passas, N. (2017). *Transnational Financial Crime.* London: Routledge.

Pickhardt, M., & Prinz, A. (eds.). (2012). *Tax Evasion and the Shadow Economy.* London: Edward Elgar.

Sharman, J. C. (2017). *The Despot's Guide to Wealth Management: On the International Campaign against Grand Corruption.* Ithaca, NY: Cornell University Press.

Informational Websites

Financial Action Task Force [www.fatf-gafi.org]
International Money Laundering Information Network [www.imolin.org/]
Organisation for Economic Cooperation and Development [www.oecd.org/fatf/legislation_en.htm]

Transparency International [www.transparency.org/]
US Department of Treasury [www.fincen.gov]

Annotated Documentaries

Das Erste/NDR (2016). *Panama Papers: The Shady World of Offshore Companies* [55:00 min.]. On the uncovering of thousands of documents showing leaders and criminals involved in tax evasion.

BBC (2018). *Gangsters' Dirty Money Exposed* [30:00 min.]. A Panorama series programme on criminals and their associates using offshore secrecy to launder money through the UK.

Bailout Films (2017). *All the Plenary's Men* [56:14 min.]. Investigation, prosecution and exoneration of HSBC for money laundering of drug syndicates and terrorists.

Al Jazeera (2018). *Is Dubai a Money-Laundering Hub?* [25:00 min.]. Questions whether those profiting from wars, terror and drug trafficking use Dubai's real-estate for money laundering.

CBC (2017). *KPMG and Tax Havens for the Rich: The Untouchables* [43:00 min.]. Exposé of an offshore tax haven that reveals the names of some of its wealthy clients.

General Reading

Brooks, R. (2014). *The Great Tax Robbery*. London: Oneworld Publications.

James, M. (2017). *The Glorification of Plunder: State, Power and Tax Policy*. London: Spiramus Press.

Murphy, R. (2016). *The Joy of Tax*. London: Random House.

Obermayer, B., & Obermaier, F. (2016). *The Panama Papers: Breaking the Story of How the Rich and Powerful Hide their Money*. London: Oneworld Publications.

Shaxson, N. (2018). *The Finance Curse: How Global Finance is Making us all Poorer*. London: Random House.

Endnotes

1. Schjelderup, G., & Baker, R. W. 2015). *Financial Flows and Tax Havens: Combining to Limit the Lives of Billions of People*. Oslo: Norwegian School of Economics, Global Financial Integrity, Jawaharlal Nehru University, Instituto de Estudos Socio-economicos and Nigerian Institute of Social and Economic Research.

2. Sharman, J. C. (2008). Power and discourse in policy diffusion: anti-money laundering in developing states. *International Studies Quarterly, 52*(3), 635–656.

3. Cobham, A., & Janský, P. (2017). Global distribution of revenue loss from corporate tax avoidance: re-estimation and country results. *WIDER Working Paper 201/55*. New York: United Nations University-WIDER.

4. Hampton, M. P., & Levi, M. (1999). Fast spinning into oblivion? Recent developments in money-laundering policies and offshore finance centres. *Third World Quarterly, 20*(3), 645–656.

5. Pietschmann, T., & Walker, J. (2011). *Estimating Illicit Financial Flows Resulting from Drug Trafficking and Other Transnational Organized Crimes.* New York: UNODC, United Nations Office of Drugs and Crime.

6. Financial Action Task Force (FATF) website [www.fatf-gafi.org/faq/ moneylaundering/ – accessed 03 May 2020]

7. International Association of Penal Law (2008). Combating terrorist financing: draft resolution. *International Review of Penal Law,* 371.

8. Corporate Finance Institute website [https://corporatefinanceinstitute.com/ resources/ knowledge/other/what-is-tax-haven/ – accessed 17 May 2020]

9. Gilligan, G. P. (2004). Whither or wither the European Union Savings Tax Directive? A case study in the political economy of taxation. *Journal of Financial Crime,* 11(1), 56–72.

10. Blickman, T. (1997). The Rothschilds of the mafia on Aruba. *Transnational Organized Crime, 3*(2), 50–89.

11. UNCTAD (2015). *World Investment Report 2015: Reforming International Investment Governance.* New York & Geneva: United Nations Conferences on Trade and Development.

12. Zucman, G. (2014). Taxing across borders: tracking personal wealth and corporate profits. *Journal of Economic Perspectives, 28*(4), 121–148.

13. Tax Justice Network (2018). *Financial Secrecy Index 2018.* [www.financialsecre cyindex.com/introduction/fsi-2018-results – accessed 20 April 2018]. Creative Commons Attribution 4.0 International License.

14. Cobham, A., Janský, P., & Consultation, U. U. E. (2017). Measurement of illicit financial flows. Background paper prepared for UNCTAD: Benefits and Costs of the IFF Targets, 187-238. *UNODC–UNCTAD Expert Consultation on the SDG Indicator on Illicit Financial Flows, 13-14 December, Geneva.*

15. Crivelli, E., De Mooij, R. A., & Keen, M. M. (2015). *Base Erosion, Profit Shifting and Developing Countries* (No. 15-118). Washington, DC: International Monetary Fund.

16. Salomon, M., & Spanjers, J. (2017). Illicit financial flows to and from developing countries: 2005–2014. *Global Financial Integrity.* Washington, DC: Center for International Policy.

17. Tax Justice Network (2011). *The Cost of Tax Abuse: A Briefing Paper on the Cost of Tax Evasion Worldwide.* Chesham, UK: Tax Justice Network.

18. Tax Justice Network (2018). *Narrative Report on the United Kingdom: Financial Secrecy Index.* Chesham, UK: Tax Justic Network.

19. Tax Justice Network (2011). *The Cost of Tax Abuse: A Briefing Paper on the Cost of Tax Evasion Worldwide.* Chesham, UK: Tax Justice Network.

20. Cobham, A., & Klees, S. (2016). Global taxation: financing education and the other sustainable development goals. *The Education Commission Background Paper: The Learning Generation.* Orpington, UK: Education Commission.

21. Grahl, J., & Lysandrou, P. (2003). Sand in the wheels or spanner in the works? The Tobin tax and global finance. *Cambridge Journal of Economics, 27*(4), 597–621.

22. Janský, P., & Prats, A. (2015). International profit-shifting out of developing countries and the role of tax havens. *Development Policy Review, 33*(3), 271–292.

23. Egger, P., Eggert, W., & Winner, H. (2010). Saving taxes through foreign plant ownership. *Journal of International Economics, 81*(1), 99–108.

24. Allen, D. (2015). What you need to know about the global business of free trade zones. *In The Black*, February.

25. FATF (2010). *Money Laundering Vulnerabilities of Free Trade Zones*. Paris: Financial Action Task Force.

26. Hetzer, W. (2003). Money laundering and financial markets. *European Journal of Crime, Criminal Law and Criminal Justice, 11*(3), 264–277.

27. Wilmarth Jr, A. E. (2008). The dark side of universal banking: financial conglomerates and the origins of the subprime financial crisis. *Connecticut Law Review, 41*, 963.

28. FATF (2004). *Report on Money Laundering Typologies 2003–2004*. Paris: Financial Action Task Force.

29. De Sanctis, F. M. (2014). *Football, Gambling, and Money Laundering: A Gobal Criminal Justice Perspective*. New York: Springer.

30. FATF (2009). *Money Laundering through the Football Sector*. Paris: Financial Action Task Force.

31. FATF (2009). *Vulnerabilities of Casinos and Gaming Sector*. Paris: Financial Action Task Force.

32. OECD (2018). *Illicit Financial Flows: The Economy of Illicit Trade in West Africa*. Paris: OECD Publishing.

33. Schneider, F. (2011). *The Financial Flows of the Transnational Crime: Some Preliminary Empirical Results* (No. 53). Economics of Security Working Paper. Berlin: EUSECON.

34. Lilley, P. (2003). *Dirty Dealing: The Untold Truth about Global Money Laundering, International Crime and Terrorism*. London: Kogan Page.

35. Lilley, P. (2003). *Dirty Dealing: The Untold Truth about Global Money Laundering, International Crime and Terrorism*. London: Kogan Page.

36. UNODC (2011). *Estimating Illicit Financial Flows Resulting from Drug Trafficking and Other Transnational Crimes*. Vienna: United Nations Office on Drugs and Crime.

37. Qureshi, W. A. (2017). An overview of money laundering in Pakistan and worldwide: causes, methods, and socioeconomic effects. *University of Bologna Law Review, 2*, 300.

38. Malm, A., & Bichler, G. (2013). Using friends for money: the positional importance of money-launderers in organized crime. *Trends in Organized Crime, 16*(4), 365–381.

39. FATF (2004). *Report on Money Laundering Typologies 2003–2004*. Paris: Financial Action Task Force.

40. Zucman, G. (2014). Taxing across borders: tracking personal wealth and corporate profits. *Journal of Economic Perspectives, 28*(4), 121–148.

41. FATF (2010). *Money Laundering Using Trust and Company Service Providers*. Paris: Financial Action Task Force.

42. Morris-Cotterill, N. (1999). Use and abuse of the internet in fraud and money laundering. *International Review of Law, Computers & Technology, 13*(2), 211–228.

43. FATF (2009). *Money Laundering Using New Payment Methods*. Paris: Financial Action Task Force.

44. Bryans, D. (2014). Bitcoin and money laundering: mining for an effective solution. *Indiana Law Journal, 89*, 441.

45. Protess, B., Silver-Greenberg, J., & Drucker, J. (2017). Big German bank, key to Trump's finances, faces new scrutiny. *The New York Times*, 19 July.

46. Cooper, S., Bell, S., & Russell, A. (2018) *Fentanyl: Making a Killing*. Vancouver: Globalnews Report [https://globalnews.ca/news/4658157/... – accessed 06 May 2019].

47. Fergusion, Doug, et al. (2016). *Demystifying Chinese Investments in Australia*. Sydney, NSW: KPMG/University of Sydney [http://demystifyingchina.com.au/reports/...-april-2016.pdf – accessed 04 March 2019].

48. C4ADS (Center for Advanced Defense Studies) (2018). *Sandcastles: Tracing Sanctions Evasions through Dubai's Luxury Real-Estate Market*. Washington, DC: C4ADS [www.c4reports.org/sandcastles – accessed 26 June 2020].

49. Hülsse, R. (2007). Creating demand for global governance: the making of a global money-laundering problem. *Global Society, 21*(2), 155–178.

50. Dickinson, B. (2014). Illicit financial flows and development. *Revue d'économie du développement, 22*(HS02), 125–130.

51. GAO (1998). *Money Laundering: Regulatory Oversight of Offshore Private Banking Activities*. United States General Accounting Office Report 98-154. Washington, DC: General Accounting Office.

52. Salomon, M., & Spanjers, J. (2017). *Illicit Financial Flows to and from Developing Countries: 2005–2014*. Washington, DC: Global Financial Integrity.

53. Reider-Gordon, M., & Butler, T. K. (2013). Anti-money laundering. *International Law, 47*, 387.

54. Woodward, R. (2006). Offshore strategies in global political economy: Small islands and the case of the EU and OECD harmful tax competition initiatives. *Cambridge Review of International Affairs, 19*(4), 685–699.

55. FATF (2011). *Laundering the Proceeds of Corruption*. Paris: Financial Action Task Force.

56. Rose-Ackerman, S. (2016). Corruption, organised crime and money laundering. *World Bank Roundtable on Institutions, Governance and Corruption*, 26–27 May, Montevideo, Uruguay.

57. Sharman, J. C., & Chaikin, D. (2009). Corruption and anti-money-laundering systems: putting a luxury good to work. *Governance, 22*(1), 27–45.

58. Zdanowicz, J. S. (2004). Detecting money laundering and terrorist financing via data mining. *Communications of the ACM, 47*(5), 53–55.

59. De Boyrie, M. E., Pak, S. J., & Zdanowicz, J. S. (2005). The impact of Switzerland's money laundering law on capital flows through abnormal pricing in international trade. *Applied Financial Economics, 15*(4), 217–230.

60. Reuter, P., & Truman, E. M. (2005). Anti-money laundering overkill? *The International Economy, Winter 2005*, 56–60 [www.international-economy.com/TIE_W05_Reuter-Truman.pdf – accessed 26 June 2020].

61. Maynard, P. D. (2001). Putting international financial centres out of business: the rush to judgment and the rush to capitulation. *Annual Ocean Anti-Money Laundering Conference*, 14–17 February, Miami, Florida.

62. Maurer, B. (2008). Re-regulating offshore finance? *Geography Compass, 2*(1), 155–175.

63. Cuéllar, M. F. (2002). The tenuous relationship between the fight against money laundering and the disruption of criminal finance. *Journal of Criminal Law & Criminology, 93*, 311.

64. Murray, K. (2010). Dismantling organised crime groups through enforcement of the POCA money laundering offences. *Journal of Money Laundering Control, 13*(1), 7–14.

65. Borlini, L. S. (2008). Issues of the international criminal regulation of money laundering in the context of economic globalization. *Papers.ssrn.com*.

66. Ferwerda, J. (2009). The economics of crime and money laundering: does anti-money laundering policy reduce crime? *Review of Law & Economics, 5*(2), 903–929.

67. Alldridge, P. (2008). Money laundering and globalization. *Journal of Law and Society, 35*(4), 437–463.

68. Shaxson, N., & Christensen, J. (2014). *The Finance Curse: How Oversized Financial Centres Attack Democracy and Corrupt Economies*. Chesham, UK: Tax Justice Network.

69. Brown, E., & Cloke, J. (2007). Shadow Europe: alternative European financial geographies. *Growth and Change, 38*(2), 304–327.

70. Blickman, T. (2009). *Countering Illicit and Unregulated Money Flows: Money Laundering, Tax Evasion and Financial Regulation*. Crime and Globalisation Debate Papers. Amsterdam: Transnational Institute.

71. Stewart, H., & Frigieri, G. (2012). Wealth doesn't trickle down – it just floods offshore, research reveals. *The Guardian*, 21 July.

72. Obermayer, B., & Obermaier, F. (2017). *The Panama Papers: Breaking the Story of How the Rich and Powerful Hide their Money*. London: Oneworld Publications.

73. Obermayer, B., & Obermaier, F. (2017). *The Panama Papers: Breaking the Story of How the Rich and Powerful Hide their Money*. London: Oneworld Publications.

74. Bergin, T. (2014). Britain becomes haven for US companies keen to cut tax bills. *Reuters Business News*. [www.reuters.com/article/uk-britain-usa-tax-insight/britain-becomes-haven-for-u-s-companies-keen-to-cut-tax-bills-idUKKBN0EK0BA20140609– accessed 10 October 2017]

75. Cobham, A. (2015). UNCTAD study on corporate tax in developing countries. [http://uncounted.org/2015/03/26/unctad-study-on-corporate-tax-in-developing-countries/ – accessed 09 August 2017].

CHAPTER 9
TRACKING CROSS-CURRENTS

Credit: Kaique Rocha/Pexels

Overview in Introduction

Numerous ties exist inevitably between the shadow trades enumerated in this book, as well with other trades, legitimate or otherwise. This implies that one shadow trade cannot be tackled independently of at least some of the others, for otherwise the dynamics of their relationship may change without any effective amelioration of any. All shadow trades are fostered by social inequity within and between states, exacerbated by economic globalisation through the spread of neo-liberal capitalism. Understanding the shadow trades necessitates that some attempt be initiated at succinct aggregation of their myriad forms by levels of legitimacy. The categorisation and intersects explicated in this chapter serve as a foundation for ongoing analysis and tackling of related trades. In proposing this tentative typology, the author acknowledges that some forms could seem a stretch too far in terms of their shades of legitimacy, although perhaps the respective strategies indicated should justify the exercise. Nevertheless, citing these other intertwined businesses does illustrate the complexity of the issue of shadow trades as well as its variegated relationships. As such pure shades of black and white in global business seldom exist, as many legitimate corporations might be involved partially, indirectly or possibly unwittingly in illicit operations, and vice versa. Through exploring issues like trade directionality and intersecting borderless netrworks, this chapter addresses the shadow trades related to those in humans, resources, waste, arms, finances, and others analysed in this book in order to serve for leads to further investigation and interventions.

Intersects of Commerce

Trade-flow Directionality

As evident in the organ harvesting, toxic waste dumping and conflict resources trades, the exploitation of people involved in the shadow trades is primarily of those in poorer countries by those in the wealthier in the world economy, in a characteristic neo-colonial manner. A developing-country government might be prepared to relieve itself of its unemployed poor through trafficking and smuggling, while some industrialised and emergent economies could be desirous of their labour at low prices for their industries to be highly competitive in global markets. Nonetheless irregular migrants constitute a brain-drain that adversely affects the society of the developing country in the long term, even if they represent a surplus of labour to its economy in the short term. Indirectly the impact of the shadow trade in arms from industrialised countries, as well as some emergent economies, is felt by other emergent and developing countries diverting funding from vital social services for their citizens, even while experiencing the destruction of their own infrastructure. Money laundering is derived in part from economic kleptocracy within developing, emergent or industrialised economies, depriving them of essential tax revenues. But it is driven also from the smuggling of drugs and contraband into the industrialised world for sale at prices far higher than the costs of its production in developing countries. Hence very rarely do the benefits of the shadow trades accrue to the populace in poorer economies, and even then, only to the political-economic elite segment of those countries, thus exaggerating the already great rich–poor divide within.

Shades of Legitimacy

Understanding the shadow trades necessitates that initiative be taken at proposing some classification of their myriad forms and functions for greater clarity. The gradations of the tentative typology set out in Figure 9.1 are based on the dimensions of the legality of the means and ethics of the ends of the trades involved. It may thus be a tentative foundation for an ongoing analysis of the shadow trades thus far covered. This typology comes with the proviso that none of these categories is mutually exclusive and shadow trades invariably cross over the gradations given the nuances of which entities are involved, how the operations are conducted and what their agenda is. Its use will then be applied first to the further shadow trades that are linked with those covered thus far, then with each other, and finally with legitimate businesses equally involved in borderless networks. Their straddling of the already broad categories should serve to illustrate the complexity of the phenomenon, processes and players, along with the challenges of undermining and mitigating the shadow trades.

Many trades involve patently illegal means with unethical ends, such as contraband smugglers, human traffickers, drug processors, illegal mine-owners, toxic waste traders, corrupt officials and agencies, and so on. Being the most elusive to track, these might well be termed as Murky Trades. At the other end of the spectrum are legal borderless businesses, such as freight-forwarders, shipping lines, banks, factories, hospitals, agents and processors used regularly for unethical purposes by smugglers, money launderers and human organ sellers. As this can be with or without their knowledge, these can be classified as Tainted Trades. On the other hand, there are the legal entities or the means which can be measured in official economic data while not being totally transparent, such as arms manufacturers or waste merchants. Typically secretive under the pretext of national security or global competitiveness, such businesses are better described as Opaque Trades. Finally, there are entities conducting perfectly legal operations, such as running retail or entertainment businesses, which have owners and clients with an unethical agenda. This is certainly the case with front operations for money laundering, such as casinos or forex exchanges, and can be characterised as Camouflaged Trades.

FORM OF SHADOW TRADE	PROVISIONAL CLASSIFICATION	
Murky Trades	Irregular Migration	Labour Exploitation
(Illegal Means/Unethical Ends)	Environment Degradation	Organ Acquisition, etc.
Camouflaged Trades	Arms Transfers	Waste Shipment
(Legal Means/Unethical Ends)	Military Contracting	Money Laundering, etc.
Opaque Trades	Financial Sleight	Transplant Tourism
(Illegal Means/Ethical Ends)	Hazardous Recycling	Resource Pilferage, etc.
Tainted Trades	Tourism and Hospitality	Banking and Finance
(Legal Means/Ethical Ends)	Hospitals & Clinics	Forestry & Plantations, etc.

Figure 9.1 Shades of legitimacy in the shadow trades

Blurred Boundaries

Given the variegated nature of shadow trades, much crossing-over of categories and blurring of boundaries between illegitimate and legitimate in borderless networks admittedly occurs. An illustration of the linkage is that organ sellers can also be bonded labourers, and thus part of two shadow trades, as was the case with 66 percent of those studied in Pakistan.[1] There are airline companies in developing countries, often minimally regulated by failed states, which are primarily in the business of smuggling drugs or contraband but which carry passengers and cargo under licence.[2] As the legal business is a cover for the illicit ends, as well as a supplement of their income, their trade can be classified as either Tainted or Camouflaged, or both, depending on knowledge and intent. The arms industry in the industrialised world is involved not just in supplying governments abroad but also with national security, so their business falls under secrecy laws and thus is Opaque. But it may deal both with insurgent forces and criminal syndicates as well as other illegitimate entities through smuggling, and thus the trade can then be cited as Murky. Arguably such a classification aids the analysis of the dark side of global business and can be adopted in targeting strategies to ameliorate the impact of each form of trade. Whether the typology serves this purpose adequately for now or acts as a catalyst for a more precise classification will have to be decided through comprehensive research. While further investigation on the shadow trades touched on in this book is much needed, such endeavours will be fraught with hazard and possibly place the researchers at considerable risk.

Interventions Signposted

An evident outcome of classifying the shadow trades is clarifying the optimum strategies for alleviating their adverse consequences on society and the economy by endeavouring to undermine their operations, if not ideally to eliminate their exist-ence. As acknowledged with the typology proposed above, the categories are far from distinct because their boundaries are quite blurred, and therefore any interventions cannot be exclusive to any one of them. To start at the bottom of the spectrum of shadow trades, the Tainted Trades would provisionally be best addressed by better industry self-monitoring of constituent institutions and corporations and closer regu-latory oversight by governments as well as totally independent auditing of their supply chains. Only then could any tendency to unethical practices, or manipulation by other parties, in sectors like healthcare, tourism, agriculture and manufacturing, be curbed. With the Opaque Trades, the obvious approach would be requirements for greater transparency of the entities involved and stringent licensing by governments of – for example – organ sourcing, forest clearing, financial transactions and recycling opera-tions. Nonetheless, for credibility this would need to be authenticated by civil society, as by non-government organisations or other community bodies that are autonomous from the government, not to mention the news media via investigative journalism.

Concerning the Camouflaged Trades, the strategic interventions would of necessity have to be more strident, such as the thorough enforcement of laws by better-resourced governments and the prosecution of illicit operations by all entities and persons involved in the logistics chain. In the case of the waste shipment trade, this would encompass all those from the entities generating and selling the waste, through to the transhipment intermediaries *en route*, as well as the corrupt governments, poli-ticians and community leaders that allow export or import of such waste. However, in the business of the arms transfers and military contracting, the government is a significant player and therefore needs to be held accountable by tax-payers and citi-zens through voting, as well as by non-government organisations through research and lobbying to counter the efforts of arms manufacturers, and civil society groups by protesting subsidies and military interventions. On the Murky Trades, more so than with the other forms of trades, there needs to be a three-pronged approach: first, by addressing the antecedent factors such as poverty and conflict; secondly, by penalising severely all entities profiting in order to render them economically non-viable; and thirdly, by ameliorating the suffering of victims through the protection of their human and property rights. While applied to further such trades to be covered in the rest of this chapter, the question of pertinent strategies ought to be kept front-of-mind in addressing all the shadow trades in their diversity and complexity.

Dehumanising of Persons

Brides to Order

Online dating websites for couples, or so-called mail-order brides, usually involves males from the industrialised world being matched with women in the developing world. Superficially a legitimate service, it is arguably a form of trafficking women, some of whom eventually become unpaid domestic helpers, caregivers and sexual slaves.[3] In some cultures, which transcend national borders, child marriages are considered the norm, but typically this practice involves servitude to their in-laws, violence at the hands of their spouse, not to mention the risk to health of early child-bearing. The related aspect of bride-price and dowry reinforces the notion of buying or compensating for domestic services and more. An imbalance of sex ratios in the emerging economies of Asia, where one-child policies, pre-natal screening and infanticide favour male children, has resulted in brides being sourced from neighbouring countries of similar culture and/or of women with similar skintone. A more egregious development in certain parts of the world is the enticement, kidnap, enslavement and/or coercion of women to be the *de facto* wives of warriors involved in quasi-religious wars, such as in the Middle East, or in pseudo-ideological civil wars, as in Sub-Saharan Africa and South America.[4]

The practice of bride kidnapping in many developing and emerging countries is usually imperative due to a shortage of women of marriageable age. This is a direct result of a cultural preference for male children resulting in abortions or infanticide of female foetuses and children. The problem was historically exacerbated by government policies that promoted family planning, usually at the behest of foreign aid agencies of industrialised countries and inter-government organisation like the World Bank, as prescriptive for economic development. Typically these women are trafficked from poorer parts of the country or other countries in the region of similar ethnicity, where the sex-ratio is more balanced. But the crime persists beyond the kidnapping and trafficking because these brides are treated as virtual slaves not just within the immediate family, but also to their multi-generational extended families[5]. Thus, all these forms of marriage would seem to encompass the whole range of shadow trades, from Tainted Trades to Murky Trades, depending on the extent to which consent in the process is allowed, the intermediaries involved and the legality of the marital contracts.

Children Disowned

Persons and agencies involved in the legitimate foreign adoption of children have been known to do so in dubious ways, particularly in countries undergoing and recovering from civil strife, national wars or natural disasters. While not typically included in human trafficking, the export of children from vulnerable families, from institutions or those orphaned by circumstance is a sizeable global business which covers the whole spectrum from the fully legal and compassionate to the highly questionable and exploitative[6]. The practice of child sponsorship in developing countries, often the economic mainstay of many charities, is fraught with ethical issues. Apart from the singling out of children to aid within communities, the use of local brokers, the infrastructure of periodic communications with donors, there can even be an underlying political agenda of the industrialised country encouraging sponsorship[7]. There is a modicum of racism in the process where children in Africa and Asia, for instance, tend to be promoted by charities as needing donations for institutional care and sponsorship for education, while children from Central and Eastern Europe tend to be actively made available and more readily accepted for adoption by families in the industrialised world.

A growing trend is orphanage tourism in Asia and Africa, where paying tourists from affluent countries seeking a unique experience provide unpaid volunteer work, pay for accommodation and make donations, with dubious benefit accruing to the children themselves.[8] Regardless, all these practices are patronising, even exploitative, of the poorest in developing countries for the profitability of legitimate charitable organisations in the industrialised world, which simultaneously exploit the gullibility of their well-meaning donors. As the agencies are typically legal organisations, while individual agents may not be, international adoption and sponsorship may yet be ethical and a seemingly humanitarian practice, and so would appear to range between the Tainted and Opaque Trades in the typology set out above.

Leased Reproduction

Related to transplant tourism, but even less researched, is the global business of birth surrogacy, where a woman from a developing country is implanted with a fertilised embryo and carries it to term, though at some physical and psychological risk. Done usually on behalf of a childless or gay-male couple, often from the industrialised world, this does not count as organ sourcing but rather as organ leasing for lower remuneration than in the couple's or individual's home country. In this respect, such reproductive services should be seen in neo-colonialist light. In all cases, the sperm and/or egg may be from one or both of the intended parents, or in both cases from donors. Given the ethical and legal issues surrounding the child, such as citizenship by birth, inevitable maternal bonding and child abandonment if there is a disability, certain countries have effectively banned surrogacy.[9] Hence the recruitment of poorer women in developing countries for birth surrogacy, which arguably makes this a form of borderless labour exploitation, and thus a shadow trade. Sometimes surrogacy is done in conjunction with fertility treatment that is also carried out abroad in an emergent or industrialised economy at a considerably lower cost than where the couple reside.[10] Furthermore, certain fertility and surrogacy procedures are carried out by medical professionals abroad, or stem-cell tourism may not be considered ethically acceptable or legally approved within the communities of the prospective parents. Even greater ethical concerns may attend to related research on stem cells, embryo harvesting and human cloning, which is undertaken in developing and emerging countries where there are more liberal or absent laws on these issues. Depending on whether the practices are legal in the countries involved and the agenda considered ethical, such forms of assisted reproduction could encompass Tainted and Opaque Trades.

Panaceas and Poisons

Medical Concoctions

Another contentious aspect of global healthcare may be generic pharmaceuticals, which are typically manufactured in emerging economies with technological expertise, and then marketed to developing countries. Citizens in the latter are unable to afford expensive life-saving medicines patented in the industrialised countries where the requisite research and development is conducted. Questionably, multinational drug manufacturers insist on charging similarly high prices in developing countries as in their own industrialised countries, despite the disparity in buying power. As drugs in the industrial world are often sold to government medical services at a discount, and are in turn subsidised to patients, the pharmaceutical industry practices in the developing countries of non-subsidised provision constitute a form of discrimination in their marketing. They have also lobbied their home-country governments to insist that all foreign medical aid must take the form of their patented drugs, even when cheaper generic drugs are available locally from emergent country sources[11]. Ironically, many of the 'big pharma' oligopolies, as neo-colonists, consider themselves immune from paying royalties to indigenous peoples for tapping their traditional remedies for proprietary drug development.

In many cases the pharmaceuticals manufactured in developing and emerging economies seek to replicate the patented ones, albeit without licence or by changing the formula for active constituents that are slightly different in order to circumvent patent laws. There is even a market for such drugs among the less affluent citizens of industrialised economies without socialised healthcare, such as the US, where people travel to neighbouring developing countries like Mexico for cheaper medicines or source them online via mail-order.[12] Admittedly, some of these pharmaceuticals are fake, either in not containing any active ingredients, and thus having no benefit beyond a placebo effect; or in containing harmful chemicals that could threaten health, even life. In both these cases, considerable profits are achieved by disreputable businesses at the expense of the vulnerable, especially in developing countries, thus constituting a shadow trade. Since the pharmaceutical corporations are legal, whether their production and marketing is for ethical or unethical ends would dictate their classification as either Tainted or Camouflaged Trades, on which opinion could be divided.

Germs and Toxins

Biological and chemical agents may be banned for use in war by international convention but being low-cost and devastating weapons they continue to be produced and deployed, most notably by dictatorial regimes, to assert control over locals or in anticipation of asymmetrical warfare with powerful foreign forces. The role of arms manufacturers in causing environmental fragility in war zones through poisonous residues, and their eventual repercussions for climate change, conflict over scarce resources and migrant flows are rarely enunciated.[13] Chemicals developed for the military to destroy foliage to better track troop and arms movements have had dire consequences for civilian and animal health and reproduction long after the conflict has ended, and have also affected food production and the livelihoods of local populations. Redundant chemicals, because use in weapons is forbidden by international treaties, have been repositioned as pesticides for crops, and primarily sold to developing countries, or donated through aid agencies, because their health dangers would not meet regulations in industrialised countries.[14] Sometimes developing countries are exploited as population test laboratories for testing chemical products, both for efficacy and potential harm to health, while disguised as socio-economic development aid. Hence, legal multinational corporations that have been complicit in manufacturing and exporting harmful chemical products under the sponsorship of their home governments, are thus, arguably, participating in Camouflaged Trade.

Narcotics Logistics

Most of the profits of cocaine sales, totalling USD85 billion, are generated in North America and Western and Central Europe, much of it laundered in Caribbean tax havens. Only USD1 billion is expended on production costs in the Andean region, while Latin American cartels selling to both local and overseas markets earn about USD18 billion. Drug smuggling represents about half of all transnational organised crime income and about 0.6–0.9 percent of world GDP, although the socio-economic costs of drug abuse are estimated to be twice as high as the criminal income generated.[15] Given its location alongside Central Asian countries where the opium is grown, Pakistan facilitates smuggling across shared borders mostly towards European markets. Despite legislation prohibiting money laundering, when fuelled by the narcotics trade it involves even the political and economic elite in related corruption, real estate, informal remittances, tax evasion, and the financing of terrorist organisations.[16] While drug smugglers need to launder large amounts of cash, and more frequently than other criminals, surprisingly they tend not to use international specialists in money laundering. They prefer to self-launder through small scale businesses such as currency exchange booths or at best other business fronts within kinship networks across the world, so their practices raise further challenges for tackling this pernicious shadow trade.[17]

The reason drug smuggling *per se* has not been covered in this book is that its topicality has resulted in extensive coverage in the media and in academic publications. While undoubtedly an illicit operation, the means by which drugs are transported are not entirely clandestine. Routes include the legitimate freight-forwarding and passenger aviation industries. Measures by industrialised countries to eradicate the trade in drugs have ranged from sponsoring expensive military campaigns to harsh border controls, all of which have had implications for human rights[18]. What has been unaddressed is the primary demand for these illicit drugs in North America and Europe where addiction of citizens can be treated affordably via drug rehabilitation. Instead their focus remains the violent disruption of the supply and transit zones in the developing and emergent world. Again, this constitutes a form of neo-colonial discrimination and dominance. For years, law enforcement and military campaigns have, quite evidently, not worked because the consequence of scarcity after crop destruction and confiscation only raises prices and encourages new suppliers to enter the market. Much as it is unpalatable to many industrialised countries, a radical solution to ruin this illicit business may be through demand management and price controls. This could be done via governmental control of duly tested supply from confiscated drug stockpiles at lower prices in conjunction with rehabilitation programmes for the addicts. However such humanitarian interventions may not be strictly feasible in those neo-liberal economies which lack the social provision of healthcare. Even though the narcotics industry does use some legal logistics and financial entities, its products are unquestionably harmful and its operations illegal, and so this would constitute a Murky Trade.

Requisitioning Resources

Stormy Waters

With water being indispensable to life, its scarcity or drought has devastating consequences for countries, with land degradation curbing sustainable development and exacerbating social tensions. Given the pressures to move towards economic liberalisation or restructuring from the World Bank and the IMF, developing countries have been compelled to privatise the provision of water to citizens in order to qualify for their loans. In the case of Bolivia, the government sold the water rights of its third-largest city to a firm owned by the US multinational corporation Betchel, resulting in the tripling of prices and the appropriation of all water, including that from home collection and used for farm irrigation. Admirably, the local community resisted the firm and managed to get the firm to exit the country, after which the latter demanded sizeable compensation from the government.[19] The construction of dams to provide electricity for industry and cities geographically far away has dire consequences for the rural poor, who are arbitrarily evicted from the surrounding area. This has been the case historically and presently in India, China, Egypt and Zimbabwe, among other developing countries, and it affects the livelihoods of hundreds of thousands of citizens uninvolved in the name of progress. In accessing aquifers or subterranean chambers of water in India, Coca-Cola has been responsible for lowering water levels of local wells and ruining local agriculture, exacerbating the effects of drought.[20] The human right to water is being increasing supplanted in developing countries by multinational corporations' demands for water and electricity, with the collusion of their neo-colonialist home governments and hegemonic inter-government organisations such as the World Bank. Thus, such practices with water – which may prove more valuable in the future than oil is today – would appear to constitute an Opaque or Camouflaged Trade, according to the typology of shadow trades by relative shades of legitimacy.

Despite the fragility of environments based on water and its contribution to unmistakable climate change, the latter is focused on even less in any discussion of resource depletion, even over that of wildlife and biodiversity heritage. A related but less documented phenomenon is the mining of beach sand from developing countries for construction and land reclamation projects, mostly abroad in emerging and industrialised economies, and the dire consequences this has for eco-systems and local livelihoods.[21] So, while claims over water were previously at the sub-national level, these are increasingly becoming a global and regional issue, with an inherent risk of armed conflict. As developing and emergent countries increasingly turn to conserving national water resources and to hydro-electricity to comply with carbon emission targets, other countries further down river or sharing a lake face dire consequences. This is happening with the Nile river, involving Zimbabwe, Ethiopia, Sudan and Egypt,[22] with the Tigris and Euphrates rivers, encompassing Turkey, Iraq and Syria,[23] and with the Mekong river, affecting Laos, Thailand, Cambodia and Vietnam.[24] Given that regional conflicts have been brewing for some years, many governments of those countries affected have reached tentative though unstable resolutions, without the involvement of multinational corporations or inter-government agencies. This outcome may yet hold lessons for other countries' planning developments along shared river systems worldwide, such as the Congo, the Ganges and the Amazon, which are vital to millions of people who live below the poverty line. Reliant as health, food, life and livelihood are on access to water, the latter must be enshrined as an inalienable human right by governments and exempt from being traded as a commodity by corporations.

Loss at Sea

Illegal fishing within national waters is well documented to have caused the depletion of fish stocks for fishermen from coastal regions, even of industrialised countries, and is estimated to cost USD2–15 billion.[25] Overfishing by ocean-going trawlers, often from China and Taiwan, results in reduced fish stocks for other emerging and developing countries whose coastal communities use small boats to fish in seas closer to shore. The phenomenon of fishermen resorting to piracy can be attributed to the loss of livelihood from coastal fishing due to overfishing by trawlers from these largely emergent and industrialised countries. The underlying resource looting, not to mention the ecological damage from fishing dragnets on the sea floor and general environmental degradation, would count as Camouflaged Trade at best, if not possibly a Murky Trade.

This shadow trade has socio-economic implications for unemployment, poverty, social disruption, irregular migration, urban shantytowns and piracy. Furthermore, the crew on these trawlers are reported to be subject to verbal abuse, strain from overwork and the threat of battery and death. Sometimes these people are victims of human trafficking from poorer regions of the countries of the boat-owners or of neighbouring countries[26]. This is not altogether different from the extensive employment of low-level crew from the developing world in ships owned by industrialised countries, whether luxury passenger liners or cargo carriers. Working at sea on these ships, which are often registered in developing countries or sailing under 'flags of convenience', these crew have no recourse to justice from law enforcement or employment regulations for their plight.[27] Typically, these ships are staffed with officers from the industrialised world, overseeing crew from developing countries who are paid considerably less, in typically neo-colonial fashion. When the employers are legal, as with shipping lines, their exploitative treatment of sailors should be categorised as an Opaque Trade, and where the employers may not be legitimate, such as in criminally-owned trawlers using coerced workers, this must be considered as being a Murky Trade.

Data Monetised

Global surveillance of consumers by media, communications and information technology firms on behalf of multinational corporation clients could debatably be exploitation of an intangible resource without national regulation. Consumers of these typically-free services may have consented to having their data mined, but seldom do they have much choice in the matter. Besides, the extent to which their activities online are monetised and sold is concealed from them. Even more concerning are the growing mergers and strategic alliances of online platforms, search engines and social media apps, notably by Google, Apple, Facebook, Amazon and Alibaba, thus creating a digital equivalent of the past US railroad 'robber barons'. These oligopolistic networks are able to aggregate data on individuals for sale to corporations for marketing purposes.[28] Consequent tracking, prediction and manipulative socialisation of behaviours via bots, click-baits, decks and troll-farms is possible not just by corporations but by political interests, including hostile foreign interests. The collection of DNA and facial recognition data by governments and corporations for use via artificial intelligence – for further profiling and socio-economic discrimination – urgently requires legislation, which is as yet inadequate to control it. Arguably a form of neo-colonial domination, this appears to be a Camouflaged Trade.

The increasing number of partnerships between governments and corporations on technology and access to each other's databases represent a growing shadow trade in information, rather than a utopian vision of 'smart living' through the 'Internet of Things'. Block-chain technology is said to revolutionise the way business is conducted, especially the traceability of resources and other inputs into products. This would be a commendable development towards reducing related shadow trades. Yet block-chain is also the foundation of crypto-currencies that are based on the mining of information, which in turn can facilitate untraceable transactions between secretive participants as evidenced by their extensive use on the so-called Dark Web.[29] Hence these economic activities are worthy of further investigation and future regulation as a conduit in various shadow trades, and ought provisionally to be classified as a Murky Trade.

Military Machinations

Technological Terrors

Cyber-warfare remains a novel technology that is fairly well guarded by leading countries in the arms trade for now, but it is capable of being emulated rapidly in many other countries with a reasonably good education system in the sciences and technology.[30] It is also immensely affordable, in diametric contrast to nuclear and other traditional armaments, and yet is capable of devastating effect in shutting down essential services in communications, utilities and infrastructure. Furthermore, cyber-warfare is a production extension for information technology and the electronic games industries, making them willing or commandeered participants in the shadow trade of arms.[31] Drones are another relatively new technology that is capable of surreptitious use and indiscriminate harm to civilians, euphemistically termed collateral damage, as well as military targets. Recent devastating events in the Middle East suggest that the technology has been replicated by emerging economies and supplied to insurgent forces in poor countries for use in asymmetric warfare.

Both cyber-warfare and its cognate of drones raise the question of the rules of military engagement when one party can wage war rather cowardly by remote action at no risk and where the military personnel perceive their destructive actions insensitively as merely a computer game. Preferred by militaries and governments for not requiring troops to be closer to the battlefield but literally thousands of miles away in pristine offices, this does not preclude moral injury to and the mental illness of the operators.[32] To date, there is no international regulation of such warfare, which is being increasingly deployed alongside conventional warfare. This would imply that countries and non-state actors are at liberty to act without the penalty of sanctions. Therefore, use of this unregulated form of warfare by a legal entity would constitute a Camouflaged Trade, but if the user is doing so illegally it should count as a Murky Trade.

Nuclear Renegades

The development of nuclear arms continues unabated as those countries that previously signed non-proliferation treaties abandon their commitments in the name of upgrading technologies, and emerging economies develop such bombs and choose to remain outside those treaties. In the US, nuclear arms are surreptitiously included under its Department of Energy and not the Department of Defense, a practice designed to misrepresent the actual size of the arms industry in the country, which is already the largest producer, buyer and supplier of arms internationally. The warning of US President Eisenhower against the growth and influence of a military-industrial complex has certainly gone unheeded even among the US's western allies, even as their forces downsized after the Cold War. Nuclear arms, technologies and materials located in the countries previously constituting the Soviet Union are not fully accounted for and the expertise of the underemployed scientists involved has apparently been available for purchase at the right price.[33] Interest by emergent economies as well as non-state actors in acquiring these technologies, whether for clean energy or finished arms, may represent one means by which these countries hope to pre-empt imperialistic interventions. This area has still been relatively under-researched as a major shadow trade. Since the non-state actors are typically illegal entities, sale to them of nuclear technologies or arms would definitely be a case of a Murky Trade, although debatably if the same products or services are sold to nation-states it would be classified only as a Camouflaged Trade.

Revolving Lobbyists

Major manufacturers of arms receive governmental research and development grants, and themselves fund scientific research in other technologies that may have military uses. Makers of civilian passenger and freight aircraft, such as Boeing, Airbus and Embraer, are subsidised indirectly by having their technological advancement funded by government contracts for the development of military aircraft. Relatively less attention has been paid to major US firms like the privately-listed Betchel and Halliburton, led by retired politicians and generals, via the 'revolving door', which have benefited from thousands of multimillion-dollar contracts from the Pentagon at the onset of regional wars.[34] This legalised corruption in industrialised countries has included lucrative contracts for the construction and operation of bases as well as reconstruction of infrastructure destroyed by war under home-government aid. More recently, the growth of private militaries, essentially mercenaries motivated financially in place of soldiers driven by patriotism, has gone largely unheeded. Arguably, lobbying by the arms industry for greater spending by their own hegemonic governments and their marketing of products and services to foreign governments have considerable impact on decisions to maintain a belligerent stance with other countries, if not a predisposition to go to war rather than explore diplomatic solutions. World peace would be detrimental to the shadow trade in arms, which could be said to have a vested financial interest in fomenting and sustaining conflict by countries and insurgent groups, and so their lobbying ought to be reckoned as a Camouflaged Trade.

Financial Siphonage

Institutionalised Fraud

Tax regulations have been redesigned deliberately by the respective governments to attract investments from each other. European countries like Switzerland, Luxembourg, the Netherlands, Ireland and the United Kingdom are demonstrably instrumental in tax avoidance through currency swaps, tax domicile rules and financial incentive zones. Ironically, in the UK this phenomenon of casino capitalism is duly supported by academic research from the Oxford Centre for Business Taxation, which is funded by businesses like HSBC, AstraZeneca, Cadbury and Rolls Royce. Availing themselves of such opportunities are other multinational corporations, such as insurance institutions like Prudential, liquor makers like Diageo, pharmaceutical developers like GlaxoSmithKline and AstraZeneca, and information technology giants like Microsoft, Google and Apple, not to mention Russian and other oligarchs, Swiss hedge fund managers, and famed UK soccer players.[35] Among the intermediaries in the process are banks like Barclays, HSBC, Citibank and Royal Bank of Scotland, and others among the global financial institutions that have unabashedly felt entitled to government bail-outs whenever in distress from their own investment speculation without incurring prosecutions for their financial shenanigans.

Despite the efforts of the US government to clamp down on money laundering and tax evasion worldwide, its own Caribbean territories, such as the Virgin Islands, are just as complicit in those shadow trades as British territories like the Cayman Islands. Both shadow trades deserve to be investigated. The institution and imposition of anti-laundering and anti-tax haven measures through the Financial Action Task Force (FATF) programme would be commendable except for the fact that a number of its fully-fledged member states offer financial secrecy. The FATF has been hypocritical in targeting banking secrecy from Panama and Hong Kong to Vanuatu and Guernsey, while overlooking US states such as Delaware and South Dakota, which allow secret trusts along with no personal and corporate income taxes for wealthy families worldwide, amounting to about USD800 billion.[36] Unethical creative accounting under the guise of tax planning is regrettably an entrenched practice among leading multinational accounting consultancies like KPMG, Deloitte, PwC and Ernst & Young, which act in the service of multinational corporations and wealthy individuals. Thus, these legal banks, consultancies and jurisdictions which are active in promoting unethical practices to the detriment of the governments and societies where they operate, should be categorised as participants in the Camouflaged Trades.

Payments Ransomed

While sometimes distinct in their operations and the criminals involved, maritime piracy and the kidnapping of persons are used as a means for raising funds which are then laundered for personal gain or for terrorism purposes. However, they are difficult to trace since the transactions are made in cash. Sea piracy may also be classified as a form of resource plunder, particularly when the cargo of the commandeered ships, which are mostly headed to the developed world, are filled with primary resources and agricultural produce from developing and emerging countries which are critically valuable for earning foreign exchange. The Somalian criminal syndicates comprise investors, shareholders, clan chiefs, local militia and various maritime professionals plus guards, translators and intermediaries who between themselves share the ransoms, which on average per ship had risen as high at USD9.2 million by 2010. Thus about 40–60 percent of the ransom funds tend to stay in Somalia.[37] While military resources have been directed by the EU and NATO to reduce the incidence of piracy off the Somalian coast, there has been no clear attempt to track the laundering of the proceeds from this crime through the global financial system and its possible funnelling towards terrorism finance.[38] Piracy for ransom has become a lucrative activity in certain parts of the world, but because the crews, management companies, ship owners, country of registry and insurers are based throughout the world, its resolution has become a multi-jurisdictional issue. Certainly, this enterprise, conducted by illegal entities via illegal means for unethical ends, is a Murky Trade.

Citizenship Sale

Another form of financial outflow is that of the trading of citizenship by developing countries to wealthy individuals for either a donation to the national government or to make an investment supposedly to create jobs and contribute to economic development.[39] Where investments are made, these can range from simply making a deposit with a local bank, purchasing an existing enterprise and/or starting a new business. In the latter two cases, there are no repercussions for their failure to create jobs, support local enterprises, bring in export income, pay the minimalist taxes (if any), or even to remain in business past a generous minimum period.

Predictably these citizenship schemes attract many who are involved more rigorously in illicit operations, corruption and embezzlement, who are keen to launder their funds as well as to be beyond the reach of law enforcement by their home countries and those in which they operate their borderless networks. Understandably, these countries prefer not to disclose how many citizenships were granted for donations, since this would require political accounting for the funds, which are often corruptly misappropriated.[40] Although an entrenched form of tax evasion and a conduit for money laundering related to shadow trades, citizenship sale has rarely been investigated. The government involved and its scheme are of course legal, and the beneficiaries may or may not have unethical purposes in mind, so this could be either a Tainted or a Camouflaged Trade.

Commentary in Conclusion

As this book has sought to demonstrate, corporations are complicit in the shadow trades at various levels of legitimacy but choose not to highlight it and largely ignore the dark side of their global businesses. In fact, these sectors go further to distract by promoting a consumerist lifestyle that is unquestioning about the people exploited, the resources used, the conflicts engendered, the waste created and other issues of unethical, if not illegal, practices. The prevalent promotion by the Washington Consensus institutions of public-private partnerships is a debatable prescription economic development. What is needed is neither glib denials of culpability by governments for socio-economic injustice nor tinkering around the edges by corporations in the name of social responsibility, but radical transformation of perspective, attitude and actions towards the shadow trades. This demands not just unilateral advocacy by isolated corporations against any specific shadow trade impinging on their own business, but also a concerted effort at corporate activism against all the shadow trades, at the very least those tainting their respective industries. Addressing the moral deficit in the neo-liberal capitalism *vis-à-vis* the borderless shadow trades could well mean reduced business profitability in the short term in the cause of ethical action towards environmental sustainability in consultation with governments and civil society.

───────────────── DIM DOMAIN ─────────────────

UNTANGLING THE DARK WEB

This book on shadow trades would undoubtedly invite the assumption that it is about all the hidden activity that resides on the Dark Web, which would be a tenuous link at best. Sometimes mistakenly conflated with the Deep Web, the Dark Web's primary

(Continued)

characteristic is being an extensive network of websites that are not accessible by the mainstream browsers and search engines. Requiring passwords to access them securely and not being searchable via the more common browsers, these sorts of sites are not necessarily of an illegal nature and often have a commonplace purpose. While increasing numbers of the world population have come to depend on the internet for news, information, communication and entertainment, they are also discovering that less of the data online is readily accessible.

Above and Underground

Strictly speaking, the Deep Web encompasses the Dark Web but also confidential databases, encrypted email services, web forums requiring registration, internet banking, scientific raw data and web pages behind paywalls, altogether said to be hundreds of times larger than the public internet. The Deep Web is also essential for political dissidents in authoritarian countries, whistle-blowers on corporate crime, citizen journalists and bloggers and human rights activists to deliver the truth and bring about justice. Some have developed or cloned social media sites on the Deep Web to circumvent the surveillance and data mining that is routinely carried out for marketing purposes. Confusingly, the benign part of the Deep Web is correctly identified also as the Dark Internet, but the latter term is unfortunately used in the mass media and social media as a synonym for the Dark Web. For the purposes of this section, only the term Dark Web will be used because it will be concerned with the nefarious trading that takes place there.

For security reasons government agencies have endeavoured to gather data via the Dark Web on terrorist groups and drug syndicates, and have shared these data with academics to enable research. Social networks analysis and text mining have been applied to understanding these websites in order to develop counter-measures. But often visual representation of the topic-based information gathered proved ineffectual because it did not elucidate any patterns, apart from identifying key members of networks.[41] Nonetheless, being able to identify the key members who orchestrate malicious activities is invaluable in the effort to shut down certain Dark Web networks. These players are typically characterised as being well connected to other suspicious sites while not being connected with legitimate ones.[42] Still, assumptions made about the proximity of their current links are not necessarily conclusive proof of alliances across networks. Furthermore, these linkages are difficult to ascertain with certainty given the fact that there may be missing links through communications outside the networks, either 'live' or at another part of the Dark Web, or even fake links to deliberately mislead.[43]

Suspicious Services

In contrast to users of the 'surface web' or 'clear-net', most originators and patrons of the Dark Web use the Tor encryption tool to hide their identities, and hence it attracts those for whom secrecy is premium. The Tor search engine uses multiple layers of encryption that disguise the location of the user, much like a VPN but by a quantum of effectiveness. Consequently, the Dark Web is where much illegal trading is conducted involving drug trafficking, child pornography, blackmail, counterfeiting, arms smuggling, terrorism planning and other such covert activities. Although the drugs trade had a modest start on the Dark Web, it is estimated by the UN to have increased by 50 percent year-on-year between 2013 and 2016. Guns sales to private citizens in the US have shifted to the Dark Web in anticipation of more stringent regulation by their government. In Europe, arms can be bought online for home delivery. Pornography can include acts not only involving children, but also of sexualised torture and the wanton killing of animals. Quite apart from guns, drugs, pornography and the like, Dark Web markets have offered hacked personal data from literally millions of people for sale, such as credit card details from stores, user information from phone companies, log-in credentials from email providers, even the medical records of citizens from government insurance agencies, all for about USD22 each. Buyers of such data can then extract financial compensation from corporations and individuals through ransomware.[44]

Hidden Wiki is the directory to the Dark Web that provides links to services like money laundering, contract killing, cyber-attacks and restricted chemicals, including instructions on making explosives. Terrorist groups have used the Dark Web to plan attacks, publicise their exploits and recruit via propaganda and, with access to the technology, they are capable of cyber-attacks in addition to real-life ones. The Dark Web has also been implicated in assassination, not just in contracting for it to be done, but in allowing betting by others on when it will occur, although some of these have been exposed as hoaxes and scams. A now-defunct website detailed medical experiments performed on homeless people, typically unregistered citizens, who consequently died. Robbing-to-order sites on the Dark Web are run by those skilled at stealing anything that any customer of this service can ill-afford or refuses to pay a legitimate price for. It enables bitcoin-based gambling, which is banned in the US, by allowing gamblers there to disguise their IP addresses. Crypto-currencies are recognised as undergirding most of the criminal transactions on the Dark Web.

Patrolling Online

The closure of illicit marketplaces like the infamous Silk Road, which dealt with drugs, and the regular break-up of paedophilia rings have been achieved quite effectively as a result of online policing in industrialised countries. It is worth noting that participants in the Silk Road saw it as not just a market for trading drugs, but as a site for subcultural discussion from a libertarian perspective about socially stigmatised behaviours and activism against the prohibition of drug consumption.[45] But closing down all Dark Web networks may not be viable in the long term and could prove unreasonable to those who genuinely benefit from these systems. For it seems almost as if the downsides of the Dark Web mostly impact citizens of democratic countries, while the benefits tend to accrue to those under authoritarian regimes. The issue of Dark Web secrecy, and thus its oversight, must be treated as a sociological issue rather than a

(Continued)

technological one. Monitoring can be achieved through mapping the hidden services directory, as well as the semantic analysis of customer databases and social forums.

Just as real-world lives benefit from law and order through judicious policing in industrialised countries, a similar practice for policing online could be adopted worldwide.[46] Exploits are malware-based on software's vulnerabilities before they are patched by their makers, and a marketplace exists for buying and selling such exploits priced on both the popularity of the software and the difficulty of cracking its code.[47] Software piracy that is commonplace in developing countries may appear as a form of resistance against powerful corporations controlling products like computer games, movies and programs. But these are also one means for transmitting viruses and cookies which gather valuable personal and financial data. Arguably, online crime such as on the Dark Web is not substantially different from crime in the real world, except for its utilisation of a new technology as its medium.

Crucial Queries

Are shadow trades a subset of Dark Web activities or are they fundamentally different in character, and if so, how? Since all networks on the Deep Web or Dark Internet are secretive, how is it possible to differentiate the nefarious from the mundane?

While legitimate corporations might not be dependent on the Deep Web, could these organisations source scarce services or goods that are available there when necessary? Can legitimate corporations utilise the Dark Web as an extension of their e-commerce strategy? If so, how and why? And if not, why not?

Would monitoring clandestine businesses on the Dark Web be essential or just helpful for intervening to restrict all or some forms of shadow trades? Since the Dark Web is global in its reach and its participants are generally untraceable, can any one country be capable of law enforcement?

If governments gain access to data on Deep Web networks, could they eventually breach the confidentiality that is essential to legitimate business competitiveness? Will shutting down Dark Web marketplaces undermine the shadow trades, or will this only drive those trades further underground?

FURTHER RESOURCES

Research Works

Mandel, R. (2011). *Dark Logic: Transnational Criminal Tactics and Global Security*. Stanford, CA: Stanford University Press.

Reichel, P., & Albanese, J. (eds.). (2013). *Handbook of Transnational Crime and Justice*. London: Sage Publications.

Shelley, L. I. (2018). *Dark Commerce: How a New Illicit Economy is Threatening our Future*. Princeton, NJ: Princeton University Press.

Storti, C. C., & De Grauwe, P. (eds.). (2012). *Illicit Trade and the Global Economy*. Cambridge, MA: MIT Press.

Informational Websites

Council on Foreign Relations [www.cfr.org/interactives/global-governance-monitor#!/]
OECD Directorate for Public Governance [www.oecd.org/gov/risk/illicit-trade.htm]
Transnational Alliance to Combat Illicit Trade [www.tracit.org/]
World Customs Union [www.wcoomd.org/en/topics/enforcement-and-compliance]
York University [https://nathanson.osgoode.yorku.ca/]

Annotated Documentaries

Chatham House (2018). *Dark Commerce: Technology's Contribution to the Illegal Economy* [57:11 min.]. Lecture on how technological and market forces behind e-commerce have also helped in the selling of illegal goods.

The International Institute for Strategic Studies (2015). *The Shadow Economy: How Illicit Trade Impacts Development and Governance* [1 h.]. Addressing the role of the illicit economy on poverty eradication.

A&E TV Network (2017). *The Triad - Organized Crime* [44:45 min.]. Addressing the Chinese transnational organised crime syndicates based in Greater China and countries with significant diasporic populations.

General Reading

Gilman, N., Goldhammer, J., & Weber, S. (eds.). (2011). *Deviant Globalization: Black Market Economy in the 21st Century*. Edinburgh: A&C Black.

Barker, T. (2014). *Biker Gangs and Transnational Organized Crime*. London: Routledge.

Keuck, A. (2009). *Illicit Transnational Businesses in a Global Economy: How Criminals and Terrorists Pay the Bills*. Lulu.com.

Endnotes

1. Naqvi, S. A. A., Ali, B., Mazhar, F., Zafar, M. N., & Rizvi, S. A. H. (2007). A socio-economic survey of kidney vendors in Pakistan. *Transplant International, 20*(11), 934–939.

2. Verloy, A. (2014). *Making a Killing: The Merchant of Death*. Washington, DC: Center for Public Integrity.

3. Belleau, M. C. (2003). Mail-order brides in a global world. *Albany Law Review, 67*, 595.

4. McAlpine, A., Hossain, M., & Zimmerman, C. (2016). Sex trafficking and sexual exploitation in settings affected by armed conflicts in Africa, Asia and the Middle East: systematic review. *BMC International Health and Human Rights, 16*(1), 34.

5. Kaur, R. (2013). Mapping the adverse consequences of sex selection and gender imbalance in India and China. *Economic and Political Weekly*, 37–44.

6. Efrat, A., Leblang, D., Liao, S., & Pandya, S. S. (2015). Babies across borders: The political economy of international child adoption. *International Studies Quarterly, 59*(3), 615–628.

7. Fieldston, S. (2014). Little cold warriors: child sponsorship and international affairs. *Diplomatic History, 38*(2), 240–250.

8. Rotabi, K. S., Roby, J. L., & McCreery Bunkers, K. (2016). Altruistic exploitation: orphan tourism and global social work. *British Journal of Social Work, 47*(3), 648–665.

9. Mohapatra, S. (2011). Achieving reproductive justice in the international surrogacy market. *Annals of Health Law, 21*(1), 191–200.

10. Twine, F. W. (2011). *Outsourcing the Womb: Race Class and Gestational Surrogacy in a Global Market* (2nd edn). New York: Routledge.

11. Smith, R. D., Correa, C., & Oh, C. (2009). Trade, TRIPS, and pharmaceuticals. *The Lancet, 373*(9664), 684–691.

12. Hall, A., & Antonopoulos, G. A. (2016). *Fake Meds Online: The Internet and the Transnational Market in Illicit Pharmaceuticals.* Basingstoke: Palgrave Macmillan.

13. Rappert, B. (2013). *Controlling the Weapons of War: Politics, Persuasion, and the Prohibition of Inhumanity.* London: Routledge.

14. Szöllösi-Janze, M. (2001). Pesticides and war: the case of Fritz Haber. *European Review, 9*(1), 97–108.

15. UNODC (2011). *Estimating Illicit Financial Flows Resulting from Drug Trafficking and other Transnational Crimes.* Vienna: United Nations Office on Drugs and Crime.

16. Qureshi, W. A. (2017). An overview of money laundering in Pakistan and worldwide: causes, methods, and socioeconomic effects. *University of Bologna Law Review, 2,* 300.

17. Malm, A., & Bichler, G. (2013). Using friends for money: the positional importance of money-launderers in organized crime. *Trends in Organized Crime, 16*(4), 365–381.

18. Comolli, V., & Hofmann, C. (2013). Drug markets, security and foreign aid. *Modernising Drug Law Enforcement Report 6.* London: International Drug Policy Consortium.

19. Otto, B., & Böhm, S. (2006). The people and resistance against international business: the case of the Bolivian 'water war'. *Critical Perspectives on International Business, 2*(4), 299–320.

20. War on Want (2007). Coca-Cola drinking the world dry. [https://waronwant.org/media/coca-cola-drinking-world-dry – accessed 18 October 2019].

21. Gavriletea, M. D. (2017). Environmental impacts of sand exploitation: analysis of the sand market. *Sustainability, 9*(7), 1118.

22. El-Fadel, M., El-Sayegh, Y., El-Fadl, K., & Khorbotly, D. (2003). The Nile river basin: a case study in surface water conflict resolution. *Journal of Natural Resources and Life Sciences Education, 32,* 107–117.

23. Akanda, A., Freeman, S., & Placht, M. (2007). The Tigris–Euphrates river basin: mediating a path towards regional water stability. *Al Nakhlah, 31.*

24. Goh, E. (2017). China in the Mekong River basin: the regional security implications of resource development on the Lancang Jiang. In R. Emmers & M. Caballero-Anthony (eds.), *Non-Traditional Security in Asia.* London: Routledge, pp. 237–258.

25. Liddick, D. (2014). The dimensions of a transnational crime problem: the case of IUU fishing. *Trends in Organized Crime, 17*(4), 290–312.

26. Chantavanich, S., Laodumrongchai, S., & Stringer, C. (2016). Under the shadow: forced labour among sea fishers in Thailand. *Marine Policy, 68*, 1–7.

27. Urbina, I. (2015). Sea slaves: the human misery that feeds pets and livestock. *The New York Times, 27*.

28. Mchawrab, S. (2016). M&A in the high-tech industry: value and valuation. *Strategic Direction, 32*(6), 12–14.

29. Fanusie, Y., & Robinson, T. (2018). Bitcoin laundering: an analysis of illicit flows into digital currency services. *Center on Sanctions & Illicit Finance*: memorandum, January.

30. Liff, A. P. (2012). Cyberwar: a new 'absolute weapon'? The proliferation of cyberwarfare capabilities and interstate war. *Journal of Strategic Studies, 35*(3), 401–428.

31. Billo, C., & Chang, W. (2004). *Cyber Warfare: An Analysis of the Means and Motivations of Selected Nation states.* Hanover, NH: Institute of Security Technology Studies, Dartmouth College.

32. Wallace, D., & Costello, J. (2017). Eye in the sky: understanding the mental health of unmanned aerial vehicle operators. *Journal of Military and Veterans' Health, 25*(3), 36.

33. Lee, R. W. (2000). *Smuggling Armageddon: The Nuclear Black Market in the former Soviet Union and Europe.* New York: St Martin's/Griffin/Palgrave Macmillan.

34. Maogoto, J. N. (2006). Subcontracting sovereignty: commodification of military force and fragmentation of state authority. *Brown Journal. World Affairs, 13*, 147.

35. Brooks, R. (2014). *The Great Tax Robbery: How Britain Became a Tax Haven for Fat Cats and Big Business.* London: Oneworld Publications.

36. Scannell, K., & Houlder, V. (2016). US tax havens: the new Switzerland. *FT. com*, 19 May.

37. FATF (2011). *Organised Maritime Piracy and Related Kidnapping for Ransom.* Paris: Financial Action Task Force.

38. House of Lords (2009). Money laundering and the financing of terrorism. London: The Stationery Office.

39. van Fossen, A. (2007). Citizenship for sale: passports of convenience from Pacific island tax havens. *Commonwealth & Comparative Politics, 45*(2), 138–163.

40. van Fossen, A. (2018). Passport sales: how island microstates use strategic management to organise the new economic citizenship industry. *Island Studies Journal, 13*(1).

41. L'huillier, G., Alvarez, H., Ríos, S. A., & Aguilera, F. (2011). Topic-based social network analysis for virtual communities of interests in the dark web. *ACM SIGKDD Explorations Newsletter, 12*(2), 66–73.

42. Li, Z., Alrwais, S., Xie, Y., Yu, F., & Wang, X. (2013). Finding the linchpins of the dark web: A study on topologically dedicated hosts on malicious web infrastructures. In *2013 IEEE Symposium on Security and Privacy*, 19–22 May 2013, San Franciso. pp. 112–126.

43. Xu, J., & Chen, H. (2008). The topology of dark networks. *Communications of the ACM, 51*(10), 58–65.

44. Reilly, C. (2017). *Dark Web 101: Your Guide to the Badlands of the Internet* [www.cnet. com/news/darknet-dark-web-101-your-guide-to-the-badlands-of-the-internet-tor-bitcoin/ – accessed 10 October 2017].

45. Maddox, A., Barratt, M. J., Allen, M., & Lenton, S. (2016). Constructive activism in the dark web: cryptomarkets and illicit drugs in the digital 'demimonde'. *Information, Communication & Society, 19*(1), 111–126.

46. Jardine, E. (2015). The Dark Web dilemma: Tor, anonymity and online policing. *Global Commission on Internet Governance Paper Series,* 21.

47. Chertoff, M., & Simon, T. (2015). The impact of the dark web on internet governance and cyber security. Global Commission on Internet Governance, Paper No. 6. [www. cigionline.org/publications/impact-dark-web-internet-governance-and-cyber-security – accessed 05 May 2019].

CHAPTER 10
IMPERATIVE OF ENGAGEMENT

Credit: Kelly Lacy/Pexels

Retrospective and Prospective

While the shadow trades might exploit ambiguities in the politico-legal systems governing global business, there is a near-universality of moral standards that should apply to their victims. The consequences of such trades affect people around the world differentially, with the bottom strata in lesser developing countries among the most vulnerable to exploitation. This book is aimed at enabling citizens, consumers, workers, union officials, government policy-makers, business executives, civil society and academic researchers alike to collaborate at addressing the very real human fallout from the shadow trades. Through proposing a typology, the author intends that all concerned may be sensitised to how legitimate products and services in the global marketplace may have a symbiotic relationship with illegitimate businesses and illicit operations. This chapter revisits various concepts and ideas raised throughout the book, namely intersecting business, illegal organisations, illicit operations, government negligence, market re-regulation, neo-colonialism, stakeholder sensitisation, moral values, ethical practice and socio-economic justice. In concluding this book, a clarion call is made for the re-regulation of global business, legitimacy discernment, demand de-marketing, unsustainable consumption, activist research and corporate advocacy, among other antidotes to the shadow trades.

Appraising the Concomitants

Globalised Economy

Deregulated markets

The burgeoning of the shadow trades documented in this book is certainly attributable to the lowering of barriers to international trade, just as the inability of governments to constrain them is due to the weakening of the powers of individual countries through their membership in regional and international economic groupings. Furthermore, the rise of capitalist free-market ideology inhibits government intervention in the economy in any way that might affect businesses, whether legal or otherwise.[1] The resultant shrinking of public funding makes it prohibitive for governments, even those which have the political will, to regulate, investigate and prosecute corporate crimes. Arguably neo-liberal globalisation has fostered the growing socioeconomic inequity between countries as well as within them that has resulted in the conditions conducive to many shadow trades. Organised crime's ascendancy in formerly planned economies such as in Eastern Europe, the former Soviet Union and other politically unstable regions is an exemplar of the cost of marketisation without attendant institutions for corporate oversight, the rule of law, an independent media and the establishment of civil society groups. New communications technologies, like the internet and mobile telephony, have been a boon to legitimate global businesses, but are likewise of benefit to illicit ones, and make it far more challenging for governments to track down their operations.

Inequitable investment

While protection of local industry in the industrialised world via tariff and non-tariff barriers might seem politically astute, it can have dire consequences in the developing world. What is rarely acknowledged is that such social injustice and economic violence on a global scale can and does come back to haunt the industrialised world, through the problems of human trafficking, drug smuggling and terrorism. Much publicity may have attended the launch of the UN Millennium Development Goals (MDGs), but the momentum seems to have lapsed as the world economic downturns place at risk commitments made by industrialised countries even as the prospects for developing countries worsen. The more comprehensive UN Sustainable Development Goals (SDGs) is an arena where economists in academia, government, the private sector and non-government organisations might advocate and lobby for needful changes in economic trade policies that can address the poverty that feeds labour exploitation. Even though host countries might prefer to attract the highly skilled, it is the low-skilled who are in demand abroad to do jobs which their own citizens may not be willing to do, even if unemployed themselves. Still, migrant workers, especially the undocumented, keep jobs at a low wage for citizens of the industrialised country as well, and industry has little incentive to mechanise, computerise and otherwise increase the labour productivity of locals through investment in training. The dominance of the globalised free-market economy, characterised by the interdependence of all countries, industrialised, emergent and developing, has the potential for neo-colonialism, of which the shadow trades are a symptom.

Shortsighted protectionism

The lack of access of legitimate agricultural or horticultural products in developing countries to industrialised countries is due to high tariffs barriers and farming subsidies in the latter, such as the US and EU, although these are often disguised as non-tariff barriers requiring compliance with phytosanitary and quality standards. Low and declining commodity prices set largely by institutional buyers in the industrialised world threaten the livelihoods of millions in agriculture and mining in the developing world, in a form of neo-colonialism. This often leaves the citizens of the latter countries with little recourse but to grow cash crops such as coca and poppy plants, which can be converted into illicit drugs to be smuggled for lucrative sale into the former countries. Alternatively, these peasants have themselves smuggled or are trafficked into industrialised countries to work in unsustainable agriculture, sweat-shop factories or the criminal underworld. So industrialised countries could find it more cost-effective to ease their import barriers to agricultural and other products or to raise the prices paid for resources, rather than to spend on border controls and other social programmes for migrants, legal or otherwise, or even on generic aid to their home countries. Policies based on political expedience and economic avarice in the industrialised world actually work to the detriment of their own societies and economies too, and ought to be lobbied against by their citizenry, once they are better-informed and ethically challenged about these shadow trade linkages.

Governmental Delinquency

Abdication of sovereignty

Ironically, countries that would go to war to defend their sovereignty over peripheral territories, which are usually laden with natural resources, are only too ready to declare urban or coastal areas free from their jurisdiction so that their own citizens might be employed under conditions that are otherwise illegal. Labour is patently exploitable in free-trade zones where neither the laws of the host country or the home coun-try apply, ostensibly to create employment at the cost of foregoing tax revenue and denying social services. Employment in free-trade zones is one magnet for the poor from deprived parts of the country or region, and thus a catalyst for trafficked, smug-gled, bonded or otherwise exploited labour. The disenfranchisement of citizens from legitimate opportunities to improve their economic lot compels them to create or participate in the quasi-legal, extra-legal or illegal parallel economy, at home or abroad via irregular migration. There has been evidence of exploited labour on fishing ves-sels operating in international waters far from their home countries. Furthermore, by fishing near or in national waters, these often breach maritime resource rights granted to developing governments that are delinquent and powerless to enforce sovereignty. Worse yet are the conflict zones where government forces, rival armed groups or for-eign occupiers exploit people and resources because the rule of law no longer operates.

Civil and regional conflict

The onset of violent conflict in a country is usually the culmination of an extended political struggle in which the economic rights of one or more of its constituent groups have been denied full fruition. Unfortunately, this can be unethically sponsored in post-colonial countries by former colonial powers, including via arms and military forces, with a vested interest in having one pliable group gain control over another for strategic reasons. Research has demonstrated that prolonged conflict is a trap that keeps countries poor long after the initial cause has passed.[2] The resultant state of war between rival claimants to civil authority provides the critical ingredients for an illegitimate economy to develop and the shadow trades to prosper. Under the barrel of the gun, slave labour and stolen minerals result, which in turn feed into the jewellery industry, industrial processes, food chains and household electronics globally. In reality, most buyers are unaware of a product's supply chain. They tend not to enquire about the origins of their purchases or else find any shadow trades hard to connect with the end-product. Whatever their salutary intentions, embargoes imposed by countries that are in conflict on one another, or by hegemonic powers, invariably spawn large-scale smuggling, another shadow trade, ironically at times with the collusion or at least the knowledge of both sets of countries concerned.

Corruption of officialdom

In many developing and emergent countries where government officials are underpaid and law enforcement weak, whole sections of the economy are actively involved in the shadow trades. These include unethical diamond mining in West Africa, hardwood timber harvesting in Southeast Asia, trafficking women in Eastern Europe and drug smuggling in Latin America, often for the markets of their post-colonial powers. Trafficked and smuggled peoples, for instance, are not always able to seek protection in the countries to which they are transported since often, on being rescued or detected, they are repatriated to their countries of origin. Once home they can be subject to retribution from all the parties complicit in their trafficking, including corrupt police and other government departments.[3] Most transnational threats to countries from their black or grey economy come from individuals and groups within, not from other nation-states, unless the latter are thoroughly corrupted by the former.[4] Sometimes government officials, political leaders or other influential persons in a country are indirect participants in the shadow trades, by being paid to overlook or facilitate, just as they had done in historic imperialism with immoral slavery, looting, violence and smuggling. More often than not, they facilitate it unwittingly either by incompetent inaction or misguided policies such as trade embargoes, industry subsidies, and prison labour or armed conflicts within or outside their countries. Failure to tackle state capture by the wealthy and to promote socio-economic development eventually leads to post-colonial citizens voting with their feet to leave for imperialistic economies, thus undermining the nationalist rhetoric of political independence.

Corporate Culpability

Production problematic

Global supply chains involving child labour or forced labour, minerals from war zones, the dumping of toxic wastes from manufacturing processes or discarded products and pollutants left in the country of production often result in or from products that are marketed legitimately in industrialised, emergent and developing economies. Many legitimate businesses share the same supply chains, use the inputs of or are used by shadow trades, with or without their knowledge, and are thus tainted. Human trafficking and organ harvesting, for instance, uses travel agencies, ships and airlines, some of which might treat it as a lucrative if immoral sideline. Legitimate logistics may be done on behalf of corporations which might be in ethically questionable trades, such as in arms or waste disposal. Even perfectly legitimate businesses may have owners or managers that use trade mis-invoicing as a cover for illicit operations, as in money laundering and tax evasion. Their consumer or industrial clients are invariably made complicit, with or without consent, for it is reasonable to expect that a number would withdraw their custom on realising the whole context of the practice. Often it is the consequences of adverse publicity or consumer boycotts for revenue streams, profitability and stock value that drive a corporation towards corporate social responsibility, rather than the moral compass of its leadership. Espousing subscription to the principle of corporate citizenship needs to encompass taking note of societal consensus, instead of seeking to ignore, undermine or overturn it.

Consumerist propaganda

The capitalist economic system is highly dependent on persuading consumers via the soft power of media of their need for the goods and services produced by the free market. Advertising and programming, then, must share some responsibility for fostering dissatisfaction among citizens of developing and transitional countries with their standard of living, constituting a form of cultural imperialism. One consequence of such propaganda for capitalist consumerism is oftentimes that lower economic classes in developing countries in Asia, Africa and Latin America are prepared to undertake risky economic migration to the industrialised world. Thus, they are particularly vulnerable for injustice by traffickers and smugglers and face the attendant hardships of living at the margins of societies in Europe, Australasia and North America. Rather too late do these economic migrants realise that the grass is not always greener on the other side of the industrialised/developing border, particularly as newcomers and illegal aliens. Public education ought decisively to be directed to highlighting the downside of the various forms of exploited labour, whether trafficked, forced or otherwise illegal, in the societies of origin, transit and destination.

Mediated messages

The commercial media, advertising and public relations industries today constitute the propaganda arm of the capitalist economic system, for the corporations as well as the governments of neo-liberal persuasion, in much the same way that government media were and are still used in totalitarian societies to promote ideology. This misinformation and disinformation are especially so with the burgeoning of commercial television channels, domestic, regional and global, under the dictates of deregulation and marketisation. Even publicly funded media, if these continue to exist at all, are increasingly dependent on advertising and sponsorship revenue. As governments reduce their funding, these media abdicate their journalistic mandate to inform and educate society, especially for the next generation of citizens, and adopt editorial content favourable to marketers. Often multinational corporations outsource production and marketing to, or are in joint ventures with, local firms that have strong connections to the regime in power. These firms are owned by the political and economic elite who may also own commercial media or be able to apply unjust pressure on public media. Imperative instead is the fostering of a global counter-culture of sustainable living to counteract the dominance of consumerism that is promoted by the market-dominant media.

Catalysts for Remediation

Ethical Economics

Fairer trade

Just as there was a revolution over the bankruptcy of the communist economic system some 30 years ago, symbolised by the fall of the Berlin Wall, it now seems a matter of time before contemporary societies seek at least an evolutionary reform of the hyper-capitalist system pervasive in the US and promoted worldwide. Fairer trade terms in the longer term, along with targeted funding in the short term, would have arguably far better consequences in fast-tracking the achievement of sustainable development, a just peace and the security of the whole world – industrialised, emergent and developing alike.[5] The way that citizens commute, live, work, produce and consume in a world with finite resources can only lead to collective destitution and environments conducive for the illegitimate and illicit. For too long now, economics has trumped ethics in strategy and policy, while corporations have forgotten their roots in the historic guilds which professed no conflict between their civic responsibility and enterprise performance. Rather than denials of culpability in or just token addressing of the shadow trades in their businesses under the guise of corporate social responsibility, a progressive transformation of perspective, attitude and actions is needed, even if it is incremental over time. Neo-liberals who are quick to cite Adam Smith's notion of the 'invisible hand' of the market in their deification of profit ought to be mindful that as a political economist Smith also advocated strongly for the equitable redistribution of wealth.

Sustainable business

Given economic globalisation, governments are constrained by neo-liberal capitalism from instituting regulations on corporations such as those to protect the human rights of workers, the conservation of resources or the taxing of finances. Hence there is a growing dependency between governments and corporations – nationally, regionally and internationally – for mutual existence and endurance, often at the expense of their citizens of from the lower and middle classes. Consumerism becomes endemic, driven by market trends, media propaganda, unsustainable production and technological obsolescence. The destruction of forests for industrial-scale agriculture and conflict-zone mining for manufacture harm land and waterways, while dumping and recycling of waste pollute the air and cause other forms of environmental degradation.[6] Climate change is an imminent threat to the sustainability of this planet, which has potential for social unrest and conflict. The arms trade often fuels conflict over scarce resources. Refugees, whether as a consequence of war or of climate change, in turn create demand for human trafficking and people smuggling. All of these contribute to the resource depletion, armed conflict, exploited labour and generation of waste, among other related shadow trades, with all their implications for global issues of climate change, health epidemics, intractable poverty, social unrest, armed conflicts, and so on. Thus all shadow trades are causally interrelated and mutually reinforcing, and their negative impact cannot be mitigated singly.

Accountable responsibility

Currently corporations are required to declare their societal and environmental impact, but it seems to be a token compliance to protect their public reputation, government relations, brand equity and customer loyalty. More cynical is the propensity of corporations to co-opt social responsibility concerns through such measures as cause marketing and purpose marketing to their own economic advantage. There are no structures and systems to test the veracity of those claims, much less to penalise misleading information and deliberate misrepresentation. For instance, despite attempts by government to regulate disclosure and require consent, consumers are not in a position to decline electronic monitoring, in order to be able to use online services. Consequently, this represents pseudo-transparency because there are legal and financial consequences, which seem to be all that matter as far as share prices and management bonuses go. Until there is criminalisation for even tenuous participation in the shadow trades, corporate audits and governmental pronouncements may well be insufficient at reversing the growth trends. Hence alongside non-government organisations, political leadership and civil society groups, the academic disciplines and the related professions have a role to play in demonstrating how borderless business networks may perpetuate socio-economic injustice via involvement the various shadow trades, and how these might be mitigated through interventions (Figure 10.1).

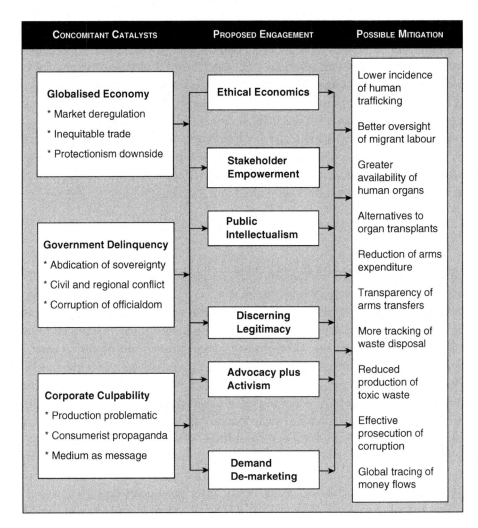

Figure 10.1   Catalysts, engagement and mitigation of the shadow trades

Demand De-marketing

Promoted ignorance

Most consumers are blissfully unaware that the products and services they use have the taint of questionable global business or shadow trades. Medical clients of transplant tourism are kept from full knowledge of the organ harvesting, invariably involving the poor. Patrons of the adult or pleasure industry at home and abroad tend to be rendered oblivious to the plight of the trafficked sex workers under the fantasy marketing involved. Salutary achievements have been made in the marketing of products certified not to utilise child labour, although more needs be done to ensure that this does not drive children counter-productively into labouring less visibly as domestic help, or even more exploitatively into the local sex trade or pushing their families into destitution. Regardless of criticism for neo-colonial paternalism, the use of global certification in the garment, precious-stone and furniture markets has gone a long way towards creating consumer awareness of the sources of these products in conflict zones, of protected rainforests illegally harvested, of countries under repressive regimes, of products made with prison labour and the like. On the other hand, all such commendable measures, including tracking via block-chain technologies, could prove ineffectual if the socio-economic conditions of the home countries of these potential economic migrants remain desperate due to war, civil strife, climate change, trade barriers, land acquisition, financial exploitation and the like.

Strategic awareness

Raising awareness of the socio-economic complexities undergirding the shadow trades is an arena where academics and practitioners in corporate communications, public relations, advertising, social marketing and related fields might contribute their expertise. Moreover, consumers might be assumed to be reasonable human beings when faced with the facts, instead of misinformation or disinformation. There ought to be creative communications and investigative media that seeks to trigger cognitive dissonance and pangs of moral conscience at transacting for such services, for which the best marketing minds might apply themselves. Campaigns against sex trafficking or human organ harvesting might be co-sponsored by the regulated medical and entertainment industries. More radically, laws ought to be amended in order that any industry, its suppliers and its clients could be charged with implicit complicity in the crimes involved, along with the various actual traffickers, brokers and facilitators, even if the latter group can only be charged in absentia and/or remain out of legal reach abroad. Again, academics in management, ethics, communications, media and law can be at the forefront of urging corporations and governments into sponsoring such social marketing campaigns to change attitudes towards and dampen demand for various shadow trades through synergistic carrot-and-stick approaches.

Stakeholder Empowerment

Agenda setting

Profound political-economic, technological, ecological and cultural change in recent decades has fostered dialogue and collaboration between industry and civil society on such issues as human rights and labour conditions.[7] The movement towards quality production and certification to global standards ought to be extended to include stringent monitoring of manufacturing for the ethical sourcing of all inputs, not just their nominal supply and end-processes. Such certification of legitimate production could prove attractive to multinational corporations in terms of brand image, risk management and cost reduction for profitability, while its value to NGOs would include verifiable change, poverty alleviation and cost-effective lobbying.[8] The key motivation for in-depth research into the shadow trades must surely be greater accountability by governments and corporations for any symbiosis between legitimate and illegitimate business, even if this may jeopardise funding from both public and private sources. Policy-makers and officials objecting to counter-productive measures advocated by politicians and party platforms, which are often at odds with the relevant physical or social sciences and international treaties, need to be heeded and not accused of constituting a dissident 'deep-state', possibly influenced by other governments. Further, governments and corporations will have to be nudged behaviourally and economically[9] by citizens and consumers rather than vice versa into moral action by widespread investigative journalism, adverse publicity and targeted activism, since they seem not to be persuaded otherwise by dispassionate discourse confined to scholarly conferences, journals and books.

Boundary staking

The link between the shadow trades and legitimate corporations in the industrialised world needs to be more clearly demarcated. While the growth of electric cars in industrialised economies is widely applauded as being an environmental boon, nickel incorporated in their batteries is mined in developing countries such as in Guatemala, which has a high incidence of organised crime and exploitative labour. Likewise, sand mining to support the construction industry of booming cities of the emergent economies involves dredging beaches and seas of neighbouring developing countries that destroys their eco-systems, marine resources, health and livelihoods. Bonded labour has been found in the sand mining and the construction industry, as well as its workers being vulnerable to kidney harvesting. One of the largest industries in the world is tourism, which is frequently cited as a cause of land degradation in the developing world as hotels, beach resorts, golf courses and other amenities encroach on public land accessible to or lived on for generations by poor communities without title. While the argument is typically made that this is compensated for by job opportunities and spending by tourists from industrialised and emergent economies, the wider social impact of such developments has had inequitable socio-cultural and political-economic costs on local communities, which need to be factored into the economic model.

Privilege shaming

The mega-rich, or the 1 percent of the world's population who reputedly own almost 80 percent of its wealth, are known for flaunting it with luxury homes, yachts, holidays and benefaction.[10] This is done without a trace of embarrassment over the means by which it was earned, from dubious business practices and governmental corruption to illicit operations, embezzlement and tax evasion. It is remarkable how business leaders are turned to by governments to lecture them on global economic policy, as annually at Davos, even while they continue to not meet their financial obligations to society. Multinational corporations and their owners have increasingly turned to charitable giving and development initiatives where they have little expertise in various countries that they have shamelessly exploited. Now they patronisingly find fault with public underfunding in areas such as health or education, and play the generous benefactor. Remarkably, celebrities have cynically taken on and been widely condoned in the role of global activists on economic development and international relations, fields in which they have little expertise but much to gain in personal brand enhancement.[11] Such contributions are not without perks in tax deductibility, non-profit status and reputational dividends, sought not altruistically but cynically by corporations and individuals who determinately fail to be transparent about all their economic affairs. In a world of increasingly scarce resources and drastic economic inequity, there ought to be societal mores towards the obscenity of mega-riches, which are conserved for generations to come via prudently structured family trusts to evade rightful taxes, flaunted in ostentatious lifestyles, made into legacy endowments and are rewarded by celebrity.

Pedagogy against Oppression

Academic Conundrum

Normative research

While researchers have documented corporate trends and analysed successful business models, few have had the gumption to propose realistic modes for reducing this economic injustice on the 99 percent of citizens who are subject to full taxes while being deprived of social benefits through corporate financial shenanigans. Social scientists need to desist from skirting around questionable practices while indulging in esoteric theorising on established topics in pursuit of highly ranked publications. Since the wealthy benefit as much as other citizens, from public infrastructure, they need to be held accountable for expecting the middle and lower classes to bear a disproportionate burden for funding these. Since corporations invariably exploit loopholes in tax regimes, social scientists must promote the adoption of public policies for assessing their income and assets on a worldwide basis. Until there are penalties beyond punitive fines to actual imprisonment for tax evasion, wealthy individuals and corporate managers will have no incentive to be compliant with existing or future laws for the social good. Likewise, unless arms makers and dealers are at joint risk of prosecution with their clients for crimes against humanity, they have no incentive to curtail their lucrative trade. Scholars need to argue with well-researched facts for why the injustices perpetuated via shadow trades ought to be subject to punishment as crimes. In essence, they need to be unafraid to speak truth to power, instead of obfuscating with academic jargon, and mobilise others to take up the cudgels of societal transformation.

Risk aversion

Many shadow trades are controlled by criminal gangs, although sometimes also by corrupt police forces or renegade armed forces, all of whom have no qualms about violence towards those who would threaten their lucrative sources of income.[12] Hence, academic researchers – much like investigative journalists and enforcement-officials are at risk of their lives, if not of physical harm or kidnapping, or at least the threat thereof.[13] Much research analysis will doubtless have to depend on secondary sources for quantitative data and trusted informants for qualitative data. Yet there are already considerable data available on the extent of the shadow trades, even though these can at times be differing 'guesstimates' that need to be triangulated or otherwise harmonised across sources, and preferably supplemented by primary data. Quite self-evidently, quantitative methodologies such as surveys, or even some qualitative ones like focus groups, would not work effectively in researching illegiti-mate, quasi-legal or otherwise highly sensitive shadow trades. This would instead call for recognition of the place of surreptitious ethnographic-style case research as an ethical, valid, if unconventional, contributor to inductive knowledge in this fraught sub-discipline of global business. Most of all, academic research evaluation needs to resist the stultifying encroachment of the market criteria of utilitarianism, funding, efficiencies, impact factors and citation counting[14] in favour of societally invaluable knowledge and engaged public intellectualism.

Re-writing education

Most books, cases and courses on business ethics deal with questions of manag-ers acting immorally, although sometimes perfectly legally, within legitimate firms, government and non-government organisations. What has not been discussed is their indirect involvement in illicit operations run by criminal gangs, officials, clans, armies, militia, rebel groups and so on, blinded by the pursuit of competi-tiveness, growth and profit in a hyper-capitalist ethos. Management literature, both academic- and practitioner-oriented, seems concerned with corporate social responsibility primarily for the enhancing of shareholder value, rather than corporate advocacy against illegitimate businesses and altruistic engagement against the socio-economic injustices these perpetuate. Rather than focusing on *post-hoc* systemisation and value-free theory, ideally education ought instead to be about problem analysis through dialogue and collaborative action to alleviate oppression and empower the exploited.[15] There needs to be a re-education of students, scholars, journalists and all thinking citizens that socialism is not as tarnished as communism and incompatible with a market system, but as evidenced by the Keynesian economy policies adopted in the aftermath of the Great Depression and World War II. Thus, critical academia in the social sciences may collectively hold the key, not just to analysing the causes of shadow trades, but also to bringing about social, political and economic change in the contexts where these trades are prevalent. In much the same way as academia as a whole was found wanting in not forewarning about the consequences of unregulated financial markets that led to the global economic crisis of the late 2000s and early 2010s, we might be seen as irrelevant to yet another critical socio-ethical issue in the world today.

Discerning Legitimacy

Identifying and distancing

By and large, advocates of neo-liberalism and free-market capitalism appear to neither address the immorality of the shadow trades that are parasitic on the world economy, nor the economic inequities resulting from the legitimate operations of multinational corporations unwittingly condoned by governments. It took solidarity between civil society activists and non-government organisations to spearhead the requisite of social responsibility now being placed on the agenda of corporations, even if it sometimes remains tokenism on the part of the latter. Perhaps legitimate corporations need likewise to be educated into distancing themselves from illicit operations that nonetheless share the same supply chains, financial institutions, communications technologies and favourable trade treaties, thus tarnishing consumers and citizens alike. Instead of lip-service by corporations about the need to be consultative to all stakeholders, radical change would require communities, governments, workers, suppliers and consumers to be represented at the board level with decision-making rights. It is not all that far-fetched as communities and cities worldwide have pioneered such equitable structures, typically following conflict and crisis. Far more than corporate social responsibility narrowly defined and practised, the need is for corporate advocacy, activism and action against all forms of shadow trade – including those at some geographic or economic distance from one's own corporation and industry. The uncritical promotion of international trade as the means of co-opting developing and emergent economies into the neo-liberal capitalist world economy on the questionable promise of equitable trade terms and sustainable economic growth needs to be proactively challenged as demonstrating elements of neo-colonialism by the industrialised world.

Extrication and reformation

The shadow trades are inextricably entwined with and parasitic on legitimate business in the world economy, and thus cannot be eliminated without severe, somewhat unpredictable consequences to the latter. In fact, some suggest such deviant globalisation may be the only means by which many in the developing economies can participate in and profit from the global free market, largely by meeting pent-up demand by circumventing the regulatory environment of trading nations.[16] If these trades are facilitated by the same factors as legitimate borderless business, then policies designed to impact one would be quite certain to affect the other. But what if their relationship can be transformed from being symbiotic to being competitive business sectors, such that market forces are harnessed to favour the legitimate business over the shadow trades and be ethically sensitised to demand accountability of businesses. Perhaps the catalyst could be consumers, once they are made more aware of the shadow trades in the supply chains of products, and convinced of their agency through boycotting corporations that do not comply with ethical standards as a form of civil disobedience, while rewarding those that do so stringently with greater demand despite higher prices. Or is it best achieved by governments individually or cooperatively penalising multinational corporations with suspicious links to the shadow trades, while compensating with subsidies and tax breaks businesses that endeavour scrupulously not to have such contact? Ultimately all these interventions may only work if not just corporations and industries are prosecuted for contravention of laws committed abroad, since these have the financial means to fund litigation or public relations. Instead individual managers and directors have to be held jointly and severally legally liable with their corporations for failing to act against the shadow trades if the undergirding moral imperative is to be taken seriously by all.

Critique for Intervention

Public Intellectualism

Inter-disciplinary collaboration

The first step to tackling the shadow trades has certainly to be mapping their transnational operations and the extent to which they impinge on legitimate business. More than just the de-marketing of products with dubious origins, comprehensive disincentives need to be placed all along the entire supply chain of each trade.

That moral effort would need to engage the various social science disciplines that global business typically draws on, such as political science, sociology, economics and geography as well as its own intersecting business sub-disciplines of marketing, operations, economics, organisational behaviour, human resources, tourism and finance (Figure 10.2). Thus, there appears to be work enough for scholars from a plethora of backgrounds, and the applied research stands to benefit from truly inter-disciplinary perspectives, as opposed to lip-service to the latter while pursuing recognition in one's field of specialisation. Rather than ignorance of, or worse yet disparagement of, other research, the clarion call is for mutual learning and active debate, without shying away from expressing informed opinion instead of proposing sterile models. While some other academic disciplines have begun addressing these issues, it remains critical for strategic management and global business scholars to consolidate these insights as well as bring their own expertise to bear on the workings of the dark side of global business.

Action orientation

The critical objective for any advocate against the shadow trades must surely be to identify the means to inhibit them effectively, not just explicate their workings. Some lessons might be clearly drawn from the de-marketing of tobacco consumption, excessive liquor imbibing, drug addiction and problem gambling. Besides, the disenfranchising of all the shadow trades is not just a case of dampening demand for goods and services that are in short supply, but those that might be plentiful from legitimate industry yet nevertheless morally objectionable in their sources and processes. If management concepts of competitive advantage, production outsourcing and strategic alliances are as valid in the marketplace of the shadow trades as they are in the legitimate global marketplace, then the business processes involved must be just as worthy of academic investigation and policy intervention. In analysing how and why such illegitimate businesses thrive, it is obligatory for all concerned to address the wider context of war, civil strife, natural disasters, political corruption, climate change, trade barriers and the like which legitimate global business also endure. Otherwise, platitudes and pronouncements without engagement on the dire causes and consequences of the shadow trades will ultimately result in more costly societal breakdown and greater conflict worldwide.

Advocacy plus Activism

Political clout

Multinational corporations are undoubtedly in an influential position to lobby host-country governments to act against the shadow trades, and to support legislation in

SHADOW TRADES	SELECTED INDUSTRIES INVOLVED	SAMPLE PROFESSIONAL SPECIALISATIONS
Irregular Migration & Labour Exploitation	Manufacturing	Employment Relations
	Farming & Forestry	Migration Lawyers
	Passenger Transport	Agri-Business
	Entertainment	Tourism & Hospitality
Transplant Tourism & Organ Acquisition	Hospitals	Healthcare Management
	Medical Insurance	Marketing Communications
	Travel Agencies	Tourism & Hospitality
	Prisons	Social Work
Resource Pilferage & Environment Degrading	Mining	Operations Management
	Exploration	Investment Consulting
	Logistics	Supply-Chain Management
	Antiquities	Agri-Business
Waste Transhipment & Hazardous Recycling	Manufacturing	Operations Management
	Chemical Engineering	Production Engineering
	Recycling & Garbage	Waste Treatment
	Logistics	Logistics Management
Arms Conveyance & Military Contracting	Manufacturing	Marketing Strategy
	Shipping	International Relations
	Airfreight	Public Administration
	Exhibitions	Strategic Studies
Finance Sleight & Money Laundering	Banking & Insurance	Accounting & Tax Advisory
	Investment Brokers	Financial Planning
	Retailing	Macro-Economics
	Consultancy Services	Commercial Law

Figure 10.2   Industry and professional junctures with the shadow trades

their home countries that would extend protections of victims worldwide, even at some cost to their own operations. Yet, few corporations do so, preferring instead to proclaim their legal compliance with less stringent host-country laws, rather than adhere to higher ethical standards on socio-economic justice. Nor has academia published critical research to nudge practitioner consciousness on this neglected aspect of business ethics and hold them accountable to higher standards of corporate social responsibility. As long as there is a preoccupation in management studies about job satisfaction, work stress, fair remuneration, occupational health and safety, and employee rights, there ought to be at least some attention directed at working with the hidden underclass of trafficked and exploited labour for whom such concerns remain totally absent. Ought not professors as researcher-lecturers to be at the forefront of educating our societies, its politicians, officials, managers, consumers, citizens and students about, and galvanising them to act morally against, present-day manifestations of the shadow trades towards which our capitalist economies display myopia? Addressing the shadow trades may require collaboration of institutional outsiders and insiders, including minority shareholders, to act in concert. Just as entrepreneurship within corporations is encouraged by nurturing innovative teams of employees, perhaps activism and action against the shadow trades and action by corporations needs to be driven by teams of what might be coined as 'intra-activists', whether formally organisationally-promoted or informally self-organised. Where their efforts at reform are ignored or undermined by their corporations and governments, there needs to be societal acceptance for them to turn whistle-blowers under the full protection of the law.

Cultural confrontation

If activist shareholders are not able to bring corporate practices and policies to heel, then citizens need to be mobilised to act through their votes to hold politicians and government officials to account for appropriate legislations and regulatory oversight on the shadow trades. Governments will have to reorient themselves from being influenced by the industry rhetoric about economic growth, development and job creation, and recommit themselves to be primarily the representatives of citizen aspirations and supporters of community concerns. In those cultures that are noted for a propensity to circumvent laws, especially when there is lax implementation through state capture or incompetence, there may be strong religious or even superstitious traditions. Where the law may fail to enforce compliance, spiritual leaders who are much revered may be co-opted to dissuade participants in one way or another in the shadow trades through appeals to a divinely ordained moral code. Commendably, Pope Francis has been exemplary in advocating against corruption, resource looting, climate change, poverty and the like.[17] Perhaps religious sanctions ought to be on pain of retribution in this life, in the next via rebirth or for all eternity, which all the benefaction to religious causes, individuals and organisations cannot absolve. In essence, this calls for societies, corporations and governments to be preoccupied with the political economy and cease to treat the global market unquestionably as god.[18] Instead of celebrating wealthy entrepreneurs and corporations as well as condoning corrupt politicians and oligarchs, these should be subject to close scrutiny by governments, civil society and the intelligentsia as stakeholders, followed by naming-and-shaming for misbegotten wealth and ostentatious living, if found to be so deserving. Given the surfeit of awards for individual and corporate achievement, allowing for self-congratulation on social and mass media, there ought to be annual citations for global worst performance by legitimate corporations, governments and their leaders on addressing each shadow trade.

Solidarity towards Justice

Any interim challenges to arriving at definitive solutions ought to be no barrier to raising queries and generating possible alternatives for resolution, which comprise the archetypal role of the intelligentsia of any society, particularly those who inhabit its academic institutions. Whenever comprehensive, accurate and definitive information is still lacking, as with the shadow trades, the precautionary principle ought to be adopted for public policy if their potential harm is to be minimised and the risk managed. Besides the moral outrage habitually expressed by the intelligentsia of the industrialised economies, any expectation that regulation along with enforcement will, in and of itself, limit if not eliminate the shadow trades might well be futile. If multinational corporations seem recalcitrant in distancing themselves from the shadow trades and governments negligent in monitoring them, then civil society and non-government organisations doubtless have a vital role to play in being agents of change, nudging the former entities into responsible action. In time, corporations could actually become powerful instruments of societies in diminishing the shadow trades, rather than being unwitting participants. That the present approach of regulation, law enforcement and charity to victims does not adequately address the growth of the shadow trades is manifestly evident.

Analysing the business models that lead to immense profits could be crucial to shedding light on the dark side of global business, and undermining them will be essential to eradicating or at least diminishing the socio-economic injustices. It would make for a refreshing change if business scholars and other social scientists would be radically outspoken on the adherence by corporations and governments to equity ideals, and proactively involved in the empowerment and emancipation of disadvantaged citizens throughout the world. Rather than focusing on corporate leadership, marketing innovation, operational efficiencies and financial modelling, there ought to be commensurate emphasis on business ethics, corporate social responsibility and environmental sustainability. A theme running through this book has been that the roadmap to intervention will take both systemic-structural change by governments and corporations as well as individual and collective ethical courage if there is to be lasting impact in tackling these pernicious businesses. May we all come to realise that restorative justice worldwide is not achieved by remaining ignorant or failing to acknowledge unethical practices perpetuated surreptitiously, but by making ourselves more aware, and then working collectively as agents of incremental change to set wrongs right. Idealistic as it may appear presently, there must surely be a place for inspired vision and passionate conviction, even moral outrage, to be embodied by managers, regulators, citizens, consumers, media professionals and researchers alike, and translated into sustained collaboration on advocacy, activism and action against the scourge of the shadow trades still ongoing in our 21st-century world.

Endnotes

1. Koslowski, R. (2001). Economic globalization, human smuggling, and global governance. *Global Human Smuggling: Comparative Perspectives, 338*, 340–342.
2. Collier, P., Hoeffler, A., & Söderbom, M. (2008). Post-conflict risks. *Journal of Peace Research, 45*(4), 461–478.
3. Miko, F. T. (2007). International human trafficking. In K. L. Thachuk (ed.), *Transnational Threats: Smuggling and Trafficking in Arms, Drugs, and Human Life*. Westport, CT: Praeger Security International, Chapter 2.
4. Thachuk, K. L. (2007). An introduction to transnational threats. In K. L. Thachuk (ed.), *Transnational Threats: Smuggling and Trafficking in Arms, Drugs, and Human Life*. Westport, CT: Praeger Security International, pp. 3–22.
5. Sachs, J. (2005). *The End of Poverty: How We can Make it Happen in Our Lifetime*. Harmondsworth: Penguin UK.
6. Raleigh, C., & Urdal, H. (2007). Climate change, environmental degradation and armed conflict. *Political Geography, 26*(6), 674–694.
7. Mark-Ungericht, B. (2001). Business and newly emerging civil society actors: between conflict and new forms of social dialogue. *Global Business Review, 2*(1), 55–69.
8. Conroy, M. (2009). *Branded! How the 'Certification Revolution' is Transforming Global Corporations*. London: New Society Publishers.
9. Leggett, W. (2014). The politics of behaviour change: nudge, neoliberalism and the state. *Policy & Politics, 42*(1), 3–19.
10. Beaverstock, J. V., & Faulconbridge, J. R. (2014). Wealth segmentation and the mobilities of the super-rich. In Birtchnell, T. and Caletrío, J. (eds.), *Elite Mobilities*. London: Routledge. pp. 40–61.
11. Tsaliki, L., Frangonikolopoulos, C. A., & Huliaras, A. (2014). *Transnational Celebrity Activism in Global Politics*. Bristol & New York: Intellect Books.
12. Saviano, R. (2019). *Gomorrah: Italy's Other Mafia*. London: Pan Macmillan.
13. Tondo, L., Kirchgaessner, S., & Henley, J. (2017). Death of Maltese journalist could be linked to fuel-smuggling network. *The Guardian*, 24 October.
14. Watermeyer, R., & Olssen, M. (2016). 'Excellence' and exclusion: the individual costs of institutional competitiveness. *Minerva, 54*(2), 201–218.
15. Freire, P. (1996). *Pedagogy of the Oppressed* (revised edn). New York: Continuum.
16. Gilman, N., Goldhammer, J., & Weber, S. (eds.). (2011). *Deviant Globalization: Black Market Economy in the 21st Century*. Edinburgh: A&C Black.
17. Pullela, P. (2019). Environment, poverty, corruption on agenda for Pope's Africa trip. *Reuters*, 1 February.
18. Cox, H. (2016). *The Market as God*. Cambridge, MA: Harvard University Press.

APPENDIX
ABBREVIATIONS & ACRONYMS CITED

AI	artificial intelligence
AML	Anti-Money Laundering programme
ATT	Arms Trade Treaty
AU	African Union, formerly Organisation for African Unity (OAU)
AUD	Australian dollar
BEM	big emerging markets
BRI	Belt and Road Initiative
BRICS	Brazil, Russia, India, China, South Africa (economic grouping)
CAAT	Campaign Against the Arms Trade
CAD	Canadian dollar
CFS	Conflict Free Smelter programme
CITES	Convention on International Trade in Endangered Species
CSR	corporate social responsibility
CTF	Combating Terrorism Financing programme
DRC	Democratic Republic of Congo (formerly Zaire)
EFT	electronic funds transfer
EPZ	export processing zone

EPR	extended producer responsibility
EU	European Union
EUR	Euro (common currency within European Union)
FATF	Financial Action Task Force
FDI	foreign direct investment
FSU	Former Soviet Union
FTZ	free trade zone
G7	Group of seven largest industrialised economies
GATT	General Agreement on Tariffs and Trade
GBP	Great Britain pound/UK sterling
GDP	gross domestic product
GNI	gross national income
GPAT	Global Programme Against Trafficking
IEDs	improvised explosive devices
IFF	illicit financial flows
IGOs	inter-government organisations
ILO	International Labour Organization
IMF	International Monetary Fund
IOM	International Organisation for Migration
ISIS	Islamic State in Iraq and Syria (also known as IS and ISIL)
iTSCi	International Tin Supply Chain Initiative
MDGs	Millennium Development Goals (set by the UN)
MENA	Middle East and North Africa
MICs	middle-income countries
MNCs	multinational corporations
Mt	million metric tonnes
NATO	North Atlantic Treaty Organisation
NGOs	non-government organisations
NICs	newly industrialising countries
NIEO	New International Economic Order

NPT	Nuclear Non-Proliferation Treaty
NRI	non-resident Indian
OECD	Organisation for Economic Cooperation and Development
OFC	offshore financial centre
PCBs	polychlorinated biphenyls, a toxic chemical
R&D	research and development
RPG	rocket-propelled grenade
RSC	responsibility to socialise corporations
SDGs	Sustainable Development Goals (set by the UN)
SIPRI	Stockholm International Peace Research Institute
SMEs	small-to-medium enterprises
StEP	Solving the E-Waste Problem Initiative
TI	Transparency International
TJN	Tax Justice Network
UAE	United Arab Emirates
UNCTAD	United Nations Conference on Trade and Development
UNDP	United Nations Development Programme
UNEP	United Nations Environmental Programme
UNESCO	United Nations Educational, Scientific and Cultural Organisation
UNHCR	United Nations High Commissioner for Refugees
UNODC	United Nations Office for Drugs and Crime
UNU	United Nations University
USD	United States dollar
WB	World Bank
WEF	World Economic Forum
WHO	World Health Organisation
WMDs	weapons of mass destruction
WTO	World Trade Organisation
ZAR	South African rand

INDEX